THE BIRTH OF POLITICS

MELISSA LANE

The Birth of Politics

EIGHT GREEK AND ROMAN POLITICAL
IDEAS AND WHY THEY MATTER

PRINCETON
PRINCETON AND OXFORD

Copyright © Melissa Lane, 2014

Published in the United States by
Princeton University Press,
41 William Street,
Princeton, NJ 08540

press.princeton.edu

First published in the United Kingdom
as *Greek and Roman Political Ideas: A Pelican Introduction*
by the Penguin Group
Penguin Books Ltd, 80 Strand, London
WC2R ORL, England

ISBN: 978-0-691-16647-6

Library of Congress Control Number: 2014951472

Book design by Matthew Young
Set in 10/14.664 pt FreightText Pro
Typeset by Jouve (UK), Milton Keynes

Printed on acid-free paper. ∞
Printed in the United States of America

1 3 5 7 9 10 8 6 4 2

In memory of Peter Lipton, whose unparalleled skill and enthusiasm for the communication of philosophical ideas are an enduring inspiration

Contents

Figures

Maps

Possibilities of Power and Purpose

Politics is a spectrum of the possibilities of power. It defines relations among humans and the purposes they pursue. At one end of the spectrum is sheer exploitative domination, where the only question is, as Lenin said, 'Who [is able to dominate] whom?' There was no single birth of the idea of domination; all too many societies in human history have been marked by it. At the other end of the spectrum of politics is a much rarer ideal: that of a regime of free and equal citizens with the power to decide and act. There is no monopoly on this practice either; it has evolved in many places and in many forms. Yet one set of ideas, from one particular era and one part of the world, has been enormously influential in delineating a vision of that ideal that continues to resonate powerfully in our own times. The ancient Greeks and Romans gave birth to a vocabulary still at work in the analyses and aspirations of many of those concerned with politics across the globe today.

One important dimension of Greek and Roman political ideas includes the claims and practices of self-government, exemplified especially in Athenian democracy and the Roman republic. What makes their ideas so rich a resource for thinking politically is that those forms of self-rule were

accompanied by philosophical and literary and rhetorical challenges to them. Some orators and writers debunked political ideals of self-rule, of justice and equality, as illusory or exploitative; others argued that self-rule was better achieved in ethics than in politics, or in some form of fellowship distinct from the existing political community. In other words, Greek and Roman political philosophy embodies both those practices of self-government and the reactions to them. This makes it a resource not only for those who want to celebrate politics today, but also for those who are critical of it.

This book treats historical practices and philosophical reflections together, on the grounds that what makes Greek and Roman ideas such good resources for thinking is the remarkably wide spectrum of possibilities of power that they covered. It is hard to find a modern critique of Greek and Roman politics (on slavery, on gender, on elitism, on imperialism) that some particular Greek or Roman did not make first. For every incarnation of a political regime, there were critics scrutinizing its claims. Alongside the distinctive ideas of democracy and republic, Greeks and Romans also explored the limits of those political ideals of citizenship; investigated the claims of oligarchies, kingships and even tyrannies; and questioned whether any claim to embody justice in civic relations could be valid. Rather than confine the value of the Greeks and Romans to just one position on the spectrum of politics – as either proudly committed to popular self-rule or philosophical critics of it, for example – we can learn most by exploring the whole range of ideas that they generated.

To respond to the ranks of critics and to the plight of the outsiders, to think for ourselves about the value and limits of politics, we need to understand the development of these influential classical ideas. Why turn back to classical ideas and models rather than simply think about what these terms have come to mean today? Greek and Roman versions of these ideas are radical in the original sense of the term. They serve as the roots (the etymological meaning of 'radical') of a multitude of modern ideas, roots that have sprouted in many different ways in the intervening centuries, in the West but also beyond it. Indeed, these ideas have been recovered, revised and contested in all parts of the world where the classical thinkers have been read or classical practices prevailed. They have been debated from Marseille to Ai Khanoum in Afghanistan (where a student of Aristotle inscribed celebrated Greek maxims on a funerary monument), from Tunis to Tarsus, in Byzantium and among its Ottoman conquerors; and also in the parts of the world where Greek and Roman ideas were brought by conquest and colonization, taken up by rulers and ruled alike, across other parts of Africa and Asia as well as Latin America.

Roots bear little visible resemblance to the plants that spring from them. Sometimes the Greeks and Romans are held to be too different from modern peoples to be of much use for current understandings. Perhaps they are of little use because they are too good for us: in this light they are sometimes celebrated as public-spirited citizens in comparison with our modern self-interested counterparts. Or perhaps it is because we are too smart or too lucky for them to be relevant any more: in this alternative perspective, liberal

and representative democracy in the context of capitalism is seen as a game-changing innovation that makes ancient models of only limited use.

Both points are intertwined in Enlightenment philosopher Jean-Jacques Rousseau's critique of ancient politics as irrelevant to modern circumstances, a critique that manages to be at once nostalgic in tone and uncompromising in implication. Rousseau in 1764 issued a warning to the citizens of Geneva (of whom he was one by birth) that they should not be tempted by flattering comparisons of themselves as citizens of a 'republic' with the peoples of classical times:

> Ancient Peoples are no longer a model for modern ones; they are too alien to them in every respect ... [Addressing Genevans as 'you'] You are neither Romans, nor Spartans; you are not even Athenians. Leave aside these great names that do not suit you. You are Merchants, Artisans, Bourgeois, always occupied with their [*sic*] private interests, with their work, with their trafficking, with their gain; people for whom even liberty is only a means for acquiring without obstacle and for possessing in safety.[1]

The fundamental political implication of this contrast, Rousseau concludes, is that 'Not being idle as the ancient Peoples were, you cannot ceaselessly occupy yourselves with the Government as they did.'[2] In other words, Rousseau implies that without the slaves and the wartime spoils that allowed Greek and Roman citizens to be idle, their distinctive brand of political involvement is impossible, and so there is little or nothing to be learned from it. But, in fact, against his insinuation, the allocation of effort and leisure is a political

allocation that both classical and modern societies have made, one that is not wholly determined by economic forces. Slavery was one (brutal and important) form of exploitative wealth-appropriation, but it was not the pivotal or dominant form of wealth accumulation in Greek or Roman societies outside certain specialized sectors; conversely, plenty of similar societies had slaves without devoting themselves to politics. Meanwhile, modern societies have accumulated sources of wealth, energy and capacity (through the division of labour, non-animal energy sources and new media, among others) that could be used to allow more people to devote time to politics, if they (we) so chose.

Certainly there are striking differences between ancient and modern societies in terms of economics, technology, religion and bureaucracy. The Greeks and Romans had productive economies based on agriculture, mining and artisanal production as well as trade and wartime plunder, but no exponential economic or technological growth, nor any idea of a capitalist market relatively emancipated from other aspects of the social order. They had communal religious rites honouring a range of deities, rather than monotheistic religions that could be divorced from public control. And they had no notion of a state as an abstract separate entity, distinct from the particular personnel who govern it and also from the people who compose it.

These differences are real, but the very differences can reveal certain important points about politics more clearly. Without an extensively bureaucratized and specialized state apparatus, the Greeks and Romans conceived of politics as fundamentally about relations among those in the political

community, and about relations with those who were inside or outside its boundaries without full membership. Indeed, this is why it is sometimes even said that they had no special idea of 'politics' at all as something distinct from general community concerns: politics was not separate and specialized, but a pervasive and abiding concern for the matters belonging to the community in common.[3] This means that classical ideas can provide a lens for focusing on the broad constitution and purposes of a community – something that is too often obscured in modernity by so many specialized aspects of the political apparatus. This is not to say that all Greeks and Romans idealized those relations among citizens (or that their societies were composed of citizens only: the politics of exclusion and inclusion were also a form of politics). On the contrary, some saw civic ties and pursuits as inherently exploitative or as less fulfilling than other ways of spending one's life. Those criticisms are as instructive as the ideas and ideals that they challenge.

This book will explore both the similarities and differences between ancient and modern politics. The point is not to come up with a net tally – are they more different or more similar? Rather, it is to reveal a range of ancient and modern preoccupations, so that common ground can be traced and light shed on those areas where they differ – and to do so in a way that is most productive for thinking about politics in whatever circumstances one finds oneself. Ancient ideas may prove radical both in the etymological sense of serving as roots, and also in the sense of offering profound challenge. For example, the internet and social media magnify the realization that politics today is dominated by rhetoric, just as it

was in Athens; we are forever searching for new mechanisms to produce the social knowledge that the Athenians enjoyed. The opinionated blogosphere makes the questions of Plato and Aristotle – whether social knowledge is enough, and how politics can take account of scientific expertise – pressing once again. And, meanwhile, rising levels of economic inequality and social immobility raise a challenge faced continually in antiquity, with fresh force: how, and in what circumstances, if at all, can the rich and the poor be enabled to act as political equals?

To explore classical ideas with an eye to their modern resonances, I have chosen eight ideas that are vital for thinking politically today and that have Greek and Roman roots (even though not always exact Greek or Latin translations). A more thoroughgoing antiquarian concerned only to represent Greek and Roman ideas in their historical contexts, with no thought of the present, would probably choose some startlingly different candidates: Polytheism, say, or Patronage. Equally, a modern philosopher guided only by contemporary politics would undoubtedly choose differently too: Rights, say, or Legitimacy. My guiding principle has been to choose ideas that can be used to illuminate key aspects of ancient thought while also informing contemporary reflections. They provide an overview of essential aspects of political thought and practice in ancient Greece and Rome over 700 years, from the late 6th century BCE to the late 2nd century CE, with a special focus on the 'classical eras' from roughly the 5th to the 1st centuries BCE (remember that BCE centuries are numbered downward to the birth of Christ, which marks the beginning of the Christian era, as in Figure 1). Each chapter is

A TIMELINE OF PEOPLE AND IDEAS

6th Century BCE = 500s BCE	Solon	
5th Century BCE = 400s BCE	Socrates	HEYDAY OF GREEK DEMOCRACY
5th–4th Century BCE	Plato	
4th Century BCE = 300s BCE	Aristotle	
4th–3rd Century BCE	Zeno, Epicurus	
2nd Century BCE = 100s BCE	Polybius	HEYDAY OF ROMAN REPUBLIC
1st Century BCE = 99–1 BCE	Cicero	
1st Century CE = 1–99 CE	Seneca, Epictetus	
1st–2nd Century CE	Plutarch	HEYDAY OF IMPERIAL ROME
2nd Century CE = 100s CE	Marcus Aurelius	

centred around an idea, while each idea in turn is presented as emblematic of a particular time, place or author, notwithstanding the fact that each was also explored in many others.

Across such a vast chronological range, a short book must necessarily be far from comprehensive, even in its coverage of the chosen eight ideas. For example, it leaves out the Jewish and Christian thinkers who remade crucial aspects of political thought in Greece and Rome. It focuses primarily on 5th- and 4th-century Greece and on the latter half of the history of the Roman republic, with only a brief and partial survey of aspects of the early imperial period of Roman history. And even within the classical eras of Greek democracy and the Roman republic, it is highly selective, aimed at informing readers who are interested in better understanding the politics of Greek and Roman antiquity both in themselves and also as a way of understanding the contemporary world. To explain how those two projects might be connected, I consider now five dimensions of politics, along the axes of which power is related to possibility, illustrating them primarily by reference to the Greek societies in which our story begins.

What is Politics? Five Questions

Every idea of politics must answer five questions about how power can be mobilized to shape certain possible outcomes: Who? Where? Why? How? When? While the Greeks lacked a special notion of 'politics' as something clearly different from, say, economics or military affairs, they certainly recognized and responded to what have been called the

'circumstances of politics'. They developed ideas that for us count as political ideas, addressing what they themselves called *ta politika*: the things or matters of concern to a certain – we would say political – community. To flesh out the range of ideas that they developed, let us consider how those varying ideas addressed each of the five questions in turn.

Who were those who concerned themselves with *ta politika*? Answer: the citizens (*politai*, plural of *polites*),* understood as sharing in a common condition and concern that made them equals, even though some were rich, others poor. That equality was Janus-faced. Some lucky few were included as citizens by means of excluding all others (foreigners and slaves) from their common privileges. Most harshly excluded were those whom Greek societies enslaved. Citizens could count themselves as equals even under a tyrant, at least in the sense that even a tyrant would treat citizens and slaves differently. For the Romans, the common concern would be called *res publica*, literally the people's thing or affair, from which derives the English word 'republic'. A Roman citizen was someone who was free, as opposed to a slave, who was protected in his private affairs and who enjoyed important powers related to the welfare of the common thing, the common concerns. The place of women as (passive) citizens in the classical regimes – with certain privileges and duties, but no voice in key political forums,

---

* To sound out Greek and Latin words as you read them, pronounce every syllable (so a 'citizen' is *ho po-li-tes*, as opposed to the plural of the English pronunciation of the word 'polite'). More information about Greek and Latin spelling and pronunciation is given in the glossary.

albeit sometimes dramatic political agency in a broader sense – will be considered in the chapters that follow.

Where did concern for *ta politika* take place? In Greece, primarily, though not always, in a *polis*. A *polis* was a particular kind of territory and settlement, combining an urban core, often walled, with a region of agricultural hinterland. About 1,000 separate *polis* communities have been counted in archaic and classical Greece. In size of territory, they ranged from less than 12 square kilometres in size to several thousand – with Sparta as an outlier at about 8,000 square kilometres (and with a relatively small population). In size of population, a *polis* might include anything from a few thousand upward – with Athens as the outlier at about 250,000 inhabitants, of whom about 60,000 were male citizens at its zenith in the time of the 5th-century statesman and general Pericles (in a relatively large territory of about 2,500 square kilometres).[4]

While land was important to a *polis*'s identity, both practically and symbolically, it was ultimately secondary to the identity of its inhabitants. A *polis* was defined most fundamentally in terms of its people. The Greeks never spoke of 'Athens' or 'Sparta' as political actors in the way that we speak of 'France' or even 'Paris'; they spoke always of 'the Athenians' or 'the Spartans'. And, in desperate moments, the survival of the *polis* meant the survival of the people holding *ta politika* in common, even at the cost of sacrificing some of their land. (Famously, at one stage in their 5th-century wars with Sparta, the Athenians followed the advice of the general and orator Pericles and abandoned their countryside to the pillagers, crowding together in the urban core of the *polis* under the

protection of the Long Walls, where they continued to care for *ta politika* together.) *Polis* is often translated as 'city-state', because it was in the urban civic centre that politics was concentrated. Indeed, it can even be translated as 'citizen-state', since it was the people, more than the place, who made the *polis*.[5] As we will see throughout the course of the book, this idea of politics as taking place within city walls would later become subject to philosophical critiques that opened up potentially wider and more inclusive ideas of how and where ethical and political communities might arise.

Rome, for its part, also began as an urban centre with a rural hinterland. But it soon grew beyond all recognition into a very different kind of place, a huge geographical expanse incorporating pre-existing political communities by conquest or treaty. After recurrent bouts of conflict, the Romans gradually and sometimes grudgingly extended the condition of citizenship to the inhabitants of their expanded domains: first, to almost all those who were not slaves living in what is now Italy south of the Po River; and, eventually, in 212 CE, to all the free men living in any Roman territory. In the earlier expansion, citizenship was sometimes extended to new groups *sine suffragio* (without the vote).

In another way, too, Roman citizenship was dramatically expansive and inclusive, because slaves who were freed by means of recognized civic procedures thereby became citizens (unlike in Greece).[6] Still, relatively few of these new citizens created by manumission (i.e., by being freed) or incorporation could come to Rome in practice to attend the assemblies where officials were elected and laws passed. So a gulf opened up between the condition of citizenship and the

actual practice of politics – a gulf that is likewise alarmingly wide in many parts of the world today.

Why did Greek citizens so prize the *polis* and the possibility of caring together for *ta politika*? They valued being respected as equals (as well as the possibility of being esteemed differentially as individuals), and they valued collective flourishing. The *polis* was a space in which the collective well-being could be defined, pursued and shared. Each *polis* community was vulnerable to invasion and so was constantly jockeying for advantage and sometimes even permanent domination over its neighbours. The political community could marshal its men (along with non-citizen residents and mercenaries, and sometimes slaves) to fight others, Greeks and non-Greeks alike: offensively, with the prospect of winning booty and tribute; and defensively, to protect their people and resources against domination – which could mean despoliation, enslavement or death.

Though a good number of adventurous spirits chose to hazard their personal fortunes as merchants or travellers, living abroad to teach, trade or advise, the personal safety and welfare of most Greeks depended crucially on the fate of their *polis*. In Rome, the standing of a Roman citizen in the republic meant protection from outrage of one's person, in the form of arbitrary flogging, illegal imprisonment and the like. Many citizens also had the duty of serving in the military if conscripted – with the prospect of gain and glory, but also the danger of defeat and the horrors that might bring.

It is perhaps in their answer to *how* that the Greeks innovated most dramatically: by developing mechanisms of decision-making and accountability that allowed *ta politika*

to be considered and determined collectively. These included practices of formal voting in assemblies and courts, sometimes using written ballots; the use of lottery and election to choose officials on a rotating annual basis; and scrutinizing the accounts of those officials to hold them accountable for their actions. Some democracies, most conspicuously Athens, innovated further in using large popular juries to decide almost all legal cases and eschewing professional judges, taking such power out of the hands of archaic aristocratic bodies. These mechanisms were both protective and productive, seeking to protect the *polis* and its institutions against damage or corruption, and to marshal its collective powers in pursuit of prosperity.

In Rome, the election of officials and the making of laws became a peculiar form of art, with elaborate group voting procedures and a key role for certain elected officials in proposing laws to those assembled for the purpose of approving them. The Athenian poor defended their interests themselves, especially in the law-courts that they controlled by force of numbers; the Roman commoners forced the establishment of special elected officials ('tribunes') to protect them. These practices also give us a clue as to *when* Greek and Roman politics happened: for if politics is the domain of power and possibility, it must happen in time as well as in space. That is, while political institutions are bounded by space, the pursuit of actions and decisions within them is done in time. To practise politics is to decide and to act, or to authorize action: using forms of power to make certain possibilities real. The Greeks and Romans controlled the timing of political actions in diverse and complex ways: the Athenians

timed the speeches in jury trials by means of a water-clock, for example; while the Romans consulted augurs, priests who were charged with determining when crucial political or military actions should be taken in accordance with divine favour.[7] Within institutions, opportunities to act were carefully prescribed and allocated; outside them, an ambitious man might perceive and seize the opportunity to rewrite the rules and take power as a tyrant or as one of a group of oligarchs. Inside and outside established institutions, in classical antiquity and today, politics is in large part an art of timing.

Eight Political Ideas

Eight ideas will constitute the core of this book, and will help us envision what politics might be. All arise at the levels identified earlier: the level of philosophical reflection and the level of political practice. Two ideas address what power might possibly achieve: Justice (especially a concern in the histories of the classical regimes) and Virtue (especially a concern for the philosophers, who incorporated their own special ideas of justice into it). Six address how to organize and tame the relations of power among people, and the extent to which varying kinds of control should be brought to bear upon these relations: Constitution, Democracy, Citizenship, Cosmopolitanism, Republic and Sovereignty.

All these ideas took special and distinctive forms in Greece or Rome, or both, though similar families of ideas may be found in other societies. While all were developed by a wide range of thinkers, my presentation focuses on

each one primarily in the context of one or a few thinkers at a certain time period, chosen because they contributed rich material to the development of that idea. This approach will help to guide readers who are less familiar with Greece and Rome on what will be a broadly chronological journey, while at the same time highlighting the thematic power of the ideas.

Of course, a case could be made for other ideas over those I have chosen. A list of the most important political ideas of the Greeks and Romans from some absolute standpoint would surely include Equality, Liberty and Law (these three thread throughout most of the chapters here, in fact), and we will also have occasion to think about ideas like Friendship and Sociability. My claim is not that these eight are exclusively or pre-eminently important. It is rather that they offer the best way I have found of telling a story in these pages that illuminates classical ideas while also resonating with contemporary readers.

The eight ideas begin in Chapter 1 with Justice as the fundamental – and contested – basis of common citizenship for all. For if the rich can exploit and even enslave the poor, if the poor are always afraid of the violence or fraud that might be perpetrated upon them by the rich, the extreme of domination reigns, with little hope that power might be used for any other possibility. To establish justice requires a *politeia*, often translated in English as 'constitution', meaning in Greek a condition of citizenship that involves the broad ordering of the way of life of a society. The Greeks were acutely aware of the merits and demerits of rival constitutions in this sense, as we will see in Chapter 2.

Chapter 3 looks at the specific Athenian idea, and constitution, of Democracy. Here the comparison between ancient and modern is most direct. While the people played far more extensive and diverse roles in ancient democracy than they do in modern forms of government, central ideas, including accountability, control and judgement, are common to both, though institutionally manifest in different ways. Appreciating the special qualities of Athenian democracy – a task that will involve dispelling a number of myths about it – allows us to think hard about how well modern democracies achieve, or could achieve, the ideas that they value most. It proves that a political system can exist in which the richest citizens cannot use their wealth to dominate the poor or to accumulate a lasting and far-reaching power base in politics. While the rich had certain opportunities and responsibilities in Athens and could make the most of those, they were always subject to the judgements of the wider political community and so restricted, for the most part, to the pursuit of the interests of that wider community, as the dominant group within it saw them.

The Greek menu of constitutions was arguably far wider than that served up in polite international society today. But, to a lineage of philosophers living in Athens across three generations, that menu did not go far enough, for it did not include any genuinely valuable regimes. In different ways, these philosophers all argued that existing regimes were marred by greed and lust for power, producing endemic conflicts without actually making their inhabitants truly better off. As we will see in Chapter 4, the lineage began with Socrates, who questioned his fellow Athenians incessantly

about the nature of justice, knowledge and virtue; it continued with Plato, his pupil, born to a privileged family but in thrall to the ugly plebeian Socrates, and the source of our most scintillating writings about him; and then, turning to Chapter 5, it was passed on to Aristotle, who came from a family serving the Macedonian court in northern Greece to join the Academy that Plato had established in Athens, later setting up a rival school of his own. Each of these philosophers envisaged another form of politics, even an ideal *politeia* (this is the title of what we call in English Plato's *Republic*), which would be based on a deeper idea of justice and achieve a more genuine human good. For Plato and Aristotle, Virtue and Citizenship would ideally coincide in a good *politeia*.

For some of Socrates' followers in subsequent generations, however, the vision of an ideal *politeia* was radicalized to constitute a permanent ethical fellowship that might never take any conventional political form. This was the birth of the idea of Cosmopolitanism (Chapter 6), referring to the entire universe (*Kosmos*) as a realm of citizens (*politai*), an idea that we will find turned to a dizzyingly wide range of ethical and political purposes. Alongside the debate about Cosmopolitanism in the post-classical Hellenistic period of Greek politics following the death of Alexander the Great in the late 4th century BCE was a related discussion about the naturalness of politics and of human fellowship. Was politics truly natural, a feature of human nature, as Aristotle especially would define it? Or might it be a makeshift tool, a useful social contract that does not answer to our highest capabilities of forming relationships?

The tensions between politics as rooted in natural sociability and politics as rooted in utility, and between a polity limited in space to one's actual fellow citizens and one in which one's fellow citizens were one's true peers in virtue wherever they might reside, were played out again and again in the schools that either followed Socrates or rejected his example in the post-classical era. As we shall see, one school of Hellenistic philosophers, the Stoics, argued for natural sociability and saw politics as a healthy outgrowth of that, though perfected in the republic of fellow sages; a rival school, the Epicureans, argued for politics as a matter of utility rooted not in nature but in contract, contrasting it with a higher human ideal of friendship. In such ways, the philosophers of the late 4th to 1st centuries BCE mapped out basic terms of political debate that set the stage for Roman politics. For the Romans came to dominate Greece politically, only to reappropriate Greek philosophical distinctions, which they then put to work in governing the expanding republic and empire – a story we will trace forward into the 2nd century CE.

Chapter 7 tells the story of the constitution of the Roman republic, seen through the lenses of an analyst of its rise and a participant in its decline. 'Republic' is a transliteration of the Latin term (*res publica*) at the core of the constitution that the Romans developed. Polybius, a hostage Greek historian who analysed the Roman constitution, viewed that constitution as a balance among three elements – consuls, Senate, and people – each representing one of the simplest three forms of constitution known to the Greeks (kingship, oligarchy and democracy). This idea of powers of government

that are in varying ways divided and balanced (and, for some, mixed) would evolve into the republican ideal of 'checks and balances' adopted by the American founders and their followers. Animating this recurrent tension was the struggle to attain equal liberty, involving respect for even the commonest and poorest citizen in his person, property and powers. Respect for the poor, however, went alongside special privileges for a meritocratic elite, one largely overlapping with inherited or earned wealth. Whereas the Athenians used democratic powers to constrain their elites, the Romans allowed theirs a more significant and independent set of political powers. The Romans balanced the role of the political elite (overlapping with the economic elite) against the role of ordinary Romans, whereas the Athenian democrats had enabled the poor to control and adjudicate, in crucial ways, the claims of the elite.

Writing in the 2nd century BCE, Polybius, an historian of Rome's rise who wrote his account in Greek, witnessed republican Rome at its height – but he prophesied that it could not last. Public devotion to duty, to the Roman understanding of the virtues that must be exercised if the 'common thing' (the *res publica*) is to be protected, would eventually and inevitably lapse. That undermining was witnessed a century later by the philosopher and statesman Marcus Tullius Cicero, who had clambered up the ladder of power and honour by sheer exertion of public speaking, but at the same time studied and debated zealously with philosophers of many schools in Rome and also in Athens. Like Plato and Aristotle before him, Cicero found that his reflections on politics took him in the direction of imagining a better

republic, with a better set of laws, which he set down in his writings just as the integrity of the actual republic was slipping away in a series of bloody struggles for power – in the course of which he himself would be one of those murdered. That vision put a particular understanding of what liberty required at its centre, an understanding giving pride of place to the roles of private property, law, and virtue in supporting the republican constitution.

Cicero died in one of the last convulsions of the republic before the appointment of a 'first citizen' – a *princeps* – who was, in 27 BCE, elevated to the new status of 'Augustus Caesar'. By the time of the Stoic philosopher Lucius Annaeus Seneca, in the next century, the 'first citizen' had become what we would today recognize as a full-blown emperor – though the title *dominus* (master or lord) would be officially accorded to the emperor only in 284 CE. With the mutation of republican practices in a new era of imperial leadership (Chapter 8: Sovereignty) came a change in political imagination.

Seneca, like Cicero, was a statesman, author and man of affairs who was made to suffer a violent death. Instead of writing of an ideal republic, he dreamed of an ideal prince. Within Rome, he embellished the original Greek idea of the monarchical constitution, envisioning how the virtues of mercy and liberality could be fostered in the *princeps*. So we see that Greek and Roman ideals of politics were not limited to democratic or republican models alone. Through the 'mirror for princes', Seneca and other writers of the imperial age initiated centuries of debate about the values and virtues of monarchical rule.

*

Those who trek to Rome to study the ruins of antiquity will find that the Senate House now standing was not built by the Roman republic. It is a building constructed for that purpose and on that site by a later emperor. The distant past of classical antiquity is like many of the mosaics that have been bequeathed to our museums: broken and reset, or refashioned with elements of the original pattern still clearly visible. When officials today count votes or make speeches, when voters elect 'senators' or 'presidents', when the United Nations debates how to establish the rule of law in a war-torn society, we see at work both ancient models and more recent rethinking, old ideas and new ways of putting them into practice. By engaging with the political ideas of the Greeks and Romans, we can equip and empower ourselves to develop our own ideas anew.

Justice

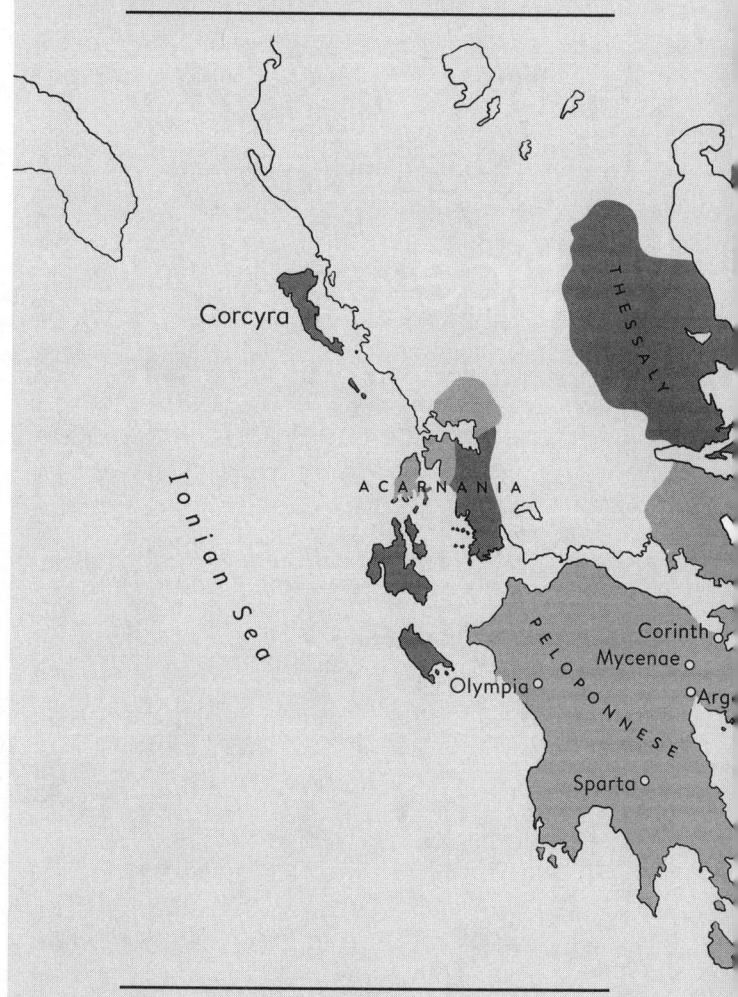

Classical Greece (circa 430 BCE)

Corcyra

Ionian Sea

ACARNANIA

THESSALY

PELOPONNESE

Corinth

Mycenae

Olympia

Argo

Sparta

Athenian Empire or allies

Peloponnesian League or Spartan allies

0   100 miles

0   100 km

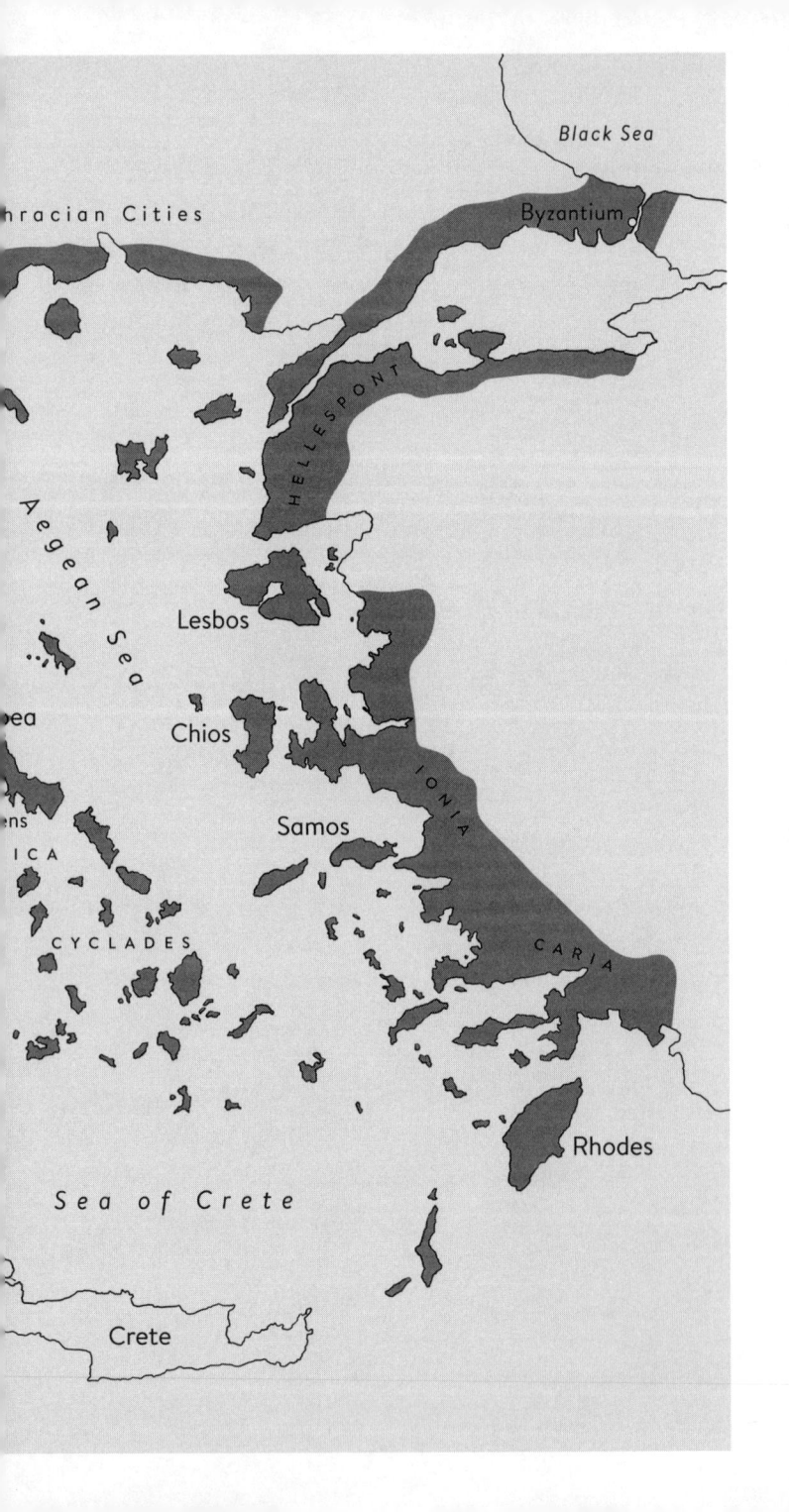

Civilizing *hubris*

'Their justice is violence.'[1] So the Greek poet Hesiod, some-time about 700 BCE, scathingly described the peasants among whom he lived in the mountainous region of Thebes, and indeed the whole generation to which he belonged. A small farmer embittered by losing a tussle over family land to his brother, Hesiod claims to have risen above his loss by taking the high road, writing an ambitious poem, *Erga kai Hemerai* (*Works and Days*), to instruct his brother in how to farm. Meanwhile he records his harsh assessment of the injustices practised by the likes of his brother in their generation, comparing their contemporaries unfavourably with the idealized justice of a legendary golden age.

Hesiod is one of the two major epic poets, with Homer, who wrote during what is called the archaic period of Greek history, from roughly the 8th through the 6th centuries BCE. Both Homer and Hesiod recount the doings of the panoply of gods whom the Greeks acknowledged in various hierarchies. (One set of gods, the Olympian gods headed by Zeus, had won a power struggle with an earlier set headed by Kronos; complex familial and affective ties existed among each set of gods, and between gods and favoured mortals.) These two poets likewise recount generations of human politics,

interwoven with divine interventions. While Homer, considered as the author of poems composed somewhat earlier than those of Hesiod, looked back to earlier centuries dominated by Bronze Age kings, Hesiod centred *Works and Days* on the politics of the archaic period itself, which was dominated by alliances of aristocratic families as well as by internal power struggles among them. These 'oligarchical' polities, interrupted by bouts of tyranny when one family or individual would obtain the upper hand, were the crucibles in which dramatic changes in technology and social organization – such as the development and spread of coinage, writing and new military tactics – were forged. Struggles for power, among these polities and within them, came to include a new set of players: the non-elite multitude who were relatively poor, and who first asserted themselves in Athens in the 5th century BCE (the century most often counted as the beginning of classical Greek history) in the establishment of a democratic regime.

The fundamental political idea of justice can already be found in archaic poetry, and it is there that we will first explore it, moving on to some of its subsequent developments in poetry and philosophy, especially those in classical Athens. Setting the terms of right or fair treatment, justice was widely seen by the Greeks as the key to civilization. Living in over 1,000 separate communities of different sizes, scattered across a mountainous mainland with its Peloponnese peninsula as well as hundreds of islands, calling themselves Hellenes but speaking diverse dialects, the Greeks were acutely aware of how recently human societies

had become civilized and how precarious the fruits of civilization remained. They knew themselves to be relative latecomers in comparison with the long-settled communities of Mesopotamia or Egypt from which they had learned much. Civilization freed humans from bare subsistence by developing arts and sciences such as agriculture, metallurgy, navigation, architecture and the very poetry that Hesiod composed. For Hesiod, whose poetic voice gave substance to archaic Greek ideas, it was justice that made all this possible. Why? Because without it, humans would be in the same position as the nightingale seized by a hawk, described in Hesiod's poetic fable. 'As I wish, I will make my meal of you, or let you go,' says the hawk to his hapless victim clutched in his talons (WD 209). Without justice, human society could never have risen beyond such an incessant struggle to kill or be killed.

We can think of justice as opposed to the idea of *hubris*, which in Greek signified a form of status violation, a disrespecting of what is owed to someone. Justice is giving people what they are owed. The disrespect involved in *hubris*, by contrast, upsets the natural order and threatens to bring down divine retribution. In the bitterness of Hesiod's words quoted at the outset of this chapter, we find evidence that the Greek attachment to justice was as vulnerable as it was deep. Justice is not an idea unique to the Greeks, but they developed powerful understandings of what it might require, especially between the rich and the poor, alongside corrosive challenges to the claim that it merits being followed at all. We will explore their statements of aspiration to justice, as well as their challenges to its nature and value.

Rich and Poor

In ancient societies, justice among citizens was as important as it was regularly threatened in the relations between rich and poor. Each Greek city-state harboured a small but powerful group of wealthy families, together with a much larger body of the poor. Some of the rich had inherited their wealth, largely in land and in the harvests of grain, grapes or olives that it could provide. Others would engage in trade, financing ships sailing to trading posts like Persia and Egypt, or (especially from the 5th century onwards) investing in industries like shipbuilding. Greek vases depict the good life that the rich enjoyed: wining and dining, listening to the music of hired musicians, adorning themselves with jewellery. By contrast, many of the poor lived at the margin of survival – as landless peasants or urban scavengers – although others made a decent living as artisans or small farmers. Whatever their actual income or wealth, all of those considered members of the 'many' lacked the luxury and status possessed by the 'few' and bestowed by wealth, especially the relatively secure wealth of the landed elites.

The elites thought of themselves as *hoi aristoi*, the best men, from which we get our word 'aristocracy'; in Athens, their families were known as the *Eupatridae*, the well-born.[2] Sometimes they simply called themselves, or were called by others, *hoi oligoi*, the few, contrasted with *hoi polloi*, the many. That so few are rich that the rich can even be defined as 'the few', while the vast multitude are destined to be relatively or absolutely poor – such an equation is not a matter of strict logic, for why, in principle, can't there be more than

a few who are rich? Yet it was endemic in ancient Greek history, and it remains a powerful description of many societies today. A society based on a class between rich and poor – on a middling class – would be an alternative, as Aristotle would come to recognize, and as Americans especially would demonstrate in the 20th-century post-war boom. But as many societies currently slide into further polarization of wealth, the key question of Greek politics from 600 BCE onwards is increasingly resonant again: on what terms can the rich and the poor live together in a single polity?

The poor must not routinely threaten the lives or property of the rich; otherwise, social peace is impossible. But unless the laws are fair enough to the poor, why should they respect them? (History shows that the margin of fairness required has often been far less than an impartial observer would have imagined necessary.) In seeking that balancing act, some regimes simply imposed terms by force. But even then the rulers had to define 'justice' and present their laws as embodying it. The struggle to establish justice between rich and poor – or to label the arrangements that were imposed *as* just – was the fundamental point of intersection between economic and political power, then as now.

We find a perfect vantage point from which to view this process in the work of Solon (*c.* 630–*c.* 560 BCE), an Athenian aristocrat who made a name for himself as a 'wise man' and poet, but most of all as a legislator called on by his countrymen to help quell the bitter struggles between rich and poor and set his city on a new just path. Solon wrote new laws that amounted to what we might call a new constitution

(the idea of a constitution is discussed in Chapter 2).[3] By giving the poor a defined role in politics, Solon put an end to exclusive aristocratic domination and so marks a crucial point in the transition from archaic towards classical Greek politics.

How did Solon achieve civic peace? By focusing on economic relations. Like certain lawgivers and rulers in other ancient societies, including the Near Eastern societies of Egypt and Phoenicia with which the Greeks traded goods, stories and ideas, he abolished the right of the poor to pledge their bodies as security for debt and so, upon defaulting, to be seized or sold as slaves by their creditors.[4] This was clearly a restriction on the contractual liberty of the poor: they were not to be allowed to incur debts with such security, even should their children starve for want of cash. But it was a restriction of their contractual liberty for the sake of protecting their political liberty: as Solon explained it, for the sake of justice. Wherever the poor are vulnerable to contracts that make them potentially liable to be used or sold as slaves, they cannot be equal citizens, because they cannot be secure in their status as citizens at all. They are in those circumstances always at risk of falling into some form of bondage. The abolition of bodily security for default on debt among citizens, then, was crucial to the establishment of the justice that could make poor and rich alike full citizens of Athens.

Without a balanced regime that gives the poor some political clout, they will always be at the mercy of the rich. Law is the most important way in which a city can achieve justice. Solon claimed to have combated *hubris* – the violence

and insolence that threaten justice – by the establishment of *eunomia*, or a condition of good laws and law-abidingness. He boasts in his poetry: 'These things prevail, power and justice [*dike*] having been fit together by me, and I saw it through as I had undertaken. I wrote laws [*thesmoi*] too, the same for the poor and the rich, and inscribed straight justice fitly for each' (W 36). Indeed, while both sides agreed to abide by Solon's proposed constitution in order to put an end to civil strife, neither side liked it. That is a good measure of his success: as Solon himself describes it, he established 'a strong shield' for each side against the other, 'not allowing victory to either unjustly' (W 5).

Justice for Whom?

Some people in the Greek world lacked the full protection that justice offered. That was true above all for the slaves, who in Greek societies were mainly non-Greek (though Greeks were liable to be seized as slaves should they find themselves on the losing side of battles abroad, or simply unlucky in their encounters there: the philosopher Plato is said to have been put up for sale as a result of his unhappy experiences with a tyrant in Syracuse). Most slaves were captured in warfare or piracy, sold either en masse from conquered cities (often women and children, all of whose menfolk had been massacred) or as individual prisoners (though many of these were ransomed by remaining friends or family).

A slave was the conceptual opposite of a free person. Indeed, it has been argued that it was in Greek reactions to

the social role and experience of slavery that the concept of freedom was fully born.[5] The conceptual opposition between slavery and freedom would become enshrined in the first title of the *Digest* of Roman Law, which made no effort to conceal the conventional, rather than natural, origin of the status of slaves (adapting the original Greek contrast between *nomos* and *phusis*): 'Slavery is an institution of the *ius gentium* [the law common to all peoples], whereby someone is against nature made subject to the ownership of another.'[6] In the Greek and Roman legal systems, while certain legal provisions for slaves varied, slaves were nonetheless broadly conceived as chattel. They were property, not persons. Justice was left behind, or almost so, in the near-absence of any legal protections or secure entitlements for slaves.

Athenian slaves, for example, were almost entirely excluded from the very site of justice, the law-courts. They could not generally bring suit or serve as witnesses, and their testimony was admitted only if obtained under torture and if both contending parties agreed.[7] They could not marry without their master's consent; in this sense Athenian slaves were as Roman slaves would later be described, under an alien jurisdiction (*alieni iuris*) rather than their own (*sui iuris*). Their labour was more varied: while some slaves worked the city's silver mines in nightmarish conditions, others ran households for their masters or were even deployed by the city as public administrators.

Alongside the formal public role of some slaves, the crowded and informal collective life of Athens led to slaves in general being accorded some legal protections in practice even though they were deprived of them in theory.[8] For

example, in classical Athens, as in republican Rome, slaves wore clothes that were indistinguishable from those of free persons.[9] Likewise, Athens, like most Greek cities, prohibited by religious customary law the killing of a slave (or of anyone), in that case in stark contrast to Rome, where the lives of all members of the household – wives, slaves and children – were in the absolute power of its head, or *paterfamilias*. Still, while such maximally harsh (capital) punishment of slaves was allowed in Rome, a Roman master might mourn a slave boy's accidental death, as a bust of 'the dearest Martial, a slave child, who lived two years, ten months and eight days', commissioned by his master sometime between 98 and 117 CE, suggests.[10] Yet, overall, the fundamental point remains: slavery was conceptually alien to justice.

What did it mean for the Greeks to tolerate such an abrogation of justice as slavery, at the same time that they celebrated justice as one of the foundations of civilized society? We can follow the lead of the late British moral philosopher Bernard Williams here, in seeing slavery as having been understood at the time as the imposition of necessity.[11] The Greek view of slavery seems generally to have been not that it was *un*-just, but that it was *non*-just. It marked the limits of where justice could apply. Beyond that was a matter of sheer necessity. Williams pointed out that those in wealthy democratic societies today tolerate gross abrogations of justice too. The existence of the global poor is seen as a regrettable by-product of capitalism, or of feudal economic relations, but too often it is not seen as something that can be made just. It is tolerated as if it were a necessity, or at least an inevitability, as an institution.[12] For any one individual, being

enslaved was a matter of cruel and unlucky fate. Just as most slaves were indeed hapless prisoners of war, so most commentators on their lot saw it not as a matter of nature, but of misfortune, as in a fragment of Sophocles:

> One day showed us all to be one tribe of humans,
> born from father and mother; no one is by birth
>   superior to another.
> But fate nourishes some of us with misery
> and some with prosperity, while others are compelled
> to bear the yoke of slavery.[13]

By and large, the Greeks did not see slavery as a case of injustice. Rather, justice arose as a question only among those who were not slaves; slaves were outside the reach of its full protection. Although they did receive certain minimal protections in the law, these were not protections that they could themselves act legally to claim. In extraordinary circumstances however, further legal protections could be bestowed, as in the case of the personal freedom and political citizenship bestowed by the grateful Athenians upon their slaves who had helped to man the fleet in the battle of Arginusae in 406 BCE.[14]

Other groups in the *polis* also stood at a certain distance from justice, but they were not as wholly alienated from it as were slaves. Athens, for example, harboured an especially large population of free-born foreigners, mainly from other Greek cities. Some, like the travelling 'sophists' (intellectuals and orators) or visiting merchants, were merely passing through. But other foreigners settled in the city and could, if sponsored by a citizen, gain the legal status of 'metic', which

was, broadly speaking, in between that of slave and full citizen. Metics paid special taxes and were obliged to serve in the military; they were recognized in certain religious processions, as an honoured foreign contingent in the city; and they could trade on equal terms with citizens (apart from having to pay a special fee for establishing a market stall).[15] But they could not vote in the assembly, hold office or serve as court jurors. They could use the courts to bring lawsuits seeking justice, but they could also be subjected to torture to elicit evidence, and certain crimes against metics were punished less severely than those against citizens.

Plato's *Republic* is set at the house of one of the wealthiest and most prominent metic families; one son would die fighting for the restoration of the democracy and another would become famous as a speechwriter. As shown by the dialogue's depiction of the patriarch of that family (Cephalus, originally from Syracuse), metics could conceive of justice in their economic relationships with other men (paying their debts) and in their relationship with the gods (paying the debts, as it were, of their sacrifices), even though they were aliens to political justice in its fullest form. Perhaps the most famous metic in Athenian history is Aristotle, who wrote his account of man as a political animal while living outside his own political community, unable there to fully exercise his own nature as a citizen.

Last but not least on the list of those systematically excluded from full political justice were women and children. Women were in one sense citizens – in Periclean Athens, Sparta and Rome, only a child born to a married citizen-mother and citizen-father was straightforwardly

counted as a citizen. Spartan women were educated and trained publicly as citizens until puberty; in all cities of the ancient world, women played special civic and religious roles as priestesses and in various forms of religious cult. Spartan women and Roman women could own property, though their ability to conduct legal transactions was limited, whereas Athenian women could not own property and played a less visible role in the economy outside of the household than would many Roman women. But, from the standpoint of politics, while Athenian and Roman women played important roles in religious practices and in giving birth to citizen children (in marriages to male citizens), they had no voice in the institutional forums of civic decision-making.

While the Athenians may have silenced their adult women in the 'agora' (marketplace) and assembly, their playwrights gave their traumatic vulnerabilities unforgettable voice – even though female characters were played on stage by male actors. The ethical perils of women's passivity – and the risk that they would eventually lash out, like Medea, against the cruel and arbitrary way in which they were treated – preoccupied the tragic playwrights. We see the centrality of concern with the peculiar and painful status of women threaded through the titles and characters of Greek tragedy: *Suppliant Women*, *Phoenician Women*, Medea, Phaedra, Antigone. Yet it remained true that women's peculiar status of citizenship, even in Sparta and Rome, where women could (for the most part) inherit and own property, was largely insulated from justice. Lawsuits might be held about them, their status might be legally defined and circumscribed (as in the obsession with female heiresses in certain periods in Sparta and Rome),

but they were not active participants in politically defining
the justice of the terms on which they were treated. As for
children, male children entitled to full citizenship would of
course claim it in due course. Yet their exclusion during their
minority was severe. Roman fathers had in theory the power
of life and death over their children, a power that Athenian
masters did not have even over their slaves.

Justice: Natural or Conventional?

Return to Hesiod, the poet with whom this chapter began.
Like other poets of his day, perched between archaic and
classical Greece, writing epic or didactic poems to educate
and shape the values of his fellows, Hesiod sought to explain
the origins of justice by connecting it to the intentions and
laws given by the gods. He proclaimed justice to be sponsored by the gods: first, the pre-Olympian head of the gods,
Kronos, and then his Olympian supplanter, Zeus:

> This is the *nomos*[16] Kronos laid down for human beings;
> to fish and beasts and winged birds it is allowed to eat
>   one another,
> since there is no justice among them;
> but to human beings he gave justice, which is become
>   far superior.
> For if someone is willing, knowingly, to say what is just,
> wide-eyed Zeus gives him well-being,
> but if someone lies, voluntarily, while testifying as a
>   witness,

so wounding justice, he shall be irremediably damaged
himself (*WD* 276–83).[17]

The gods come off well in this presentation, as the
sources and defenders of justice. But in the myths and poems
of traditional Greek religion, while the gods were officially
assigned the role of upholding justice and were acknowledged in religious rites for that purpose, many stories were
told of their exploits that could undermine human trust in
their reliability in that role. Described in anthropomorphic
ways as engaging in passionate love affairs and attendant
quarrels, with one another and with mortals, the gods' influence on human affairs had the potential to disturb justice
as much as to ensure it. If Zeus raped women like Leda and
Europa, if the god Poseidon inflicted shipwrecks out of vengeance and the goddess Athena sided with the Greeks against
the Trojans in the Trojan War out of pique, could humans
put full faith in divine punishment of the unjust and reward
of the just?

As Greek societies struggled with political unrest and
military and economic changes from roughly the 8th into
the 6th and 5th centuries, this kind of question started to
become unsettling. In response, a few thinkers scattered
across the mainland and islands began to place justice on a
broader and so potentially more secure canvas: not merely
as a gift of the gods to humans, but as inscribed in the order
of the universe itself (the Greek word translated as 'universe', *kosmos*, means literally 'order'). If archaic poets like
Hesiod and Homer had propounded mythic and sometimes
problematic narratives of the gods' doings and sayings, these

new 'wise men' developed arguments in more abstract terms, rethinking divinity and nature in relation to the basic workings of elemental forces. Rather than recount the deeds and misdeeds of anthropomorphic gods, they devised accounts of the natural world as governed by principles of symmetry and balance, of the same kind as those by which human societies were ideally governed.

Consider Anaximander, one of the early Greek philosophers, born in Miletus, in Asia Minor, in the 6th century BCE. He claimed that the forces of the cosmos 'pay penalty and retribution to each other for their injustice, according to the assessment of time'.[18] Working out the balance of such cosmic scales led other Greeks – such as the followers of Pythagoras, who set up communities in cities across southern Italy in the 5th and 4th centuries BCE – to delve further into mathematical formulations of harmonious relations that could structure music and politics alike.[19] In the works of these pioneering philosophers, men and women could find a new form of reassurance that the universe was indeed fundamentally steered by justice. If hubristic or greedy humans violated its equilibrium, they would suffer for it.

Yet the assurances of these philosophers, like those of the poets, did not succeed in settling the issue. Again, the Greeks were not unique in the dissatisfaction that began to be felt with traditional assurances about justice. At about the same time that Hesiod wrote, the assurance that the unjust man will suffer for his vice rang hollow to the author or compiler of the book of Job. While the Hebrew scriptures address the question of justice through sacred histories and laws, classical Greece developed a different genre of writing and

performance in which to probe the origins of justice. This was the tragic drama, first institutionally staged at civic-religious festivals in Athens in the late 6th century BCE and spreading from there throughout Greece and later to Rome. In the dramatic representation of the fates of legendary and historical figures, and in the musings of the choruses that offered reflection on the action, these plays emphasize how some humans desire to act unjustly, others do so all unwittingly, and the just often suffer fates that are as bad as, or worse than, those that befall the unjust.[20] The tragic playwrights also raised questions about the boundaries of justice: who is excluded from its sphere? And, while some playwrights insisted on the divine sponsorship of justice and its fundamental human importance, others began to challenge the sacred origins and the naturalness of justice that had so long underwritten its role in society.

Three tragic plays produced in Athens in the 5th century BCE – in the beginning of the classical epoch and during the flourishing of its democratic politics – illustrate these themes. Building on the poet Hesiod's ascription of the general origins of justice among humans to Zeus, the playwright Aeschylus describes its specific origins in Athens as sponsored by Athena, daughter of Zeus and patron deity of the city that bore her name. The final play of Aeschylus' *Oresteia* trilogy, produced in 458 BCE, called the *Eumenides*, portrays how justice was established there in the form of the 'Areopagus', the aristocratic court that served religious as well as judicial functions. In the play, Athena sets up the court and serves in its first case as one of the twelve jurors, sitting alongside eleven Athenian mortals, to try the prince

of Argos, Orestes, for the murder of his mother and her lover. Although Orestes had in fact committed this murder to avenge his father, Agamemnon, Athena casts the deciding vote to acquit him in order to break the cycle of vengeance and instead establish new terms of justice.[21] The image of a goddess deliberating as one member of an otherwise human jury underscored the divine nimbus attached to the idea of justice, the awe with which it had to be surrounded if social ties were to withstand the many breakdowns and violations of justice that everyday life inevitably entailed.

The *Oresteia* shows that even when justice was believed to be sponsored by the gods or rooted in nature, humans still had to act politically to reach and impose just verdicts. It also shows how important procedures, and in particular judicial decisions, were in Greek law. If law can generally be understood as a public and formal procedure to settle a dispute, early Greek law is unusual in focusing more on procedures than on substantive laws.[22] There was a 'deeply rooted Greek view, going back to Homer, that a fair procedure for litigation is an essential requirement of justice'.[23] Inscribed on blocks of stone or wood or on bronze tablets (the earliest archaeological record of a written law in Greece is an 8th-century stone inscription in Dreros), the laws might be recognized as made by humans – ascribed to a lawgiver, a king or an assembly – but they were also often regarded as having some kind of ultimate divine sanction or source. Whatever their sources, it was vital, though not necessarily guaranteed, that laws should be fairly applied in human courtrooms. It was no accident that Hesiod's definition of an unjust man was someone who testified falsely in court. One mark of a good

society for ancient Greek philosophers from Plato onwards would be a lack of lawsuits.

Fifty years after Aeschylus' play was performed, a playwright of the next generation – Euripides (c. 484–406 BCE), who won prizes in the Athenian dramatic festivals more than twenty times, expressing a more disabused view of the gods than his dramatic predecessors – wrote a play – *Phoinissai* (*The Phoenician Women*) – that recapitulates the view of justice as rooted in nature, and shows how vulnerable it can nevertheless be to abuse. Its chorus is a group of women from Phoenicia on their way to sacrifice at the shrine of Delphi. Unable to make their way out of Thebes on account of war, they witness the main action of the play, which centres on the mythical figure of the Theban queen Jocasta, the mother of Oedipus, who had unwittingly also become his wife, and the fate of the children born to that incestuous and so god-offending marriage.

Despite her unhappy fate in life so far, Jocasta attests to the natural source and value of justice, praising 'Fairness, [which] binds together friends with friends, cities to cities, and allies to allies'.[24] But the dramatic action soon shows how vulnerable just bonds are to unravelling through neglect or violence. The brotherly bond between the two sons of her marriage to Oedipus is ripped apart by a breach of fairness of one towards the other in the breaking of an agreement to alternate in ruling Thebes each year. This breach of fairness leads to a double murder: each brother dies while simultaneously inflicting a mortal wound upon the other. As this play shows, justice was all too often undone by greed or lust, by ruptures of faith not inhibited by the fragile civilizing

emotions of awe and justice. Yet justice was still honoured, in a sense, even in the breach. Euripides dramatized its importance by demonstrating the bleak consequences of its failure.

In Euripides' play, one of the daughters of Jocasta and Oedipus survives to accompany her blinded and stricken father out of the city. That account of Antigone's fate is less well known than a different version told earlier in the *Antigone* of Sophocles, the third of the great Athenian tragic playwrights. It was this play that, in about 441 BCE, pressed an unforgettable case against the arbitrariness of human law in comparison with divine law. It did so by challenging the primacy of the city's public justice when set against the natural bonds of kinship and the divine sanction underpinning them.

Sophocles begins his play after Antigone's two brothers have killed one another. Ironically, the one (Eteocles) who had broken his word to share power has been buried by the city with full honours; having been its ruler at the time of his death, he (or rather his corpse) benefits from the determination of the new ruler, Creon, to connect his legitimacy with the former regime. But the other brother (Polyneices), who suffered the injustice of his brother's breach of faith, is lying indecently unburied in the dust, Creon having forbidden the dignity of a proper religious burial or of any interment at all on the grounds of his having rebelled against the city's prior ruler. Is Polyneices' mistreatment unjust? Not according to Creon's law, or, rather, to the decree that he has issued as the self-appointed ruler of the city. But it is unjust – avers Antigone – according to the 'unwritten laws' of the gods, which prescribe a profound and inviolable obligation to bury one's kin.[25]

47

Antigone's description of divine laws as 'unwritten' reflects debates at the time that Sophocles wrote. The Athenians were beginning to write down more and more laws passed by the relatively newly democratic regime; but such new laws might – so the *Antigone* implies – not be worth the stone or bronze on which they were inscribed. They might readily appear as the puffed-up and self-important orders of a hubristic political community, which, as with Creon's commands, fail to acknowledge that the power and validity of human laws pales in comparison with the older laws embodied in the religious customs of hearth and home. Antigone dies a heroine. The arrogant Creon suffers a worse fate, as Antigone's death prompts the suicides of his son (her betrothed) and then his wife from successive waves of grief. His political power to give orders is shown to be hollow, mocked for its *hubris* in contesting the inexorable ordinances of the gods and fates. *Antigone* reinforces faith in a divine order of justice. But it does so by casting doubt on the merits of the cadre of merely human laws and decrees.

The Sophistic Challenge: Is Justice Natural?

Sophocles' *Antigone* makes human law seem paltry in comparison with divine law. But it does not question the nature or value of the justice that it finds rooted in divine law. The public teachings of a new breed of 'sophistic' thinkers and teachers, questioning whether law and justice were anything more than arbitrary human conventions, offered an even sharper attack on the verities of the older poets. These new sophists were not the students of nature who had made

up previous generations of philosophers. Rather, they were specifically students of human society, who took it upon themselves to become teachers. This puts them among the earliest contributors to political theory, focusing their attention primarily on human affairs rather than on the constituents of cosmic order. The sophists were not unique in thinking about politics, but they were unusual in the proto-professional ways in which they positioned themselves and sought to profit from their reflections.

As well as offering their knowledge and advice free to their own cities and assemblies, these sophists travelled the Greek world seeking rich fathers who would pay for their advice to be transmitted to their sons, in the hope especially that a training in rhetoric – the art that many sophists claimed to have mastered – could help their sons to win power and fame. The spectacle of men seeking to influence politics not by playing their parts in the appointed duties and established institutions of their own cities, but by showing off their ability to train others to do so for a fee, was controversial. Men like the Sicilian sophist and teacher Gorgias (c. 483–c. 376 BCE), who toured the Greek world showing off a set-piece speech arguing that Helen of Troy was not to blame for having caused the Trojan War, disturbed the conservative assumption that rhetoric would always lead to just decisions.

Central to the teaching of many sophists was the drawing of a distinction between *nomos* and *phusis*, between law and nature.[26] In that context, they used *nomoi* (plural of *nomos*) to refer not to divine laws, as had Antigone, but to the kinds of laws passed by humans, by rulers, whether individual or

in groups. Man-made *nomoi* were human conventions. 'Law' in that sense, born of the happenstance of human contrivance, whether a tyrant's whims or an assembly's close-run vote, was presented as contrasting with the real nature of things – a nature that might be governed by a justice or law that is altogether different from the laws passed by humans. To contrast *nomos* and *phusis* was to call attention to the conventions of human contrivance, in comparison with the unalterable nature of reality – and, for the most part, *nomos* came off worse.

The most controversial sophists interpreted the claim that *nomoi* were man-made as the claim that they were made by *some* men for imposition upon *others* – that they offered the dominators all the advantage, and their hapless victims only disadvantage. These thinkers presented 'nature' as something like the red-in-tooth-and-claw view that early social Darwinists would later propose: they contended that it was natural for the strong to pursue their ends with impunity, making prey of the weak to suit their own desires. The Athenian character Callicles in one of Plato's dialogues is an example of someone who has imbibed these arguments and presents them in an indelible form.

Even then, if what was natural was the rule of the strong, that left open the question of how human conventions should respond, and how their merits should be evaluated. Should one respond by attacking the strong for exploiting the weak, using natural justice as a critical tool to expose the exploitative dimension of human laws? The first recorded criticism of the injustice of slavery as an institution (rather than of particular abuses) is framed in these terms. It treats

JUSTICE

slavery as a merely human law that violates the divinely sponsored and natural condition of liberty: 'The deity gave liberty to all men, and nature created no one a slave' is a saying of Alkidamas recorded by an anonymous note-taker in the margin of Aristotle's *Rhetoric*.[27]

Using the *nomos/phusis* distinction to advance that radical critique of slavery or of any other particular law did not find many takers, however. More common was the argument that the bulk of laws do serve human interests in general – but they do so only as a kind of second-best, not serving them to the fullest possible extent.[28] Individual humans would be best served by pursuing the justice of nature, which is a justice in which the strong rule the weak, but only if they are assuredly among the strong. The difficulty of being sure that one would win out leads to a second-best solution, of accepting human law as a way of ensuring that one gets something rather than nothing. The best thing for each individual would be to dominate others without being punished. But the worst thing for him would be to try to dominate, and get caught and punished. So justice was the middle of the road, the second-best option. Forgo the fruits of being a dominator, but thereby ensure that you don't suffer the pains of being dominated.[29] Plato has the character Glaucon lay out this view – while distancing himself from endorsing it – in the *Republic*: justice is 'intermediate between the best and the worst. The best is to do injustice without paying the penalty; the worst is to suffer it without being able to take revenge. Justice is a mean between these two extremes. People value it not as a good but because they are too weak to do injustice with impunity.'[30]

According to this view, justice is a good fallback, but not inherently the most advantageous path to take. It may be achieved by using law as a 'guarantor' that people will treat each other justly, even though this will not make them more inherently good or just. Yet this solution is itself unstable. If justice is only a second-best solution to the problem of how to live with others, why shouldn't you act unjustly whenever you can get away with it – thereby reaping the best possible benefits brought by injustice, while benefiting too from everyone else obeying the laws?

Such a relativizing of the value of justice – making it something we put up with when necessary, but not what is most beneficial or advantageous for our own happiness – marks an important challenge to the full-throated (if wistful) defences of justice in the poets with which this chapter began. We have seen that as new figures came on to the public stages of Greek society – from the older poets and philosophers, to the tragic playwrights and then the sophists – the consensus on the meaning of justice began to fray. Was justice central to the survival of civilization, or a swindle practised by the rich upon the poor? Greek thinkers put these questions on the table; the passionate debates, dramatic stories and tragic fates of real people and literary characters alike proved their testing ground.

The Powerful and the Weak

As we have seen, only a limited form of justice was available to slaves, resident foreigners, women and children within the *polis*. But what about justice beyond its borders, in the

relations between one *polis* and another, or between a *polis* and other kinds of political entities, such as the Persian empire to the east of the Greek cities, where a powerful empire had been ruled since the 6th century BCE by descendants of its founding king, Cyrus the Great? Where there were treaties and alliances binding political units together, justice was a recognizable way of talking about keeping to agreed terms – though, even then, the question of whether the actions of a *polis* should be governed by justice and injustice, or rather by advantage, was far from settled. In a situation of no alliances and the prospect of force, the question of whether justice even obtained could be made to appear quixotic.

That was the view taken by ambassadors who were sent by the Athenians to negotiate the surrender of the inhabitants of the island of Melos in 416 BCE, in the midst of the Peloponnesian War between democratic Athens and the oligarchically leaning regime of Sparta, even though the Melians had done the Athenians no harm and had announced their neutrality. (The Athenians considered themselves to be at war with the Melians nevertheless.) As presented by the historian Thucydides, the Athenian ambassadors advance what they claim to be a stark truth of human affairs:

> we both know that it is necessary to decide what is just in human debates only when the sides are equal, but decisions about justice are made in human discussions only when both sides are under equal compulsion; but those who are able to take advantage, get what they are able to get, while those who are weaker must acquiesce (5.89).

Most discussions of this so-called 'Melian Dialogue', a set-piece in Thucydides' history, home in on its international context, arguing that justice has no place either in any war or at least between an imperial power and those brought (even by circumstance) under its sway. Indeed the willingness of the democratic Athenians to act as tyrants in their empire, while celebrating their maintenance of justice at home, was shocking to some observers and participants at the time. But consider an even more unsettling feature of the Athenians' ultimatum to the Melians: their claim that justice cannot obtain in any situation in which one side is stronger. If one side is stronger, that side will get whatever it can, while the weaker side will simply have to bear its exploitation.

Can this be true? This chapter has argued that the Greeks saw justice as especially crucial in the setting of terms between rich and poor. One would think that Melos was precisely a situation where one party is stronger, the other weaker, so that the Athenian ambassadors' dictum would in this case overturn not only the prospect of international justice, but also the prospect of justice at home, or in any context in which it might actually be needed. Yet, at the same time, the Athenian ambassadors provide us with a clue to a resolution. For we might rethink the hasty assumption that the rich are the stronger and the poor the weaker. In individual encounters between a rich man and a poor one, the poor person will almost always be more vulnerable. But with the abolition of debt-bondage to protect him and his fellow poor – the 'many', after all – with whom he makes common cause, there is a sense in which the poor may at least sometimes be able to assert a collectively greater strength. The

poor have numerical power, and, if properly armed (sometimes even without proper arms), military power.

We should not think of this as simply mob-rule. Rather, the greater strength of the many arises not merely from numbers, but from their capacity to organize themselves in their numbers for productive collective action. The very name of democracy (*demo – kratia*) may refer to the power (*kratos*: literally, 'grip') of the *demos* in the sense of its capacity to act and not merely in the sense of brute force.[31] So, in setting fair terms between rich and poor, the poor need to be protected against individual dependence and subordination, but, equally, the rich need to acknowledge the collective power of action of the poor. Justice protects the weak against the strong, but the weak may be able to muster a strength of their own.

If we picture the 'Melian Dialogue' as a clear-cut case of overwhelming force on one side, we see in this light that it is a rather unusual military situation, rather than a paradigm of the human condition. Even in empire, the dominated have forms of economic, political and moral power, though they may be subject to partisan suasion and arbitrary coercion by the ruling few. And in all regimes the potential power of the multitude (however cowed, fragmented and undermined it may be) is as much a threat to unjust contracts as it is a prod to the formation of fair ones. Justice is a radical idea, because if people's sense of fairness is strained too far, their very sense of belonging and commitment to a common political community may snap.

This chapter has explored how archaic Greeks valued justice as part of the divine order governed by the gods, and how, in archaic and increasingly in classical times, a range of challenges to the human trust in divine justice was explored in poetic, sophistic and philosophical writings – engendering new ways to explore the relation between human and divine justice. The idea of Justice is one that, for Greek thinkers, underpins human civilization; yet it is vulnerable to divine and human misdeeds and misconstruals. To establish justice, therefore, requires not only divine sanction, but also human institutions capable of upholding justice for the most vulnerable participants in them – especially, as we saw, the poor in the face of economic and political dominance by the rich. We will next consider the ways in which different Greek constitutions sought to respect or to restrain the power of the multitude, and their treatment of the claims of the elite: to see how justice was put into action in constitutional thinking.

Constitution

Constitutions, Political and Otherwise

What is a constitution? Today we think of it as the basic laws defining the distribution of power in a regime, sometimes collected in a single document. The original handwritten Constitution of the United States of America is on display in the rotunda of the National Archives Building in Washington, D.C. By contrast there is no such single document embodying the British Constitution, which is instead understood to be a combination of important laws, conventions and treaties that have evolved over time.

No 'constitution', even in the uncodified British sense, can be found in the political languages of classical Greece and republican Rome. The word in English derives from the Latin *constitutio*, referring, in post-republican Rome, to an edict issued by an emperor, rather than to a comprehensive and fundamental body of laws.[1] Nevertheless, 'constitution' is widely used to translate what the classical Greeks called *politeia*. This translation, and the title of the present chapter, can be justified by thinking about a meaning of 'constitution' that is more fundamental than its current primarily political usages. That deeper sense is of a constitution as a specific kind of ordering and structure – what in French is called *regimen* – the characteristic make-up that maintains a

body in good health. The philosopher Aristotle would eventually employ *politeia* in both its most comprehensive sense and its most narrow political sense. He refers at one point to *politeia* as meaning the general 'way of life' of a city.[2] But he also at another point defines it narrowly as 'an arrangement of offices'.[3]

The broad sense of constitution as a specific kind of ordered regime applies to natural bodies as much as to political bodies. The comparison shows why 'constitution' may go beyond the narrowly political to mean a way of life. A person has a strong constitution if she is able to maintain her internal balance and order, warding off disorganization by rogue cells and invasion by harmful foreign bodies. A political body has a strong constitution if it is able to maintain its internal balance and order, warding off disorganization by rogue disaffected groups and invasion by harmful foreign bodies. And there is a connection between the two. Only a certain ordering of the habits and values of a group of citizens will serve to maintain the customs and principles animating a particular way of life.

This is why the Greek word *politeia* – the word most often translated as 'constitution' – is, in its earliest surviving reference, used to describe a condition of what we might call being a citizen. The word is used by the historian Herodotus (who will shortly be introduced in more detail) in describing the demands of a foreigner in 5th-century Sparta. The foreigner declares himself willing to take up a post in the Spartan army only if he and his brother are made Spartan citizens.[4] It is significant that the word is used here for the particular case of citizenship of Sparta. For Sparta, above all

other Greek constitutions, dramatized the importance of 'constitution' in connecting together its narrow political and wider way-of-life meanings. Being a Spartan citizen meant not only being granted certain privileges and duties, but also being enrolled in a comprehensive way of life, one that was noticeably distinct from that of other Greek city-states. Studies of the Spartan constitution, in works entitled *Politeia of the Spartans*, from the late 5th century onwards were pre-occupied by this way of life: concerned with the demands of military readiness, they examined extreme physical training as well as common meals and other distinctive customs for producing and rearing children. The idea of the broad consti-tution as going beyond political organization to include the social division of labour generally – how people are procre-ated, educated and trained to contribute to society – would become characteristic of many Greek discussions of the 'best *politeia*'.[5]

It is the connection between *politeia* in the sense of citi-zenness, way of life, and *politeia* as a specific political struc-ture that is the topic of this chapter. What is the relationship between a regime's way of life and its characteristic political organization in particular? For the Greeks of the classical period, there was no single answer to that question. Rather, each kind of regime – each different *politeia* – gave its own distinctive response, produced and tested especially in the two major bouts of convulsion that shook the Aegean world in the 5th century BCE. Those convulsions arose from the violent confrontations of different constitutional models. For those Greeks who participated in these battles or chronicled them soon after the fact, what modern scholars translate as

the clash of constitutions was at the forefront of ideological claims as well as more sober analyses. In the dramatic course of Greek wars as chronicled by historians, we find rival cities displaying the merits, or the flaws, in their constitutions; we also find constitutional analysis dividing regimes into three basic types of one, few and many. Exploring constitutional clashes in practice, and then in theory, are tasks to be pursued in this chapter.

Herodotus and the Politics of the Persian Wars

The first major set of conflicts involving 5th-century Greek societies was the Persian Wars (499–479 BCE, with battles continuing for years afterward), in which a diverse group of Greek polities banded together to ward off invasions by the king of Persia, who controlled a vast territory across the Aegean Sea from the Greek mainland. This story would be recounted by Greek historians as a battle of liberty against servility, of free Greek states against the slavish and despotic Persian monarchy, though we will investigate ways in which their descriptions were not quite so simple as this summary makes them seem.

The second set of conflicts in the same century was the Peloponnesian War (a preliminary set of conflicts 460–c. 445, then what is called the war proper 431–404 BCE), in which the Greek alliance that had successfully repelled Persia tore itself apart, splintering into two main groupings led by Sparta and by Athens. Historians would describe this as a war between oligarchies led by Sparta and democracies led

by Athens, though, again, their descriptions and the course of the conflict were not quite as simple as that summary would suggest.

In reflecting on these conflicts, the historians and playwrights of the day saw them in terms of a conflict of constitutions. They alternately idealized or excoriated those regimes for the political choices that they fostered and for the ways of life that they promoted. To understand the basic political choices facing 5th- and 4th-century classical Greeks, we need to understand the ideas at the centre of those recurrent clashes of constitutions – the ideas that animated the ongoing competitions between very different ways of life in the regimes of different cities and empires. And we do that best by focusing on the story of the Persian Wars – and the constitutional analysis offered in the course of that story – told by the historian Herodotus.

Born in about 484 and dying probably soon after 430 (the latest events he mentions in his *Histories* are in that year), Herodotus hailed from the city of Halicarnassus (now the Turkish city of Bodrum) on the mainland of Asia Minor.[6] Coming from this eastern edge of the far-flung Greek settlements, while later living in its western reaches in a new Panhellenic colony planted on the Italian peninsula, Herodotus was a man of wide travels, broad sympathies and multiple audiences. He was a writer with an understanding of the borderlands of Greek societies, who forged an undying account of Greek military victory in the Persian Wars (which had ended in his childhood) and cast a shrewd eye over the self-deceptions and grasping for power on all sides. And he did that as the later bout of war between alliances

OVERVIEW OF PERSIAN WARS
AND PELOPONNESIAN WAR

5TH CENTURY BCE

499–494	Revolt of Ionian Greek cities against Persian rule
490	First Persian invasion of mainland Greece; Athenians lead victory in battle of Marathon on land
480–479	Second Persian invasion: in 480, Spartans and others defeated in battle of Thermopylae, but Athenians lead Greek allies to victory in sea battle of Salamis; in 479, Athenians, Spartans and others together win land battle of Plataea and defeat Persian fleet at Mycale
465	Major earthquake in Laconia kills many Spartans; helots revolt
460–445	Military conflicts between Sparta and Athens (and their allies)
431–404	Peloponnesian War between Sparta and Athens (and their allies): in 404, Spartans win

led by Sparta and Athens was already raging, being about twenty-five when the later war began.

Herodotus tells us that he travelled widely in Egypt, as far as Memphis, and preferred the Egyptian calendar to the Greek. He describes the costumes of the Bactrians, the habits of the camel and the traditions of the Scythians, delving into foreign customs with broad-minded assessment (sometimes criticizing, sometimes praising). He draws an influential contrast between Persian despotism and Greek liberty. Yet he also points out the contradictions between Greek regimes that prized freedom at home but imposed despotism abroad, and explores how Sparta and Athens drew on very different political habits and outlooks in deploying their forces to resist Persia.

Ethnographer and moralist, historian and tale-bearing traveller, Herodotus combined all these roles in writing his great account of the Persian Wars. This is the first work of 'history' written in Greek, a name given to it by the Greek word *historia*, which meant inquiry or investigation. Herodotus invented a new discipline of history, concerned with the making of 'inquiries' among eyewitnesses and records, in order to explain and memorialize significant human actions. This was close in spirit to modern investigative journalism or contemporary history, and could be pursued only in relation to relatively recent events. It simply isn't possible to write history in this sense about the very distant past. (When Herodotus' self-appointed successor, Thucydides, would come to write about the very distant past, he cordoned it off as a prologue from his main enterprise.) In inquiring into a war that had ended in his early

childhood, questioning informants and assembling testimony, Herodotus pioneered judicious source criticism ('this I do not myself believe, but others might do otherwise', 5.86) and argumentative evaluation. At the same time, this 'prose Homer' (as his native city inscribed him three centuries after his death)[7] placed himself emphatically within the traditional role of the epic poet, inventing history while reciting it as poetry. The young Thucydides is said to have wept tears of envy on hearing Herodotus recite his work at Olympia – a revealing if possibly concocted story.[8]

Let's listen to Herodotus on the diversity of human habits and customs before concentrating on his depiction of different forms of government (one, few and many) in action in the Persian Wars. Influenced by the sophistic distinction between *nomos* (law, custom) and *phusis* (nature) introduced in Chapter 1, and by currents in medical writing about the diversity of human physiology, he highlights how many and various are human ways of living across the whole stretch of the world known to him. Most famous are his remarks criticizing the conduct of a Persian overlord in Egypt for violating local religious customs (3.37), observing that all men cling to the belief that their own laws and customs are the best. He tells a story about the earlier Persian king Darius, who staged a confrontation between a group of Greeks whose custom was to cremate bodies, and a group of Indians whose custom was to eat their dead fathers' bodies. The Greeks were revolted by Darius' asking what price they would accept to eat their dead fathers, the Indians by his asking what price they would accept to burn theirs (3.38). Centuries later Montaigne would meditate on these stories, suggesting that, in the face of such

disagreements, it is most reasonable to be sceptical as to whether there is any truth about the best or most just way to live at all. Herodotus draws on other variations in norms in explaining what had enabled the Greeks to fight victoriously over the Persians, while at the same time offering a clear-eyed view of the foibles and prejudices of all sides.

To appreciate the shape of his overarching story, we do best to consider the context in which he told it. Herodotus was writing *about* the Persian Wars of around the time of his birth (499–479 BCE), in which some thirty of the Greek polities had united against the Persians, the Spartans leading and the Athenians making decisive contributions at crucial junctures. But he was writing *during* and after the battles between Athens and Sparta and their allies that dominated his youth and maturity (460–c. 445 BCE; the Peloponnesian War proper broke out in 431 BCE shortly before his death, and would continue until the Athenian defeat in 404) – and *that* struggle pitted Athens and Sparta against each other.

That contemporary struggle makes his *Histories* all the more poignant. For, in the earlier generation he chronicled, Athens and Sparta had stood side by side in solidarity with a selective group of Greek cities in confronting the might of the Persian empire. Yet, while the Spartans had contributed significantly in memorably defiant defeats like Thermopylae and in the ultimately decisive land battle of Plataea, the Athenians had proved themselves indispensable in the important battles of Marathon on land and Salamis at sea. So, while the Spartans had officially led the Greek coalition against Persia, the war actually ended up showcasing and further strengthening the power of the Athenians.

Herodotus acknowledges that his own opinion that Athens had been the saviour of Greece from Persia 'will be odious to the majority' of his contemporaries (7.139). For, unlike most of the writers whose works survive from classical Greece, Herodotus was not Athenian and was not even writing in Athens, though there is some evidence of his work influencing Athenian playwrights from the *Antigone* onwards, as it had already begun to circulate in various stages of completion during his lifetime.[9] Yet his outsider's vantage point made him better able to see how Athens' newfound dominance was feeding her citizens' arrogance and appetite for power. As the Athenians amassed an informal empire, their growing power provoked Spartan fears, which, in turn, led to the skirmishes and breakdown of trust that ended in open warfare between them.

Recounting the story of the Persian Wars as the staccato rhythm of the Peloponnesian War was unfolding was an enterprise that was necessarily loaded with complicated messages. Herodotus' history evokes a lost sense of Greek solidarity. But it also emphasizes the origins of Athenian imperialism, an imperialism that looked uncannily like the Persian aggrandizement against which that earlier generation had fought. And it further showcases a contradiction between the Spartans' devotion to liberty at home and their willingness to crush the liberty of democracies abroad. (The Peloponnesian War would end in 404 BCE with a Spartan-supported coup against democratic Athens, though the democrats successfully counter-attacked within a year and Sparta ultimately tolerated their reinstallation.) We will see below that Athens and Sparta alike emerge as dangerously

hypocritical actors in Herodotus' writing, marked by tensions between the values they claim to uphold and the actions that undermine those values for themselves or for others. But, first, we will turn to the constitutional analysis that Herodotus embeds in his history, in the course of which he articulates the fundamental categories of one/few/many that orient Greek constitutional thinking.

One / Few / Many: Three Kinds of Regime

In addition to the doubled timeframe of writing a history of the Persian Wars with implicit awareness of the later Peloponnesian War, Herodotus engages in another act of dramatic overlay: setting a 'constitutional debate' in 6th-century Persia but charging it with the vocabulary of 5th-century Athens and Greece.[10] One of the most important passages of Greek constitutional thinking, this debate (3.80–82) is described by Herodotus as taking place in 522 BCE among seven Persian aristocrats, who have just conspired to bring down a pair of royal usurpers and are choosing what form of government will rule them next. Three of them give speeches – each favouring one particular kind of constitution and attacking others – that sound in their arguments and vocabulary startlingly like the language of Greeks, especially Athenians, at the time that Herodotus is writing some seventy years later. In fact, the historian signals, perhaps tongue in cheek, that his audience may not find the account of the Persian debate to be historically accurate: 'things were said that by some Greeks are not believed to have been said, but they were' (3.80). Because our interest is in classical Greek

constitutional categories, this seeming anachronism makes them all the more relevant.

The Persian Otanes speaks first, and he begins by criticizing the regime of monarchy under which Persia has lately been governed:

> It seems to me that there can in no way any longer be one king over us, for such rule is neither pleasant or good ... [I] no longer agree to making one of us the single ruler, for rule by one man is neither pleasant nor good ... How could monarchy ever be a well-adjusted schema, since it is possible for the king to do whatever he wants, being unaccountable? (3.80)

Monarchy has two fatal faults, Otanes explains: it breeds arrogance in the ruler, while eliciting envy – said to be fundamental to human nature – in the ruled. Having become arrogant, the monarch will lord it over his subjects, ruling arbitrarily and inconsistently, so as to 'disturb' the 'ancestral customs'. The fundamental flaw in monarchy is its lack of accountability. There is no one with the power to hold the monarch to account, so requiring him to use his powers properly on pain of a penalty if he does not. The criticism is pointed, since democrats in Herodotus' day trumpeted accountability as one of the main achievements of their constitution.[11]

Having skewered monarchical pretensions, Otanes himself advocates rule by 'the majority' (*to plethos*). Because in this model of majority-rule constitution, offices (*archas*) would be assigned by lot and subject to accountability through public examination, no one would be able to

aggrandize power or to use it arbitrarily, as would a monarch. From about the 430s, a 5th-century Greek would have called this regime *demokratia*.[12] Perhaps in a bow to his choice of a 6th-century Persian setting, Herodotus does not put this word into Otanes' mouth (though the historian in his own voice uses it elsewhere, at 6.131). Instead Otanes is made to call the regime of rule by the majority by the name of *isonomia*.

Isonomia derives from the roots for 'equal' and for 'law', so is best understood as 'equality according to the laws'. The link between this model of rule by the majority and what 5th-century Greeks called 'democracy' is evident in the word itself and in many specific features that Otanes' description shares with 5th-century democratic institutions. In particular, the idea of a mathematically equal (*ison*) share to be accorded even to the poor, and the idea of an annual rotation of office-holding, thus preventing the accumulation of arbitrary power, are exactly the points heralded by others praising democracy from roughly the 430s onwards. In Euripides' play *Hiketides* (*Suppliant Women*), probably performed in the late 420s,[13] the legendary Athenian king Theseus (in another act of temporal overlay) speaks in praise of these very same Athenian practices, though they had, in fact, come into force several centuries after he could have lived (if he ever did). Theseus declares:

> There is no rule of one man here: it is a free city.
> The people [*demos*] are lord here, taking turns
> In annual succession, not giving too much to the rich.
> Even a poor man has an equal share [*ison*] (404–8).[14]

And he adds further conditions for such fairness and equality:

> When the laws are written down, then he who is weak
> And he who is rich have equal [*isen*] justice:
> The weaker ones may speak as ill of the fortunate
> As they hear of themselves, and a lesser man
> Can overcome a great one, if he has justice [*dikai*]
> on his side (433–7).[15]

Herodotus' Persian Otanes celebrates an ideal of majority rule as similarly embodying equal justice for rich and poor, the same ideal taken to be quintessentially democratic by 5th- and 4th-century Athenian writers (and ascribed by them also to figures of an earlier time). When Herodotus elsewhere in his writing speaks in his own voice (not that of a Persian aristocrat) in describing 5th-century democratic Athens, he highlights its power as based on *isegorie*, or 'equal speech'.[16] So we see that he understands democracy as very closely connected to the *isonomia* celebrated in his rendering of Otanes' speech.

Otanes' valorization of rule by the many as a non-arbitrary and equal rule of law is immediately attacked by a second Persian debater, Megabyzos. He challenges the virtue of the 'majority' to whom Otanes wished to assign power. For Megabyzos, the majority is a 'useless crowd, than which nothing is more stupid or more arrogant' (3.81). Otanes had charged that the monarch is arrogant and arbitrary; Megabyzos deflects that charge from the monarch and applies it to the *demos*. Why so? Because the mob (as he sees them) 'have not been taught, and do not know what is best and proper'. The

ignorance of the many, compared with the cultivation of the few, would be a recurrent trope in elite arguments, central to the Greek version of the 'rhetoric of reaction'.[17] Herodotus once again puts this trope of 5th-century Greeks in the mouth of a Persian aristocrat – though the elite self-confidence he voices is somewhat timeless. Megabyzos concludes, voicing that recurrent elite pride, that 'it is likely that the best policy should come from the best men' (3.81).

The final Persian speaker is Darius, who changes tack. Each of the three regimes, he says, can make an argument to be the best (3.82). But monarchy is best in practice – if and only the one man ruling is himself 'that one of the good than whom there is no one better' (3.82). For, in that case, his character will equal his judgement, so that Otanes' fears about arrogance and arbitrariness can be set aside. Moreover, the rule of one person has structural advantages over that of any plural group, whether few or many: for groups are inherently subject to division. In oligarchies, this takes the form of 'faction' (*stasis*) among elite rivals; a scourge of the Greek world, this led to the 'heart-eating faction and civil conflict' that one archaic poet had lamented in late 7th-century Mytilene.[18] In democracies, *stasis* characteristically takes the form of a struggle between rich and poor, as the poor work to gain or to maintain political and ideological power in the face of the fatter purses giving significant advantages to the rich. 'Rule by one' could be idealized as a way of avoiding those characteristic conflicts. We turn now to explore rule by one and rule by few in turn – setting aside democracy for a fuller consideration in the next chapter.

RULE BY ONE

The idea of 'rule by one' had several very different associations for Greek thinkers, depending in part on when and where they lived. Certainly they could see an ideal of monarchy on display across the Hellespont in Persia, where hereditary kings wielded plenipotentiary powers over an empire from the 6th century onwards. And they could look back to the legendary kings of the archaic Homeric age, men like Agamemnon and Odysseus, or tell mythical stories about a 'golden age' ruled by a divine or semi-divine king, the 'Age of Kronos'.

Yet some scholars doubt whether there were ever in Greece rulers with the sort of 'absolute, hereditary power' that later generations imagined, as distinct from ritual functions.[19] Nevertheless, there were certainly influential kings scattered about the Greek world, most importantly in Sparta, where the unique, hereditary double kingship sometimes furnished a king with great influence,[20] and in northern Greece, where the kings of Macedon would burst on to a world stage in the 4th century and attract massive attention for their political and military ambitions.[21] Only then would serious Athenian thinkers like Xenophon and Isocrates dedicate treatises to monarchy: the former treating contemporary concerns about the Macedonian king Philip II by veiling them in the figure of the earlier Persian king Cyrus, the latter addressing Philip II more directly. Outside Sparta and Macedon, however, the leading Greek city-states of the classical era lacked the kind of powerful kings that students of the Bible or of later European history might expect.

Instead, in the leading Greek societies from about 650

BCE, 'rule by one' was primarily associated in practice with a ruler described as 'tyrant' (*turannos*, perhaps a loan word from Lydian or another language of Asia Minor). *Turannos* is of course the source of the English word 'tyrant', and by the mid 4th century the pejorative meaning of 'tyrant' is exactly what it would predominantly come to express, in Greek as well. Yet, in the 7th century, the *turannos* was not the founder of a new form of dictatorial regime, nor was he necessarily someone to be reviled. Instead he was a figure who managed, for a time, to dominate a group of oligarchs, bringing them to heel and so taming cycles of conflict and revenge without having hereditary sanction to do so.[22] The *turannos* might even be viewed as benevolent by the people, insofar as he offered them a measure of justice, order and protection from the rapacity of the wealthy. In short, the early *turannos* was more often a figure like an Italian Renaissance doge in the Venetian republic – who assumed power among Venetian nobles as a kind of first among equals – than like a dictator trying to install himself at the pinnacle of an authoritarian regime.

Herodotus is once again an excellent source for this development, describing an older non-Greek figure in categories derived from the Greek debates of the 5th century in which he was writing. Perhaps his story is too pat, but it is instructive. According to the historian, a Mede named Deioces wanted to become a *turannos* (1.96–100; the Medes held a kingdom whose power was first supplemented by Persian dynasties and then supplanted by them). To gain this unrivalled power, he studied the laws defining justice (*dikaiosune*, 1.96) and set himself up in his village as a

judge, winning respect for his fairness. When the people had become dependent on his judicial services, he threatened to withdraw them, so manipulating them into appointing him as king (using the more honorific, ancient title). In that role he seems to have been self-promoting but still fair, maintaining his grip on power by acting as a 'severe guardian of justice' who spied on his citizens in order to ferret out and punish any breach of the laws. So here we have a self-made *turannos* who manoeuvred himself into power in order to act as much like an old-fashioned ideal king as possible (while using new-fangled techniques of surveillance to do so).

The transformation of the idea of the *turannos* into what we mean by 'tyrant' today – a practitioner of cruel, arbitrary and illegitimate government – took place roughly between 525 and 480 BCE, when we see from many sources of evidence that the *polis* community was asserting its identity and authority over the previously warring elites.[23] It was in this period that citizen armies and civic identity put paid to private cycles of vengeance and prohibited the bearing of weapons in sacred civic spaces. History was written, as so often, by the victors: only after the overthrow of a *turannos* would the word be ascribed to him with connotations of condemnation. The reputation of Dionysius I, *turannos* of Syracuse, would not survive Plato's veiled portrait of him in the *Republic* as a rapacious and greedy "tyrant" in a pejorative sense par excellence. The decadent meals of Sicilian seafood and the mixed dramatic genres, including comic performers from abroad, that he sponsored, would become paradigmatic cases for the *Republic*'s criticisms of exesses in food and drink, and poetry and music, for stirring up licentious passions in an undisciplined way[24]

In fact, Dionysius I, like his predecessor Hieron I, was, in his own time and place, a more complex figure. Hieron I triumphed in Greece-wide chariot races and attracted famous playwrights like Aeschylus to his court; Dionysius I became a playwright himself, eventually winning first place in the Lenaea festival competition in Athens (in 367 BCE), and seeking out the company of mathematicians and philosophers. (Some of the Athenians enslaved in Syracuse after their disastrous defeat there in 413 are said to have been freed if they could recite any passage of Euripides by heart – Euripides being another favourite Athenian playwright of the sophisticated Syracusan audience.)[25] In practice and in memory, as in many regimes since, the line between glorious patron of the arts and exploitative overlord was easily blurred.

The transition from benevolent *turannos* to evil tyrant is encapsulated in the history of Athens, where Solon's attempt to establish a moderate regime including rich and poor was succeeded by two generations of *turannoi*. The first, Peisistratus, is described as having been seen as a supporter of the people in a 4th-century text emanating from Aristotle's school, a study of the history and nature of the Athenian constitution called the *Constitution of the Athenians* (recovered in the 19th century, this is the source from which all quotations and citations in this and the next paragraph are drawn).[26] Peisistratus gained and lost plenary power several times, using every trick in the book. First he framed his political enemies for a wound that he had inflicted upon himself, which led the people to vote him a bodyguard; then he used the bodyguard to support him as he 'seized the Acropolis' from the people in 560 BCE (14.1); then he was driven out,

only to return accompanied by a woman dressed up as the goddess Athena, a ruse suggesting sufficient divine sanction to induce the Athenians to take him back (14.4).

Most interesting for present purposes is that he is described (in the same 4th-century source deriving from Aristotle's school) as ruling 'constitutionally rather than tyrannically' (16.2). This later judgement shows that the term 'tyrant' had by that stage accreted so much negative baggage that even the paradigmatic tyrant of Athenian history could no longer be described as such. This is because that tyrant had at the time been seen as ruling moderately and benevolently, establishing local magistrates and even advancing money to the bankrupt (16.1–10). More than a few Athenians seem to have tolerated and even enjoyed his rule at the time.

In contrast, the excoriation of tyranny would, in the memory of later Athenians, attach indelibly to one of the sons of Peisistratus, Hippias. Hippias initially ruled jointly with his brother Hipparchus, who became embroiled in an unrequited love affair leading to a violent insult and quarrel. The erstwhile beloved, who had scorned Hipparchus' advances, conspired with his lover and other citizens to overthrow the Peisistratids. In the midst of a civic procession they thought themselves betrayed, panicked and struck too soon, killing Hipparchus but being killed themselves (one immediately, one after torture) as a result. Hippias began to rule much more harshly, becoming a paradigm of tyranny in the modern pejorative sense, and the Spartans were induced by manipulated oracles to overthrow him and his family, allowing them safe conduct out of Athens once

they had handed over the Acropolis, on which the meeting and sacred places of the city were concentrated. A further struggle between supporters of the tyrants and those of a previously powerful aristocratic family ensued, the Spartan force changing sides to expel the anti-tyrannical faction. But, at that point, the people besieged the tyrannical forces on the Acropolis, recalled the exiles and gave power to one of them, Cleisthenes, who had 'befriended the people' (Hdt. 5.66).

It is with this assertion of popular power and the subsequent legal innovations promoted by Cleisthenes that 'democracy' proper in Athens is widely acknowledged to have begun.[27] The democracy would immortalize the two tyrannicides who had killed Hipparchus – putting up statues of them in the agora and commissioning new ones after the first lot were stolen (ironically, by the Persian Xerxes, a tyrant par excellence in many Greek imaginations). This inscribed an opposition to tyranny at the heart of the democracy, even as the *demos* (the people) began to act abroad – and perhaps at home – as a tyrant itself: taking power to act unaccountably even while demanding accountability of its officers and allies.[28]

By the 5th century, the *turannos* was largely a figure of a discredited past, though powerful individuals might still dream of tyranny or be assiduously suspected of doing so. Once the Persian Great Kings' invasions of the Greek mainland (first by Darius, then by his successor, Xerxes) had been rebuffed and rival alliances began to form around Sparta and Athens, the live constitutional choice was between oligarchy (of which Sparta embodied a rather peculiar kind) and democracy (for which Athens proudly stood). Before turning

to a full consideration of democracy in the next chapter, we will flesh out the oligarchical constitution and the peculiar case of Sparta, and then sum up the contrast between oligarchy and democracy drawn out by Herodotus from the course of Spartan and Athenian behaviour during the Persian Wars.

RULE BY A FEW: OLIGARCHY

Oligarchy means the rule of some or a few, which usually implies their rule over the many, in the sense of a body of poor native-born citizens whom they exclude from offices and civic honours, and sometimes even from citizenship.[29] Among themselves, oligarchs enjoyed political equality with one another, although this did not stop them from often jockeying for more subtle forms of superiority. But they were typically united in denying such equality to non-citizens at home (usually including some group of the poor) and to subjugated groups abroad. Thus they shared with democracies the ideal of equality while disputing the boundaries of those entitled to share in it.

One could be a citizen without being eligible to hold office, or, at least, every office. That distinction was especially important in oligarchies, where a sliding scale of wealth was commonly used to measure out those entitlements. In the 4th-century text *Rhetorica ad Alexandrum*, we find the following prescription for oligarchies:

> In the case of oligarchies, the laws should assign the offices on an equal footing to all those sharing in the constitution [*tois tes politeias metechousi*]. Selection for most of the offices should be by lot, but for the most important [*tas ...*

megistas] it should be by vote, under oath, with a secret
ballot and very strict regulations. The penalties enacted for
those attempting to insult any of the citizens [*ton politon*]
should in an oligarchy be very heavy, as the multitude
[*plethos*] resents insolent treatment more than it is
annoyed by exclusion from offices [*ton archon*].[30]

In other words, according to this account, the multitude in
an oligarchy should be 'citizens', but they should be excluded
from the 'offices' that are assigned 'on an equal footing to all
those sharing in the constitution', i.e., to the select few who
share in governing the oligarchy.

We see here that both oligarchies and democracies could
make use of lottery, although the next chapter will show that
lotteries for certain purposes were especially associated with
democracies. Still, in oligarchies, according to this author,
the 'most important' (*megistas*) office-holders should be
elected by vote (this was actually true of some important
offices in democratic Athens as well).[31] Both oligarchies and
democracies used property qualifications as well as election,
in different ways and degrees. The line between them could
be a fine one in terms of political mechanics. But it was more
a matter of political culture. Oligarchies cultivated greater
deference and sought to limit and restrain forms of popular participation – as in the 'Melian Dialogue' discussed in
Chapter 1, which takes place between a group of oligarchic
office-holders and the Athenian ambassadors, after the oligarchs refuse to let the ambassadors address the popular
'crowd'.[32] Democracies, by contrast, tended to insist on stringent forms of popular accountability and judgement even

when allowing some office-holders to be elected or selected from among the ranks of the wealthier alone.

Sparta: A Peculiar Oligarchy?

Whether Sparta should be classified as an oligarchy is a complex question. Certainly, in their alliances and tactics during the Peloponnesian War, the Spartans were generally far friendlier to oligarchies and supported their installation or maintenance abroad where possible. But Sparta was also a kind of monarchy – a unique dual monarchy, as noted earlier. Yet, in a further twist, its kings exercised primarily military powers, while other important powers were exercised, respectively, by: a council of elders elected (by acclamation) for life; five annually elected 'ephors' (the most important public officials) and some other officials; and a popular assembly. While Greek observers continually had recourse to the one/few/many typology, introduced by Herodotus, to explain Sparta, it was clear that the Spartan regime was unique and did not fit neatly into any one simple constitutional category in terms of its political arrangements.[33]

Nevertheless, one can argue that the Spartan regime had crucial oligarchical tendencies, including its proclivity to support oligarchies abroad. Its relatively 'few' citizens – in the 5th century, it had a remarkably small citizen body of some 8,000 for the sprawling size of its territory – regarded each other as full equals and 'similars' (*homoioi*). That small band of citizens dominated a much larger body (though we have no exact numbers) of harshly exploited agricultural labourers who were among the local peoples whom the invading Spartans had conquered (while they allowed others

to live as free but subordinated *perioikoi*, or, roughly, 'inhab-itants of the area roundabout', meaning the countryside out-side the city-centre).[34] Thus there was in a sense no 'many' in the Spartan political community, since the greatest number of inhabitants of the territories they ruled were collectively subjugated by and made subservient to the Spartan citizen body, as 'helots,' not included as citizens. Fear of their revolt fed a vicious cycle of military training to intensify and main-tain exploitation, prompting, in turn, fear of a revolt against this brutality, and so on. It was the stark, constant demand that this oppression by military power be maintained that seems to have fostered the unique Spartan way of life that so vividly embodies the link between *politeia* as political consti-tution and *politeia* as constitution in the sense of way of life.

The Spartan *politeia* was attributed in all its fundamentals to Lycurgus, a possibly legendary figure who, if he lived, did so probably in the 7th century BCE. He was the guardian and uncle of an under-age king, not a king himself, but he arro-gated the role of lawgiver to himself. Yet all our main sources for it are from centuries later (Herodotus and Thucydides in the 5th century, Xenophon – whose sons were educated in the Spartan regime – in the 4th, Plutarch in the 1st to 2nd centuries CE).[35] This is problematic for describing the classi-cal period of Sparta, for, although all generations of Spartans insisted on the total continuity of their laws with the laws of Lycurgus, in fact there is considerable evidence that many of those laws were made up after the fact in recurrent waves of political change. Still, we can safely say that the Spartan constitution centred on preparing its men – and its women – for war, including: the ongoing military campaigns to suppress

the helots; the defensive and sometimes offensive expeditions abroad; and, incidentally, mercenary military roles undertaken by many individual Spartans for other states.

Before graduating to the common meals shared by the military companies,[36] all Spartan boys underwent a long and arduous training process (*agoge*), focused especially on athletic endurance and on obedience, and directed by city officials. This emphasis on public education contrasted starkly with the private educational courses for which only the wealthiest Athenian families paid. Spartan girls, too, were trained by the city in athletic and even military pursuits, and were entitled to inherit property in their own right; their Athenian counterparts were not. As this shows, Spartans did have private property: the ideology of equality among the *homoioi* did not prevent inequalities of wealth, to the point that men lost their civic privileges when they became unable to afford to contribute to the common meals as required. But Lycurgus was said to have banned the use of gold and silver coinage to prevent the Spartans from accumulating luxuries from other cities.[37]

These varied provisions were thought to fashion remarkably self-denying citizen paragons, who would inspire awe in Plutarch and other later writers. One of the most famous tales related by Plutarch involved the Spartan practice of depriving boys of sufficient food at certain stages of their upbringing, so as to teach them to do whatever was necessary to survive, while at the same time punishing them severely if they should be caught stealing. Hence the story of a Spartan boy said to have hidden a stolen fox under his cloak, who,

rather than betray the fact that he had acquired stolen booty, let the fox gnaw his intestines until he died (*Apophth.*[38] 234a–b). Other accounts in Plutarch describe a Spartan mother whose five sons were away at war, whose first question to the messenger was not their fate, but rather whether or not the city had won; and, even more startlingly, a Spartan mother who killed her son for having returned alive to report that all the other men had (more honourably) died in battle (*Lacae.* 241c). These stories – fictional though they may be – would fascinate later ages and reinforce the image of Sparta as a uniquely politically virtuous city.

Spartan virtue was one in which the value of liberty played a central role. One Spartan woman who had the misfortune to be sold as a slave was purportedly 'asked by the auctioneer what skills she had' – to which she answered proudly: '"To be free"' (*Lacae.* 242d). That freedom was understood as combining the independence of the city with the equality enjoyed by the Spartiates among themselves. No one else could tell them what to do; they decided for themselves. Yet, paradoxically, they protected that ability to decide for themselves by subjecting themselves collectively to the most stringent forms of discipline. The liberty of the *politeia* as a constitution and the liberty of the individual citizen derived equally from the broader maintenance of the *politeia* in a certain special way of life.

The maintenance of the way of life in every detail – scrutinizing military preparedness, marriage practices, wealth possessed – was entrusted to five annually elected officials known as ephors. Their tasks included overseeing

the training of the youth, overseeing property regulations, and generally disciplining Spartans to live according to the demanding individual and collective values of their constitution. That idea – of a political constitution exercising direct oversight of values and ways of life – would become linked in the minds of later thinkers with the Roman institution of censors, who could demote men from their rank and office for flagrant violation of expected mores, insofar as they were expected to be models for the importance of virtue in public life. To the values of equality, liberty, justice and accountability at the heart of the constitutional orderings that we have been exploring so far, we may now add the idea of Virtue, to be further explored in its formulation by Socrates and Plato in Chapter 4.

RULE BY THE MANY: AN OLIGARCHICAL VIEW

While the next chapter will be devoted to the *politeia* of rule by the many, which the Greeks also called democracy, a good bridge between oligarchy and democracy is provided by the fact that some of our most eloquent analyses of Greek democracy come from its oligarchical opponents. Thus we may begin to consider rule by the many by seeing how it was viewed in the eyes of the oligarchs. An amazing text offers just this kind of perspective. It was written by an unknown sympathizer with oligarchy living in Athens, addressing kindred ideological spirits at home and abroad, perhaps around 425–424 BCE (at a time when Athens was still largely successful in its sparring with Sparta).[39] The author – now widely known as the 'Old Oligarch', though he may well not have been old in age at all – takes a firm stand on a question that

we have yet to consider. Is 'democracy' to be understood as the rule of 'all', or the rule of the 'many' – as opposed to (and potentially oppressive of) the wealthy few?

Because *demos* can mean both 'the people' as a whole and also 'the common people' (the 'many' or 'the crowd' or 'the majority', as opposed to the 'few'), the word itself is marked by this ambiguity. Democratic politicians and rhetoricians can exploit the ambiguity to argue that the interests of the people as a whole cannot be opposed to, or overlook, the interests of the common people. But oligarchic politicians and sympathizers like the 'Old Oligarch' see the ambiguity in a sharper light. They argue that, while democrats pretend to pursue the interests of all, a 'democracy' is merely a cover for using political power to advance the interests of the many at the expense of the few.

In ancient Greece, as in many regimes since then, the 'many' were, on the whole, poorer and less educated than the 'few'. (That was especially true in Athens after Solon shifted the basis of certain political privileges from birth to wealth.) Like Megabyzos in Herodotus' 'Persian Debate', the 'Old Oligarch' stresses poverty and lack of education as the reasons for the moral and political failings of the poor. These voices of elite partisanship do not naturalize the failings of the poor, but they insist that, given the economic facts, the poor simply will be less well educated and so less virtuous and moral as a result. As the 'Old Oligarch' puts it: 'within the best men there is the least amount of licentiousness and injustice, and the most scrupulousness over what is valuable; whereas within the *demos* there is the greatest ignorance, indiscipline and worthlessness'. Why? Because 'poverty

tends to lead them into shameful behaviour, and in the case of some people their lack of education and their ignorance is the result of their lack of money' (1.5).[40]

Smug elites might assume that a regime governed by such ignorant men is doomed to fail even in meeting its own goals. But the 'Old Oligarch' disagrees. Starting from the view that the goal of the democracy is to maintain the power of the common people, he insists that the democracy does remarkably well in arranging matters to achieve its goal – however much it may offend elite sensibilities in so doing. By allowing anyone to speak in the assembly, the democrats ensure that those who do speak are interested in promoting the popular advantage (1.6–7), but, meanwhile, they restrict the most important offices to the wealthy, who are better educated in choosing the means to achieve the goals set by those spokesmen for popular interests. Democracy is not doomed to fail, however much the rich may not like it – as the 'Old Oligarch' himself does not. He says squarely that he does 'not approve' of the democracy because it privileges the well-being of the low and base over the better sort, even while reluctantly admiring its longevity (1.1).[41]

To this aristocratically minded critic, the democratic relationship between rich and poor is a relationship of injustice. It is unjust for the better sort to be ruled by the worse. From the point of view of an oligarch, democracy is an oppression of the few by the many. From the point of view of a democrat, oligarchy is an oppression of the many by the few. The struggle between these two kinds of regime came to define the political choices of the Greek cities in the classical period.

Conclusion: Comparing Constitutional Strengths and Weaknesses

Let's conclude this account of constitutions by returning to Herodotus. For having laid out the set-piece 'constitutional debate' among proponents of rule by one, by some and by all that we have been examining, Herodotus in his work dramatizes the strengths and weaknesses of each kind of regime as they manifested themselves during the Persian Wars. For example, when Xerxes, the Great King of Persia, is deciding whether to send a major expedition against Greece, he is said to be 'over-persuaded' (*anapeise*) by self-serving advisers (7.6). This subtly demonstrates a weakness in the case made by Darius for monarchy in the constitutional debate, relying as it does on the monarch being a person of outstanding character and ability even while claiming to appeal to 'practice' rather than merely to 'argument'. For, as with Xerxes, monarchs who are less outstanding, or perhaps even more worryingly, the very best, may be led astray by bad advice. Yet Herodotus is alert to the very same vulnerability in democracy (in this case, the kind of bad group decision-making that Megabyzos had predicted). Having resolved to be at war with Persia, the Athenians are 'over-persuaded' (*anapeisthentes* – a form of the very same word applied to Xerxes) by a representative of Miletus – one of the eastern Greek cities at most risk of Persian domination – to send twenty ships to aid the Ionian alliance to which Miletus belongs (5.97). Vulnerability to honeyed rhetoric is a weakness of democracies as it is of monarchies.

Herodotus thus subtly suggests that no one type of regime – neither monarchy nor oligarchy nor democracy – offers a guarantee of good rule. Flattery and rhetoric are dangers of courts and closed oligarchical circles every bit as much as they are dangers of democracies – something that Herodotus, with his peripheral position in respect of each, was unusually well placed to appreciate. Yet, if democracy and monarchy both have vulnerabilities, some of them surprisingly shared, Herodotus shows us that oligarchy is at least in one respect in a weaker position still: it is beset by a fundamental contradiction. Oligarchical regimes desire liberty as independence for themselves from foreign domination. But they deny liberty to the many, at home, where they exclude them from citizenship, and abroad, where they are intolerant of democratic regimes that empower the many and subordinate the 'few' who are the oligarchs' ideological (and often actual) kin.

Herodotus puts his finger on this contradiction in the repeated behaviour of Sparta. As we saw, Sparta had been manipulated into invading Athens in 512 BCE, and again in 510, to expel the *turannos* Hippias. But when Cleisthenes put an end to the ensuing turmoil by decisively setting up new and more democratic institutions than ever before, the Spartans regretted their aid and tried twice, though ultimately unsuccessfully, to topple the new regime. When they proposed to their allies in about 504 to try for a third time to restore Hippias as tyrant, a speaker from Corinth named Socles identified a flagrant contradiction in Spartan policy: the Spartan proposal was 'destroying the rule of equals' (*isokratia* – an ideal common to Sparta and Athens, despite

their different understandings of who counted as equals). Instead the Spartans were bringing back 'tyranny' into the cities (5.92a).

For Socles, this was tantamount to inverting the order of the heavens and earth, so as to have 'men inhabit the sea and fishes inhabit the place that was previously the place of men' (5.92a), because it so contradicted the ideal of political liberty that Sparta prided itself to hold:

> For if it seems to you beneficial that the cities be ruled by tyrants, first set up a tyrant among yourselves and then aim to do so for the others. But now, you yourselves having never experienced tyrants, and guarding with the greatest care lest they should arise in Sparta, you abuse your allies [by imposing tyrants on them; the Spartan allies at this time officially included Athens] (5.92).

Liberty as a constitutional value at home too often turns into despotism abroad. This is a characteristically oligarchic failing here. It is, however, akin to a democratic one, the same one that we saw in Thucydides' presentation of the 'Melian Dialogue' discussed at the end of Chapter 1, where the democratic Athenians insist on their untrammelled power to do what they like with the Melians, claiming that justice is not binding between the weak and the strong. Greek constitutional thinking was in the hands of the historians a matter of ideology as well as reality. Regimes prided themselves on the special ways in which they controlled power and achieved justice, equality or liberty, but their victims or observers could always ask, at what price, paid by whom, and with a strategy successful for how long? The official values

trumpeted by any one regime are always likely to sit uneasily with the realities of its practice. At the same time, each regime is subject to characteristic flaws as well as characteristic features of the citizens that it fosters, in its constitutional political arrangements and in its constitutional way of life. In the next chapter we will examine in some depth the distinctive constitution (in both senses) of the Athenian democracy.

Democracy

DEMOCRACY

Greek democracy was something new under the sun – but
not in the sense that a role for the common people in government, even in the form of an assembly, was unknown
in Greece or in the wider world up to the 5th century BCE;
forms of assembly and consultation are widely attested in
Greek history and in surrounding societies with which they
interacted. What was new in 5th-century Athens was that
ordinary people, including the poorest of the citizens, came
to control (and not merely to be consulted by) the powers of
government. They did so by deciding policy in the assembly;
judging disputes among citizens in the courts; and scrutinizing (in the assembly, council and courts) the doings of
officials, many of whom were themselves selected by lottery or election among a wide swathe of the public. Putting
these functions together, the 'people' – the *demos* – exercised
a plenipotentiary 'power' (*kratos*), which explains the new
coinage of the word *demokratia*, appearing first in relation to
Athens, and then being proudly claimed as a name for dozens
of polities dotted across the Mediterranean and the Greek
mainland that adopted similar regimes. What caused these
developments is a matter for historical debate about the
relative importance of factors like changing military tactics

(naval ships that could be crewed by the poor becoming as important as the armies that had historically depended on men wealthy enough to provide their own armour and in some cases horses) and other social and economic changes at the time. Our focus here is on the political arrangements of the 'democracies' that were created, in many cases emerging from political turmoil in tyrannies or oligarchies and the assertion of popular power in the consequent struggles. What did it mean to be a regime in which the people – the common people, the poor people, the ordinary people – held the balance of power?

In the previous chapter, we met a range of Greek constitutional regimes that were named according to who held the offices (*tas archas*) and so ruled (*archein*) in the city: in a *monarchia*, one person held office (the meaning of *mon-* is 'one'); in an *oligarchia*, an elite few did so (the meaning of *oligo-* is 'few'). In democracy, by contrast, the power of the people was multifaceted and supreme, not limited to the holding of offices – and indeed there might be some offices that the people were not eligible to hold. Rather than being focused on office-holding alone, democratic power (*kratos*) stretched from direct exercise of decision-making, to judging almost all legal and political disputes, to staffing some of the offices, and finally to holding accountable all officials however chosen. Thus democracy was not just another form of constitution distributing offices to certain people; it was a new kind of constitution that distributed power in new ways.

Greek democracies may be considered popular sovereignty in a radical sense: they gave new and old forms of

power to the people, designating as citizens a wide swathe of the free male native inhabitants of a city, including most or all of the poor, low status and worst educated.[1] Equality in the means of exercising or controlling power constituted political liberty, insofar as the most important actions of the high-ups were in some way subject to popular control. And it generated new forms of creativity, as previously suppressed people began to explore and to create in unprecedented artistic and intellectual genres. Fostering ambitious aspirations for personal gain, learning and civic pride in its citizens' way of life, democracies allowed wealth inequalities to flourish while insisting that they not be convertible into untrammelled political power bases independent of democratic control. Wealthy citizens could enjoy the prestige of largesse, even of commanded largesse (in the special taxes and duties levied on the wealthiest), but they could not use their wealth to secure influence in any way that could be fully insulated from the powers of the people.

Because of its role as the original, largest and most influential democracy, and as an economic and cultural powerhouse of the Greek world – its coins were the most prized, its dramatic competitions highly prestigious – the city-state of Athens best encapsulates the story of Greek democracy.[2] Fortunately its cultural and political ferment has left us a disproportionately large record of evidence. The story starts with Athens' gradual ascendancy through the early 5th century in the aftermath of playing a crucial role in decisive battles against Persia, and then its decades-long clash with Sparta, ending with ignominious defeat in 404 BCE.

In the wake of that defeat (as also seven years earlier), oligarchic conspirators achieved a brief coup before democracy was restored. The democracy then regrouped, making important constitutional and legal changes just before and during the 4th century, until the aftershocks of Alexander the Great's imperial conquests led to its abolition (later attempts at recovery failed). At that time, the new Macedonian overlords insisted on the imposition of a high property qualification of 2,000 drachmas for citizenship, at a time when one drachma was a day's wages for an ordinary worker.[3] It was the exclusion of the poor from political citizenship that meant democracy was at an end.

The Beginnings of Athenian Democracy

If exclusion of the poor from citizenship was the end of the democracy, what does that tell us about how to understand its beginning and its development?

When did Athenian democracy begin? In Chapter 2, we gave the best short answer to that question: it began in 508/7 BCE, with the reforms of Cleisthenes following the popular revolt that swept out the tyrants and swept him into power.[4] But, in fact, that short answer is unsatisfactory for two reasons. On the one hand, the Athenians did not consider the democracy to have been set up in one fell swoop, in the way that the Spartans credited their own regime to the legislative acts of Lycurgus. When analyses of Athenian political history were offered, as in the analytical narrative history *Constitution of the Athenians*, mentioned in Chapter 2, we find enumerated not one but eleven distinct Athenian

HIGHLIGHTS OF ATHENIAN HISTORY

7TH CENTURY BCE

| 621 | Draco's written law code |

6TH CENTURY BCE

594	Solon becomes archon and begins proto-democratic reforms
c. 546–510	Peisistratids rule as tyrants, overthrown in 510 by Spartans who support establishment of an oligarchy
508	Restoration of democracy versus oligarchs; Cleisthenes' reforms

5TH CENTURY BCE

490	Athens leads a defeat of Persia in battle of Marathon (on land)
487	Archon selection by lot begins
480	Athens leads a defeat of Persia in battle of Salamis (at sea)
462	Ephialtes' democratic reforms

460–445	Wars of the Athenian Delian League versus Sparta and its allies
431–404	Peloponnesian War between Athenian- and Spartan-led alliances
430	Plague in Athens
429	Death of Pericles
404	Surrender of Athens to Sparta: Oligarchy of Thirty Tyrants
403	Democracy restored, Athenians pass amnesty

4TH CENTURY BCE

399	Trial and execution of Socrates; Plato leaves Athens
384	Plato turns forty; returns to Athens and founds Academy
370s	Plato may write the *Republic*; further wars between Sparta and Athens
338	Athens loses battle of Chaeronea; Macedonian domination
322–321	Athenian democracy extinguished by Macedonian-imposed property qualification for citizenship (though later briefly revived)

constitutions. These stretch from the legendary days of the settlement of Athens by Ion, on to Theseus, and so on through better-documented historical changes to the time of writing.

In the approach taken in that constitutional account, democracy was not achieved at any single moment. Instead, it emerged gradually, in four key stages. Solon's constitution was the one 'in which was born the beginning of democracy'; Cleisthenes' constitution 'was more democratic than that of Solon'; Ephialtes took a further step by 'putting down the Areopagus' (the elite court that had previously arrogated government to itself). The eleventh and final constitution, from 403 BCE, is described as involving 'the people taking part with one another in power', such that in the late 4th century 'the *demos* has made itself sovereign in every respect, determining everything by decrees of the *ekklesia* [assembly] and by decisions of the *dikasteria* [law-courts with popular juries], in which the *demos* is the power' (all, AP 41.2).

That sequence remains a broadly helpful guide. Solon indeed laid the basis or preconditions for democracy, above all by abolishing debt-slavery, as we saw in Chapter 1, but also by opening most prosecution and defence appeals to the popular courts in place of the Areopagus, and by according the poorest citizens' group 'a share in the *ekklesia* and the *dikasteria* only [meaning, not in holding the offices]' (AP 7.3). Having been accorded a leading role in Athens by the citizens who had expelled the tyrants (as we saw in Chapter 2), Cleisthenes established a more properly democratic

constitution primarily by reconfiguring the Athenians into a set of new political identities: ten tribes stretching from sea to city-centre and divided into local 'demes' that became administrative and cultic centres.[5] Ephialtes, for his part, was an influential Athenian who opposed elite advocacy of solidarity with Sparta in the 460s BCE and went on to undermine elite hegemony by depriving the Areopagus of most of its remaining powers before being assassinated by an unknown hand. By suppressing the powers of the Areopagus, he established, in effect, a different kind of democracy (though much about his actions is uncertain).

Ephialtes' successor as leader of the more radical democratic faction in Athens was Pericles, famous as the long-serving general and leader who encouraged Athens at the outset of the Peloponnesian War. Although he is not mentioned in the list of eleven constitutions, the *Constitution of the Athenians* tells us elsewhere that Pericles, too, introduced important democratic measures, including a new definition of Athenian citizenship requiring a citizen-mother as well as a citizen-father.[6] While that measure might sound more restricting than democratizing, it was aimed at curbing the elite's habits of inter-city kin and friendship marriages, which, in the eyes of democrats, watered down elite allegiance to Athens to suspiciously low levels. (Ironically, the Athenians would eventually make a special grant of citizenship to Pericles' illegitimate son with the brilliant foreign-born non-citizen Aspasia.)[7]

In sum, Solon instituted the foundations of Athenian democratic equality; Cleisthenes (followed by Pericles),

of democratic identity; and Ephialtes (building on laws of Solon and Cleisthenes), of democratic accountability. These names, of course, are illustrative only. None of these laws could have been passed without support among the diversity of the people, and none of these men could have held power without popular support. Acting collectively and accumulating many different kinds of power (but not all or unlimited powers), the Athenian *demos* – including a dominant voice for the poor majority but also distinct political roles for the wealthy elites – were able to resist tyranny, defeat oligarchic conspirators two times running, and, for a time, consolidate and dominate a far-flung empire. They did all this by exercising the fundamental democratic powers to decide, to judge and to hold accountable.

Democratic Ideas in Action

How and where did the people exercise these powers? The most obvious site in which the people decided was in the assembly, which was open to all (male) citizens who chose to attend and vote. While most Greek regimes, democratic as well as non-democratic, had an assembly, the remarkable thing in Athens and in certain other democracies was that assembly participation was not restricted in any way by wealth or by status among those who enjoyed citizenship. The assembly site, on the Pnyx hill, held 6,000 citizens (somewhat more than one tenth of the male citizen population at its height in the 430s, probably less than one fifth after the defeat of 404 BCE); in cases when 6,000

was the minimum quorum required for a decision on the status of particular citizens, the assembly would meet in the marketplace instead. It was open to any male citizen to attend on any day that he chose. More than that, any one of them could in principle decide to speak (or, at least, put themselves forward to be called upon if time allowed): the assembly sessions were opened by a herald asking, 'Who wishes to speak?' But it was far from the case that any and every Athenian would respond to that invitation. Most people probably never spoke once in their whole lifetime. Instead, the speakers were self-selected, drawn from a small group of ambitious men who aimed to make a name in the public arena.

These men, the 'speakers' (*rhetores*), were the closest thing to professional politicians in Athens. Their political roles were precarious: unless they were separately elected to a one-year term as a general (as were, for example, Aristides, Themistocles and Pericles) they held no formal office. Their influence and power depended in large part on their next speech, and even when the people accepted their advice, they might resent it as a bitter pill to swallow. Those who risked speaking in the assembly knew that they could be rejected, punished or cast aside at any moment by the people whom they were trying to lead. If the policies they advocated failed, they themselves were likely to suffer as a result.

One speaker in Thucydides' history, Diodotus, bitterly points out the asymmetry in the workings of the Athenian assembly (3.43): the speakers are accountable (legally) for

the advice they give, he observes, but the listeners are not accountable to anyone for the decisions they make. Speakers were accountable for the advice they gave in the sense that they were subject to possible prosecution at the hands of anyone who thought that they had given advice contrary to the laws or (in the 4th century) disadvantageous to the city. The assembled multitude, however, were not accountable for their votes. Assembly votes were counted by hand and only the total number was recorded, without names being noted except in the memory of those who happened to be sitting nearby.

Whereas anyone could turn up in the assembly to vote, the jurors in the large popular courts that gained most judicial powers from the 460s onwards had to be sworn in at the beginning of the year as prospective jurors. After that, any one of them could choose to turn up at the law-courts on the days they were sitting, and the jurors for the day (and eventually for each case) were chosen by a system of lotteries. The jurors were even less accountable for their individual votes than the assemblymen, since, from at least 458 BCE, they voted by ballots that were meant to be secret – though their having sworn an oath to the gods to judge righteously when being inducted into the panel must have enforced significant moral accountability. They did not debate or discuss their verdicts, but simply heard the speeches on both sides and cast their secret votes. This served to protect their independence of judgement while also protecting the defendants whose fate they were judging from any contamination of their judgements by social contagion.[8]

Any citizen empanelled as a juror could judge; any citizen could also prosecute. Prosecution was an open sport for those Athenians who wished to join in. Most prosecutions were brought by lay people, either by putative victims on their own behalf, or in certain cases by someone connected with them or bringing a suit for the public benefit of righting a wrong done by one person to another. In these ways, ordinary citizens had the power to initiate political action, even if most exercised the power of evaluation far more often than the power of initiation.

The agenda for the assembly, along with other matters like the reception of ambassadors and the election of certain officials, was managed by a body called the Council of 500. Each of the ten tribes supplied fifty men, chosen by lot from volunteers (who may have had their arms twisted to stand if numbers were scarce), who served for a single year. The council voted by a show of hands, like the ordinary assemblies when making general decisions; a variation of the jurors' secret ballot procedure was used when making decisions about the good standing of individuals.[9] Unlike assemblymen and jurors, councillors were deemed to be holders of offices, meaning that they had to be aged at least thirty and were liable to be scrutinized before taking office for their good standing in relation to their general civic duties, and to be audited upon leaving office for their financial and general probity in having managed its affairs.

Along with the 500 councillors, there were about 700 annually serving officials in this sense in Athens each year in the 4th century, collectively totalling about 8 per cent of those men over thirty serving at any one time.[10]

Officially, however, the ban on office-holding by the poorest Athenians, imposed by Solon, was never overturned, and a few offices were explicitly reserved for the wealthiest tiers. Whether or not the ban on the service of the poorest was entirely a 'dead letter', as some historians have suggested, its nominal persistence makes it hard to see office-holding as the ultimate key to democratic power.[11] The rotation and widespread (if not universal) participation in holding offices is certainly impressive, but still more significant is the role of the whole people, including the poorest, in judging proposals put before them in the assembly and in the courts alike.

The assembly met at its peak forty times a year; the council every day with the exception of certain holidays; the courts possibly as many as 300 times a year. Well over 100 localities, called demes, also had their own assemblies and courts, offering further sites of active political engagement for those who chose to be involved. For it was possible to be a 'quiet Athenian', largely keeping away from politics except when required by one's deme or when unwillingly embroiled in a court case.[12] Still, Athenian democracy put a premium on showing up to play one's part, or at least on being willing to do so. The assembly included all who chose to attend on a given day; the courts and the council were drawn randomly from those who had had their names put forward (so, too, were the jurors for the civic–religious drama competitions, chosen randomly from names nominated by each tribe). In each of these venues, the participating Athenians exercised the power of sovereign decision-making, free to decide however they chose, judging the speeches or performances given

by others when (as in most cases) they did not elect to venture a speech themselves.

That sovereign power of judgement meant that the multitude – including the poorest among them – were numerically and also politically and ideologically dominant over the wealthy in key respects.[13] The poor saw themselves as part of the city as a whole, but the wealthy elite were prone to seeing themselves as a special group to whom the power of the poor was characteristically opposed. Not all of those in the elite of wealth or birth shared the disdain for the common people of the 'Old Oligarch' whom we met in Chapter 2; nor were all those in the political elite wealthy or well-born. In democratic Athens, as in democracies today, such advantages tended to cluster together and foster one another, but there are always exceptions. Among important leaders of the 5th century, Aristides was born moderately wealthy but died poor; while Cleisthenes and Pericles, part of the aristocratic Alcmaeonid family that had dominated Athens before the tyranny and claimed a role in overturning it, aligned themselves politically with the poor multitude.

Others without birth or inherited wealth behind them made their names as public speakers or generals, joining this self-selected coterie of political leaders who put themselves forward for popular favour and lived or died by the people's decision. Whether self-made or landed, whether drawing on power wholly from political success or supplemented by wealth, Athenian elites had no entrenched and independent collective political base. They had special duties, and could make certain opportunities for themselves, but their fate was ultimately in crucial ways in the hands of the people.

The Athenian Democratic
politeia as a Way of Life

Just as in the rival kinds of regimes we explored in Chapter 2, in Athens, too, the *politeia* in the sense of political arrangements and the *politeia* in the sense of a way of life mutually reinforced one another. The political power of the *demos* gave meaningful freedom and equality to even the poorest landless beggar who was a citizen. It made him acutely sensitive to any form of disrespect, and made many eager to use the legal system to redress such injuries. One Athenian's speechwriter described the indignation motivating his client's prosecution of another citizen thus: 'it is not because of any physical harm from his blows, but because I suffered insult and dishonour that I am come seeking justice, for it is proper for free men to be most angered by this and for the greatest penalty to apply.'[14] Ordinary citizens were potentially vulnerable to broader charges, too, if they were accused of having neglected or mishandled civic–religious or political–military duties, though the self-selected political leaders were more vulnerable to such accusations.

Athens offered far more than its formal institutions as arenas in which to explore these questions. Political life spilled over into the marketplace, the gymnasium, the symposia or dinner parties, at the last of which some enjoyed raucous music and lewd dancing while others aspired to more elevated conversation. Citizens gathered at a whole host of annual festivals. Perhaps the greatest was the Panathenaea, where the women of Athens displayed a giant cloak woven every four years for the statue of the patron

goddess Athena. At every festival, men – and perhaps some women also – sat in rapt attention as tragic trilogies (each festooned with a fourth satyr-play) and individual comedies competed for prizes awarded by dramatic jurors chosen by procedures akin to those of the law-courts. Travelling rhapsodists regaled company gatherings with the epic poetry of Homer and Hesiod; Olympic victors were honoured at public dinners alongside visiting ambassadors.

Although women mostly stayed at home practising the domestic arts, a few courtesans consorted with leading public men at the symposia, where men gathered for entertainment ranging from the bawdy to the philosophically sublime, with music performed by male and female musicians from Athens or abroad. In the marketplace, artisans displayed their wares, slaves jostled foreigners and country farmers enjoyed their occasional rapt-eyed outings, marvelling at the glories of the Parthenon constructed with the treasures paid into a common defence league by Athens' allies. Old men sat about the entrances to the law-courts, while younger bustling men, speechwriters and rhetoricians pushed by. In all these settings, formal and informal, the power of the *demos* to set the terms of debate in the city was palpable, if sometimes – especially by elite critics – bitterly resented.[15]

The Athenian Democratic Record: Success or Failure?

The Athenians gave themselves bad press among their own contemporaries soon enough. Certainly, they had gloried in

their triumphs at Marathon and Salamis, the latter prepared by their having heeded the advice of Themistocles to invest newfound mining wealth in the building of warships – an example of the supposedly ignorant *demos* (in the eyes of the 'Old Oligarch') making a prudent and farsighted decision. But those victories sowed the seeds of further *hubris*, as the Athenians started to lord it over their allies, using common defence funds to adorn Athens architecturally, and eventually requiring the allies to use only Athenian currency, weights and measures.

In the process, a democracy acquired an empire, as the regime dedicated to freedom and equality at home confronted the temptation to exploit others abroad. The temptation was complex. The Athenians were still inclined to side with democratic regimes abroad against oligarchical interventions, for example. But they were also self-interested, easily turning vituperative against democracies and oligarchies alike that had crossed their ambitions or thwarted their will. Having gained sway over their allies and having benefited so richly from that hegemony, the Athenian democrats largely accepted that for the *demos* to live large at home meant (regularly, perhaps necessarily) the doing of injustice to others abroad.

The 'Melian Dialogue' that we considered in Chapter 1 is one example of this; the Athenian ambassadors to Melos explained that Athens was ruled in its decisions not by justice but by its own advantage, since it was strong enough to be able to enforce that. Two other examples, also from the heart of the Peloponnesian War, are also worth considering. In the pages of Thucydides, the Athenian ex-general

who turned himself into an historian of that war to learn a lesson in political understanding, we find a sober analysis of Athens' position by the general and orator Pericles, who is credited by the historian with outstanding judgement and moderation (2.65). Shortly before dying of the plague in 429 BCE, leaving Athens embroiled in the war with Sparta that he had encouraged, Pericles in his last speech (as recounted by Thucydides) acknowledged that, for the Athenians, justice in relation to other cities had been superseded by the demands of empire. He told his fellow citizens: 'your rule [over other cities, i.e., your imperial rule] is like a tyranny – to have taken it seems unjust, but to let it go now is dangerous' (2.63).

Imperial rule is 'like' a tyranny in that untrammelled power is exercised unaccountably, though it is not usually as directly pervasive as tyranny in its effects on those it dominates. Pericles is admitting the injustice of having acquired imperial rule – an acquisition in which he had eagerly colluded. But he situates that recognition in a context of regretful realpolitik. Having admitted that imperial rule is unjust, the natural inference, all things being equal, would be that it should be abandoned. But, according to Pericles, the Athenians hold a tiger by the tail. They cannot afford to let go, lest the hostility of the erstwhile allies coupled with the threat of enemies elsewhere prove a toxic combination.

Thucydides presents a striking near-echo of Pericles' words in the voice of one of the men who became influential in the assembly after Pericles died of the plague the following year. The echo is remarkable because Thucydides, in his own voice, contrasts the way in which Pericles led the *demos* by good judgement with the ways in which the dominant

speakers after his time instead merely flattered it and followed its whims. But it is also modified, and the modifications are telling. The speaker, Cleon, whom Thucydides says is the 'most violent' and 'most persuasive' of those influential at that time, in 427 BCE (3.36), is urging the assembly to stand fast in a decision it had made the day before but decided to reopen. This was to punish the failed rebellion of their erstwhile ally Mytilene brutally: by ordering all the men of military age of that city to be put to death and the rest of the inhabitants to be enslaved.

In the course of the debate, he states as a fact what Pericles had more cautiously offered as a simile: says Cleon bluntly, 'your rule [meaning, your imperial rule] is a tyranny' (3.37). A tyrant has no need to consider justice, only his own advantage, and must do the latter in a disabused way, expecting danger from every corner. Just as in a tyranny, one must expect revolts to be plotted by those who are ruled unwillingly; just as in a tyranny, one has to face up to the need to dominate them by force. Domination is not simply a sad necessity of finding oneself in the position of tyrant, as Pericles had implied (however disingenuously, since the Athenians didn't just wake up and find themselves to be tyrants: their becoming so was the result of policies that Pericles had supported). Cleon implies that domination is the very purpose and goal of rule, of amassing the power of a tyrant in the first place. Cleon loses the debate, but the arguments on the winning side, made by Diodotus, are a paler shadow of the same position. Diodotus does not argue from principles of justice, but, on the contrary, from the standpoint of Athenian advantage, which, he implies,

is the suitable standpoint for a debate about foreign affairs that is free from the shadow of legal treaty stipulations: 'we are not judging in a court of law with regard to them [the Mytileneans] where it is necessary to do justice; rather, we are deliberating about them, how they may be most useful for us' (3.44).[16]

In the glory of defeating the Persians, Athens displayed the remarkable strengths that democracy can achieve. Once inflamed with the *hubris* of empire, the Athenians also displayed some of the characteristic weaknesses of democracy as a form of collective decision-making: self-interested, short-sighted decisions, made on the basis of flattering or vindictive advice; being too hasty to act in some cases, too slow to react or anticipate in others. Defence mechanisms like scapegoating and wishful thinking are good examples of these tendencies. While the original decision to execute the men of Mytilene and sell their women and children into slavery was cancelled in the nick of time, the scapegoating, in 406, of generals who had won a naval battle at Arginusae, but failed in the face of a storm to collect all the bodies of the Athenian dead, was not;[17] nor would be the execution of Socrates in 399. The war against the Spartans and their allies was lost in 404 largely as a result of the consequences of a disastrous expedition to Sicily in 415, based on wishful thinking and ignorance about political and military conditions there. And eventually the Athenians would succumb to the whirlwind of Macedonian conquest, having been accused by some of their statesmen for decades of doing too little to counter that threat.

Yet the Athenian democrats were able to restore their

regime judiciously in 403 BCE, with a generous amnesty for the surviving participants in the oligarchic revolt against it. And, if the democracy eventually succumbed to pressures from Macedon in the wake of the conquests of Alexander the Great, it is not clear that the city could have done anything to have staved off this fate forever (though 4th-century politicians bitterly disagreed at the time about whether Macedon should be resisted or accommodated). Still, the democracy was certainly self-interested, grandiose in its ambitions and sometimes callous towards those who got in its way.

Ancient and Modern Democracies: What's in a Name?

Is ancient Athenian democracy similar to or different from democracy today? The answer to that question is both. Athenian democracy is surprisingly similar to and yet also strikingly different from modern democracies – say for example the USA and the UK (though they are of course in important ways different from each other and from other contemporary democracies). The value of considering their relationship comes not from forcing oneself to take a stand for or against (they're the same! no, they're different!) but rather from appreciating how those facts interrelate and how they can help us to appreciate the strengths and weaknesses of ancient and also modern democratic regimes.

Unlike other ideas in this book, Democracy is one whose roots in ancient Greece took considerable time to become viewed as the precursors of the positive modern ideal going by the same name. The story of how modern states came

to think of themselves as democracies as a result of late 18th-century and 19th-century developments, taking pride in that name rather than seeing it as a derogatory term of abuse, is fascinating but beyond the scope of this book.[18] Until that time, the idea of beneficial forms of rule involving the multitude were more commonly described on the Roman model: as 'republics' rather than as 'democracies', the latter term having been tainted by the severe criticisms of Plato and Aristotle and by a rather one-sided focus on the stories of Athenian democratic failings that could be found in the accounts of Thucydides, Aristophanes and other writers of the period. These failings were supposed to be arbitrariness and stupidity, illustrated by the purportedly bad Athenian decisions mentioned above (Mytilene, Arginusae, Sicily and so on), and these were taken to have issued from a radical over-inclusion of the ignorant and from an absence of sufficiently deferential and informed forms of deliberation and decision-making.

In the 18th century, during which the modern idea of the representative republic emerged, Athens still served largely as a negative contrast. Only then did the Athenian star rise with the subsequent development of the language of 'representative democracy' among thinkers and political practitioners in late 18th- and early 19th-century Britain and America, and with re-evaluations of the achievements of Athenian democracy itself, most powerfully in the work of the Victorian-era historian George Grote. It was from the mid 19th century onwards that comparisons between ancient and modern forms of democracy began to flourish, despite the historical path between them being far from

straightforward. Those comparisons have hinged largely on three points: the role of the people in lawmaking; the use of lottery as opposed to election; and the value of liberalism.

Differences between Ancient and Modern Democracies: Lawmaking, Lotteries, Liberalism?

LAWMAKING

The 18th-century revolutionary Thomas Paine – who participated in political activity in his native Britain, the British colonies in America and France – argued that 'Athens, by representation, would have surpassed her own democracy.'[19] He was drawing a contrast between the role of all Athenian male citizens – who had the right to attend and, in theory, to speak in the assembly – and the role of the people in modern representative democracies, who elected representatives to the legislature. That contrast has been fashioned in many discussions of political theory into one between 'direct' ancient democracy and 'indirect' modern democracy.

That direct versus indirect contrast between ancient and modern democracies is misleading.[20] On the one hand, it is based on the assumption that, by analogy with modern legislatures, the main thing the Athenian assembly did was to pass laws. In actuality, the normal activity of the Athenian assembly was not to pass or amend laws (something it did only occasionally in the 5th century, at the very end of which it fixed the law code and then handed the power of amending it over to a separate jury-like body). Instead, the assembly acted primarily as a decision-making body on the major

questions of public policy, such as war and peace, 'the corn supply and the security of the countryside' (*AP* 43.4), and similarly vital matters for civic survival. Ancient and modern democracies do differ in how they make laws; but the more fundamental contrast lies in the divergent roles they assign to citizens in the making of public policy.

On the other hand, Paine's contrast suggests that the Athenians had simply lacked a conception of delegating authority. As it happens, the Athenians knew very well how to have some do work on behalf of others. They chose by election or by lottery some 1,200 civic officials each year (including the 500 members of the council); they also chose jury panels by a complex system of lottery. If they chose to allow all citizens who wished to attend the assembly, that was a strategic choice about the best forum in which to make decisions that would affect the life-blood of the *polis*, rather than a consequence of institutional primitivism or a failure of the imagination. Thus, by drawing the contrast between ancient and modern democracies as one between 'direct' and 'indirect' (or 'representative') democracies, one misses out on understanding the ways in which multiple forms of Athenian popular power went beyond the question of legislation alone.

LOTTERIES

While the Athenians elected about 100 of their 1,200 officials – most importantly the board of ten generals – they made use of lottery to select most of the annually serving officials to conduct business ranging from regulation of the harbour to oversight of the coinage.[21] Here lies a second

contrast that is commonly drawn between ancient and modern democracies: it is said that the ancients used lottery, a truly democratic mechanism, as a sign of their faith that any citizen could and should be entitled to fill any role; whereas the moderns use election, which is ironically a more aristocratic or oligarchical mechanism in presupposing that some are better suited to govern than others.[22] But, again, that simplistic contrast misconstrues the real concerns and practices of the Athenians.

While it is true that the Athenians chose to use lottery for most offices, they did so in full knowledge of how to conduct elections instead – which they did for certain posts, primarily those requiring the most experience and expertise (above all the generalships). When they did use lottery, they surrounded it with prescreening mechanisms to test willingness to serve and good standing in civic affairs, ensuring that those chosen were respectable and law-abiding.[23] So the Athenians were far from using lottery as if it presupposed that just any citizen could and should be entitled to fill any role. But they did assume that most citizens were competent enough to be able to learn the ropes of the administrative offices they were asked to undertake – including those of clerks, commissioners of roads, superintendents of the market, even public executioners. And their allocation of these roles by lottery and annual rotation (for the most part) could help to prevent corruption and self-aggrandizement. Offices staffed by lot, for the duration of a single year, were no platform for the conversion of wealth to political power, and no basis for anyone aspiring to political dominance or domination to be able to do so.

One might say that Athenian lotteries were used to staff the equivalent of the civil service more than the functions of high political decision-making. Key political decisions rested in the hands of the elected generals together with the popular votes won by the self-selected speakers in the assembly, who advised on public policy. Hence the use of lottery in ancient democracies points us not to a simple contrast with modern elected officials, but rather to a complex reflection on how to distribute essentially administrative offices so as to prevent corruption while encouraging the participation of citizens who were held in good repute. The ancients had no blind faith in lottery, and, though they used it extensively, they did so with care and with limits. They valued participation, but they also valued expertise more than is often recognized, including pre-existing skills and knowledge as well as the expertise that ordinary citizens could develop in post.

LIBERALISM

The contrasts between ancient and modern democracies on lawmaking and lottery have turned out to be subtler than is widely thought. A final contrast that has often been drawn is between ancient illiberalism and modern liberalism. If Tom Paine was the tribune of representative democracy, the Swiss-born thinker (who served in several French governments) Benjamin Constant, in 1819, made himself the tribune of 'modern liberty', as opposed to a supposed 'ancient' conception. Drawing on the contrast between bourgeois moderns and warlike ancients that we saw Rousseau sketch out before him in the introduction to this book, Constant describes ancient regimes as having thrived on war and

subjugated individual concerns to collective power and aims, treating liberty as a matter of collective self-determination, while leaving the liberties of individuals vulnerable to those collective projects. He contrasts these regimes with modern representative ones, which thrive on commerce and so leave individuals alone to pursue their private aims, using their wealth to delegate politicians to manage their collective affairs.[24] In a sense, Constant is suggesting that the wider constitutions – 'the way of life' – of ancient and modern liberties are so different as to belie any institutional resemblances between them.

Yet Constant's distinction again distorts our understanding of ancient democracy and especially that of Athens. For he treats Sparta, in effect, as the paradigm of these ancient regimes, admitting that his analysis applied least well to Athens, whose scope for private individual liberties, trade and open intellectual ferment had been so notable. Pericles himself praises the Athenians for their open and tolerant political culture. The Athenians live together, Pericles proclaims, without suspicion or censoriousness, an implied contrast with the Spartan ephors, who strictly police behaviour. The Athenians are free and generous, and enjoy their lives (an implied contrast with Spartan austerity), celebrating contests like games and dramatic festivals, making the requisite sacrifices to the gods, and enjoying all the luxuries that their flourishing merchant economy has imported and produced. Instead of imposing the kind of grim secretiveness that would again have been seen as characteristic of Sparta, the Athenians, according to Pericles, put their trust in an openness to strangers and a civic courage that

are compatible with the enjoyment of a 'more relaxed life'. They simultaneously cultivate concern for public affairs with active care for private ones. Admittedly, the Athenians drew the line between public and private differently from most modern democracies: religion, for example, was a matter of public concern and public prescription. Athens was liberal in a way with regard to religion, being open to the incorporation of foreign deities, for example. But this had to be done with the city's consent.[25]

It is tempting for modern liberals nevertheless to join Constant in indicting Athens, like other Greek regimes, for having lacked secure protection of rights. Without the full apparatus of due process protecting strong individual rights claims, Athenians are easily charged with having been less than ideally liberal in leaving individuals vulnerable to collective power. Perhaps the most egregious case is the one that Constant takes to clinch the case for Athens having lacked the modern concept of liberty, despite all its quasi-bourgeois freedoms: the case of ostracism.

Established on the advice of Cleisthenes, every year a question was put to the vote in the assembly (meeting for this purpose in the marketplace): should anyone be ostracized, that is, banished from the city for ten years? If the ayes had it, every citizen would be given a shard of pottery (an *ostrakon*) on which to inscribe the name of one person. The person getting the highest number of 'votes' was summarily banished from the city for the ten-year term. Now ostracism is described in the 4th-century *Constitution of the Athenians* (22.1) as one of the defining means by which Cleisthenes democratized the city.[26] But, to modern ears, it sounds highly

illiberal. If such a lack of due process is democratic, depriving someone of liberty at the whim of a majority, without any evidence of wrongdoing or the chance to defend himself, many modern liberals would want nothing to do with that kind of democracy. So we must ask: was ostracism illiberal, and was democratic Athens guilty of illiberalism more generally?

Ostracism was carried out without evidence or due process because the Athenians did not see it as punishment for a crime, but rather as a political mechanism to ensure the survival of the democracy. It was used pre-emptively and, it has been argued, symbolically, to express the power of the *demos* over rival elites striving for influence, and so served to bolster the egalitarian sensibilities of the many on the shoulders of whom the democracy rested.[27] A general like Themistocles, who had led Athens in the vital military victory over the Persians at Salamis in 480 BCE, could be ostracized (as he was) eight or nine years later for perceived arrogance.[28] Of course, ostracism could be used for partisan purposes. But it was more than just a factional shenanigan. It was a means by which a democratic regime sought to defend itself and its own values, even at the price of limiting the very equality under the law that it sought to defend.

Before modern liberals follow Constant in convicting Athens of illiberality, they might consider that ostracism compares rather well with some of the mechanisms pressing or exceeding the limits of law that modern democracies have recently evolved to sanction individuals deemed threatening to the political order. Ostracism was not targeted killing. It was not even civic death, since the Athenians did not

deprive those whom they ostracized of civic privileges once the ten-year term of exile was completed (a length of time long enough to let antagonisms and hostility die away). The general Cimon, for example, came back quietly ten years after having been ostracized in 461 and re-entered the city as an equal, tacitly accepting the more radical democratic measures that Pericles had put in place in the meantime.

Hence in the case of ostracism, Athenian democrats afforded some measure of respect to the liberties of the individual, even though judging in some cases that it was necessary for the community to remove someone for a definite time period. And, more generally, the Athenians protected a wide range of freedoms. Indeed, their laws and legal practices afforded a wide set of protections not only to citizens, but also in some respects to non-citizens, who could in practice shelter under the same umbrella.[29] Critics of the democracy were especially affronted by the personal freedoms enjoyed by the poor and even by metics and slaves who were indistinguishable in their dress from citizens. The 'Old Oligarch' complains that 'it is not possible to strike' a slave or metic in Athens, because if this were legally allowed, one 'would often strike an Athenian, thinking that he was a slave' (1.10).[30]

One conclusion is that in a free society, it is difficult and invidious to try to draw distinctions among people based on appearance alone. Attempts to profile non-citizens all too easily result in harming the citizens whom they will closely resemble. Athenian society was more liberal in its tacit acknowledgement of this, as in many other respects, than dismissals of it as radically illiberal in modern terms would allow.

Ancient and Modern Democracies: A Reckoning

We have seen that the contrasts often drawn between ancient and modern democracies on lawmaking, lottery and liberalism are far too crudely and starkly posed. Moreover, in focusing only on such exaggerated and misconstrued differences, we lose sight of the important similarities that link ancient and modern democracies. Perhaps the deepest one is a concern for controlling officials – a concern that preoccupied the Athenians for lotteried and elected offices alike, and so which cuts across the genuine difference between the ancient and the modern in the prevalence of those mechanisms.

The Athenians controlled their officials by subjecting them to scrutiny before they entered office. They did not allow lottery to function as a way of defeating their concern for civic rectitude; instead, they followed it with the check of scrutiny to ensure this. They also, and crucially, made every official – again, whether lotteried or elected – submit accounts at the end of his tenure of office. Holding office was a public trust; and an account – an actual financial one as well as a more general inspection of performance – was demanded by the people on its completion. To the extent that modern democrats share a vision of the people as holding their leaders to account, they have a deep similarity with the ancients, but could also learn much from their institutional differences.

This chapter has set out three things that Athenian democracy stood for: it meant the power of the

people – including the poorest of the citizens – to *decide* (key policies in the assembly, and in the council and other offices, if selected by lot, as chances were they would be several times in a normal lifetime); to *judge* (in most legal cases); and to *control* (officials). We also observed the importance of the power to *initiate*: either as an individual, speaking in the assembly or bringing a prosecution in the courts, or as a lottery-selected body (the council, initiating the assembly's agenda). It was the integrated effect of those powers that constituted the *kratos* of the *demos*, giving the people freedom from being dominated by the arbitrary will of the elite, and equality in a meaningful sense despite the persistence of economic divisions.

The dramatic extent of popular judgement and decision-making, and of inclusiveness (for the time) in defining the people as all freeborn men born to citizen parents, made Athenian democracy as remarkable of its kind as was the Spartans' regime of theirs. The Athenians offered their elites certain forms of recognition and satisfaction, but they used a panoply of mechanisms to control those elites, so as to prevent them from parlaying wealth or influence into a secure basis for domination of others. They demonstrate an ideal of democracy as genuine popular sovereignty – that is, exercised in key moments of everyday control rather than only notionally as the ultimate basis of political authority. Without resorting either to plebiscitary votes limited to the common people, or to universal entitlement to office-holding, the Athenians found ways to make popular power real.

In some respects, Athenian democracy and modern democracy are very similar, in seeing the people as

controlling their officials and as the source from which all power ultimately flows. In other respects, however, Athenian democracy went much further: in its attempts to control economic as well as political power; in its allowing of popular judgement to make decisions about fundamental questions of public policy; and in its according of the ultimate judicial powers in almost all cases not to professional judges but to courts made up of ordinary people, jurors empowered to decide facts (as are modern common law juries) as well as the meaning of the law. Athenian democracy is not so far beyond our ken that it is irrelevant to ours, but nor is it merely a clumsy shadow of mechanisms that the moderns have supposedly perfected. The very discontinuities between ancient and modern practices make reflection on certain shared values – and their different institutional expressions – all the more instructive. Athenian democrats expressed a distinctive institutional and intellectual vision of the meaning of popular power and the means by which it may be exercised, one that was radical in the powers of judgement that it accorded to ordinary citizens, and radical as a result in its challenge to more recent ideas of democracy that accord those people far fewer powers. Yet not everyone living in the Athenian democracy in the 5th and 4th centuries BCE held the democratic constitution to be of unqualified value. Two of the most famous children of Athens, the philosophers Socrates and Plato, would profoundly question whether democracy was, in fact, the best path to living a good human life – a life that they took to depend on the achievement of moral and intellectual virtue. That is the subject of Chapter 4.

Virtue

Athens (circa 460 BCE)

See Athens Map Key p. 332

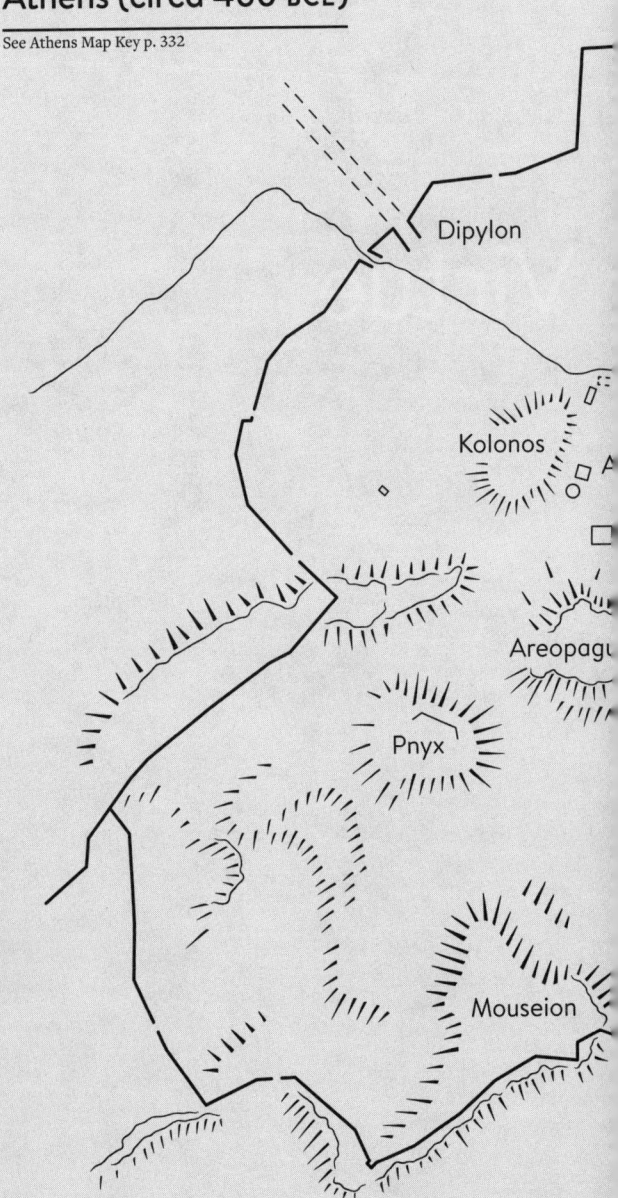

Dipylon

Kolonos

Areopagu

Pnyx

Mouseion

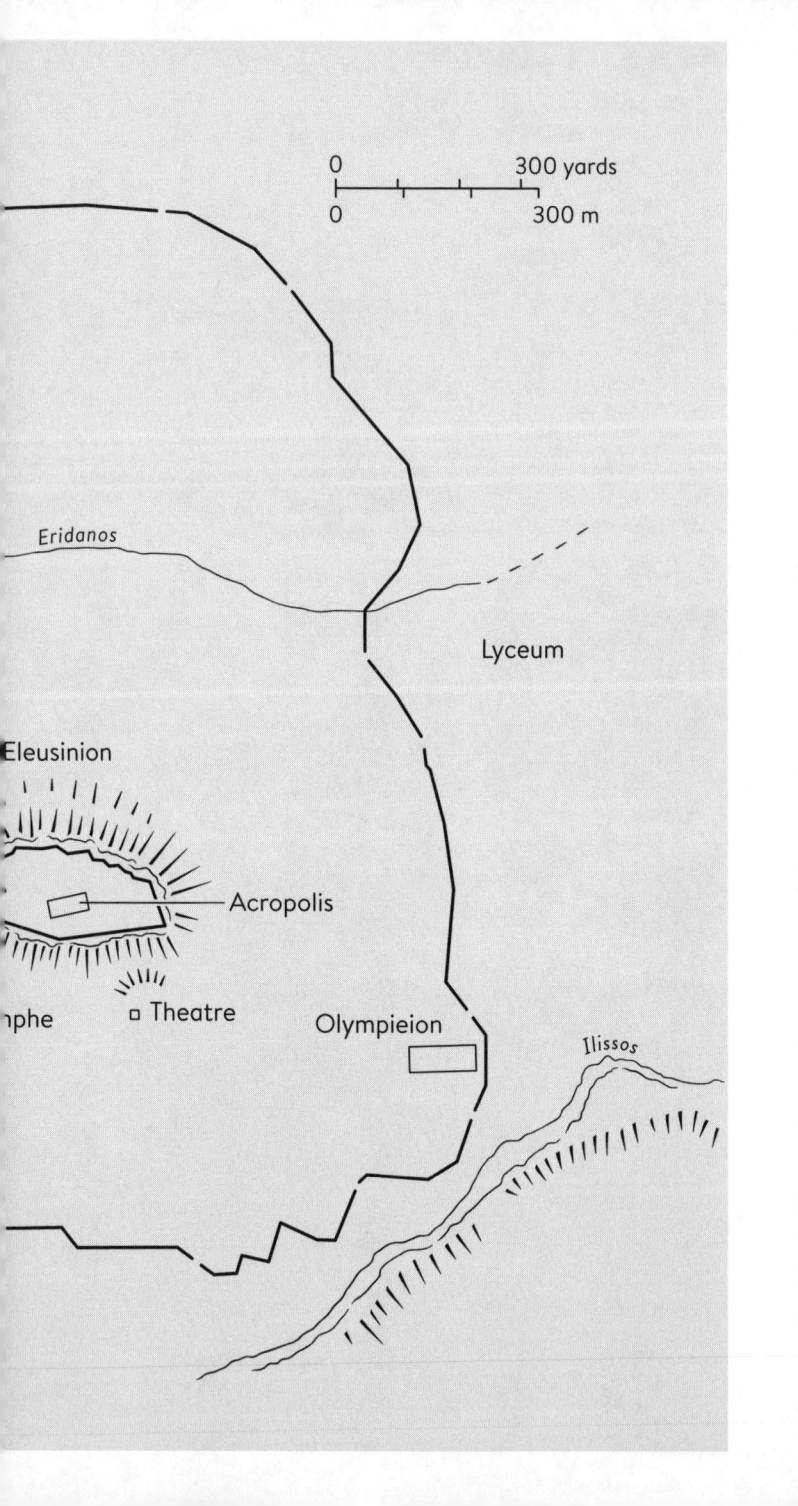

0   300 yards
0   300 m

Eridanos

Lyceum

Eleusinion

Acropolis

nphe   Theatre   Olympieion

Ilissos

This chapter will explore how the philosophers Socrates and Plato came to criticize Athenian democracy within a broader understanding of the aims of human life and the ideal place of politics in achieving them. To do so, we may begin building on the constitutional arrangements of Athenian democracy that were outlined in the last chapter, in order to ask: what were the aims, the values and the goals that the Athenian democrats used their powers to pursue? These were primarily survival, wealth and power: of the city by means of its empire, and of each individual within it, most of whom pursued wealth and power of their own. Fortune could be had through commerce, marriage or plunder, while fame, for those not talented in the arts, was available most lastingly by seeking political and military leadership. If politics was the best arena in which to win friends and a reputation, it was also a dangerous one: being held to account for bad advice or malfeasance in office could lead to financial ruin, exile or death, while any kind of prominence courted some risk of ostracism. Success or even survival of politicians and of people prominent for other reasons could come to hinge on their 'ability to persuade by speeches judges in a law-court, councillors in a council meeting, and assemblymen in

an assembly or in any other political gathering that might take place', as the sophist Gorgias – a public figure in his Sicilian hometown of Leontini who is visiting Athens as a teacher – is made to claim in Plato's writings.[1]

Despite the premium on public speaking in the Athenian democracy, the city offered no formal public education to teach young men how to do it. Thus advantage accrued to those who were able to seek private help in honing their speaking and arguing abilities, whether to pursue political ambition or simply to defend themselves should they be prosecuted. Rhetoricians and sophists flooded into Athens alongside home-grown varieties, all offering to teach ambitious young men how to speak persuasively to win power and prestige in the city. Some taught grammar, others etymology, others rhetoric – the ability to speak on either side of any question. These self-professed experts for the most part took the goals of wealth and power for granted, accepting them as the given ends for the individual and for the city alike, and focusing their attention on the clever means by which to outstrip others in achieving them. Excellence, or virtue (*arete*: the Greek word means the virtue of succeeding in carrying out an appropriate function), meant excelling in conventional political roles, getting the *demos* to accept one's advice by whatever means necessary; this would bring the pleasures, wealth and honours to which most men aspired.

This was the cosy consensus that the philosopher Socrates (469–399 BCE) attacked. The son of a sculptor, he abandoned artisanal stonemasonry to spend his time challenging leading intellectual and political figures, as well as promising young men, to give an account of the values that

they claimed to embody or wished to pursue. In so doing, he exposed blatant contradictions in the city's priorities and in those of its most prominent inhabitants. He became notorious for spending his time in such questioning in the marketplace, in the gymnasium and in banquets and gatherings in private homes, rather than choosing to give speeches in the assembly or the law-courts (though he did his military service with distinction and served one year as a member of the lottery-selected Athenian council). Young men like Plato flocked to him, seeing in him an alternative model for living a good life to those that the city officially offered and praised.

When he was seventy years old, Socrates was accused by several fellow Athenians of having violated the city's laws in ways that we will explore; he was found guilty by a jury of his peers and sentenced to drink poison. The drama of Socrates' life, with his recurrent diagnoses of the moral and political failings of Athenian and foreign elite figures, and of his trial and execution became fodder for a group of his followers who wrote up their own accounts of *Sokratikoi logoi*, or 'Socratic discourses'. None of them did so with more philosophical ambition than Plato (424–348 BCE), whose corpus of writings (almost all of which feature Socrates in a leading or minor role) has bequeathed us the description of 'Socrates' that will be the focus of this chapter. While the whole chapter draws on Plato's writings and so bears the stamp of Platonic thought, the discussion of 'Socrates' (that is, Plato's Socrates) in the first part of the chapter will look at those aspects of his life and death that several of his followers also recounted. The latter part of the chapter will discuss Plato's own life, and will provide readings of several

of Plato's major works (one of them featuring Socrates as the lead discussant) in the course of doing so.

Socrates asks his fellow Athenians some difficult questions: if the city officially excoriates tyrants, why does it act like a tyrant abroad? Conversely, if it is wrong to aim for unlimited wealth and power for oneself, why is it acceptable for the Athenians collectively to pursue that via empire? Is it really courageous to fight battles without knowing the good for which one fights? Is it just, or pious, to propitiate the gods into turning a blind eye to one's cutting of ethical corners elsewhere? He exposes the fact that hidden under the surface of what is said by sophists like Gorgias is a corrosive tension between individual success and collective flourishing. The art of rhetoric might be 'the source of freedom' for humans in general, but the sophist also presents it as 'the source of rule over others in one's own city' for an individual who can use it to master the freedom of others. Concealed in the public celebration of rhetorical skill and political service lies the potential for an unscrupulous speaker to undermine democracy itself.[2]

In stark opposition to the virtually unchallenged adulation of wealth and power in Athens and in many other regimes, Socrates proposes that the meaning of the 'virtue' that young men are admonished to cultivate in Greek societies is the most fundamental question that a human being can ask, and a prerequisite for any politician worth the name. As he tells the jurors in Plato's *Apology of Socrates* (a rendition of the speeches that Socrates had to make at his trial):

> I went to each of you privately and conferred upon him
> what I say is the greatest benefit, by trying to persuade him

not to care for any of his belongings before caring that he himself should be as good and as wise as possible, not to care for the city's possessions more than for the city itself, and to care for other things in the same way (36c–d).[3]

If politicians and sophists are not similarly aiming to make men virtuous, what is the point of their powers of persuasion? But if they do not know what virtue is, what good are they? From the standpoint of Socrates and Plato, who pressed precisely these questions, all the existing answers – the intellectual and political life paths followed by the most promising youth and influential men in the city – were bankrupt. None of those leading these lives was able to define virtue or reliably to cultivate it in others.

Socrates raised such questions throughout the Peloponnesian War, at home and while away on military service. He became notorious enough to be lampooned on the comic stage by Aristophanes in three different plays (and by at least four other playwrights, too). In the first of these plays, the *Nephelae* (*Clouds*), produced in 423 BCE, Aristophanes makes him out to be a recognizable sophist, running a school for pay; yet he hints at something different about Socrates in suggesting that his intellectual attainments don't offer his pupils any real road to the legal mastery for which they hope. Whether this was meant to be a critique of sophistry in general or a recognition that Socrates was distinctive in his abstraction from worldly measures of value, it was a lampoon that had no effect at the time on its subject's carrying on with his activities.

Socrates' notoriety, however, acquired a more sinister

edge as Athens' prospects in the war with Sparta darkened (and the later mentions by Aristophanes came in plays produced during that time, in 414 and 405). This shadow gathered with the accusations of impiety and treachery made against one of Socrates' younger friends, Alcibiades, just as the Athenians were launching the all-or-nothing military expedition to Syracuse. It intensified further when the war was lost in 404 and the 'Thirty Tyrants' (also known as the 'Thirty') were voted in under Spartan pressure to form an oligarchy, expel many of the citizens from the city's rolls, and rule by whip, force and knife. Two among them (Critias and Charmides) had been close associates of Socrates and relatives of his follower Plato. Socrates himself stayed in the city under the Thirty, seemingly having accepted enrolment in their list of purged citizens, at a time when most of those loyal to the democracy (including some of his other friends) had fled to the port.[4] After that the democratic partisans regrouped to drive out the Thirty and re-establish the democracy.

It was in 399, five years after the restoration of the democracy, that Socrates was accused by three fellow citizens of not respecting the city's laws, introducing new gods and corrupting the youth. This was not a direct reference to the coup of 404, since making a charge about responsibility for the short-lived and oppressive oligarchy would have violated a subsequent democratic amnesty barring any further prosecutions for them. But the jurors could not have forgotten the role that Critias and Charmides had played in the coup, or the various displays of impiety and treachery exhibited earlier in the war by Alcibiades. Those events made

it easier for the prosecutors to paint Socrates' distinctive life choices – reinforced, in Plato's portrayal, in his refusal during his trial to play the expected rhetorical cards of begging for his life and flattering the jury – as violations of the standards of good citizenship defined by the city's laws. He was convicted and sentenced to drink a poisonous cup of hemlock. His life and his death together served to change the agenda of what ethics and politics could mean. Socrates' legacy, as shaped and expressed by Plato, transformed 'virtue' from being an accepted prop for current ideas of success into a reflective standard for ethical and political analysis.

Socrates in Action

As observed above, while 'virtue' is one English translation of the Greek word *arete*, another is 'excellence'. In modern English, especially as inflected by centuries of Christianity, 'virtue' can sound quixotic, a trait designed to win other-worldly reward in the next life but not to gain any tangible benefit in this one. In ancient Greek, by contrast, *arete* meant the characteristic excellence that allows anything to flourish. A sharp knife has the *arete* of cutting well. Its virtue is precisely what allows it to succeed in its aims. The opposite of *arete* is not just moral vice but practical failure.

The Greek poets had praised virtue as taking several specific forms: wisdom; courage; moderation; justice; and piety. These, it was claimed, were dear to the gods and would lead to reward in this life and the next – as we saw in Chapter 1 with respect to justice in particular. But, as we also saw there, that story was becoming threadbare. It was too easy to point

to examples of moderate men who suffered from the greed of others, or to just men who were victimized by the unjust, as the poet Hesiod portrayed himself, having been bilked of a land inheritance by his brother. And the links between the virtues were also easy to question. That someone might be courageous without being smart was a familiar idea at the time: consider the rather thick warrior Ajax in Sophocles' tragic play of that name, railing against the decision to award the dead Achilles' armour to the savvier Odysseus. More disturbing still were the voices that were being raised in late 5th-century Athens to call the just and moderate and pious man not smart, but stupid, obeying the rules and making sacrifices to the gods while others less scrupulous snatched away his land or money.[5] Anxiety that the virtues might be conflicting and self-defeating raised the stakes of understanding the aims that a virtuous person might, and should, be trying to achieve.

In a city crowded with the posturing and the anxious, Socrates performs repeated acts of devastating exposé, asking those who should know best to say what the virtues are that they claim to possess. Again and again, they fail to do so, unable to state what excellence they can offer to teach or to exercise, and how it might relate to the broader aims of a good life. These failures cut to the core of the pretensions of the leading figures in the city's political and intellectual life. Plato's dialogues portray Socrates exposing two of Athens' most admired generals as unable to define courage satisfactorily. Socrates demonstrates that the leading sophists, who claim to teach virtue, can't even define it, and that self-appointed busybodies trying to enforce the laws about

piety have nothing coherent to say about the nature of the piety that they are trying to enforce (not an unfamiliar spectacle to this day).

Each of these prominent figures has built his career on claiming to know certain things, yet each fails to explain satisfactorily what they are. As Socrates puts it in Plato's version of the *Apology of Socrates* (21d), they do not know what they thought they knew. Because he himself does not indulge in such false conceits, he is motivated to seek knowledge by questioning experts who claim to possess it – even though again and again those experts disappoint him, some ruefully acknowledging their failure, others resentfully accusing him of mockery or manipulation. The knowledge that Socrates seeks is a knowledge of virtue and the good life. Without claiming to be able to define virtue himself, Socrates operates in his interrogations on certain assumptions that none of his interlocutors manage to dislodge: that to truly have one virtue, one must have them all, which means (given that wisdom is one of the virtues) that all virtue is, in fact, knowledge. One cannot be courageous without knowing what to fear, nor pious without knowing what the gods do and do not desire of humans, nor moderate without knowing what and how much to desire, nor just without knowing what one owes to others.[6]

Socrates' search for virtue and knowledge – or, rather, virtue as knowledge – was a rejection of the alternative goals that transfixed many of his contemporaries. Power and wealth are unstable and unsatisfying, he argues again and again, not least because used ignorantly they are far more likely to harm their possessor than to benefit him. Only knowledge can ensure that we pursue goals worth pursuing,

and only virtue is the possession of intrinsic and uncon-
ditional value, not contingent on the way that it is used.
Socrates' way of articulating the intrinsic value of virtue
was to focus on the *psyche*, the Greek word roughly meaning
'soul'. The *psyche* animates the body and can, according to
Greek myth, be independent of it, reincarnated into varying bodies. Socrates insists that it is the purity and health of
the *psyche* that is to be identified with a person's well-being,
the *psyche* that constitutes his very identity. What befits the
psyche is virtuous action; what harms it is vicious action. Those
who procure bodily pleasures by unjust actions – stealing or
lying to support their desires for wine or food or sex – are
making a profound mistake: they are pursuing pleasures that
cannot benefit them, because they have sacrificed the most
important and necessary good that they could possess in
order to obtain those relatively worthless pleasures.

The final twist in Socrates' conversations, as Plato depicts
them, is that he himself claims not to possess knowledge of
the most important things, and certainly does not claim to
have the full knowledge that would constitute all the virtues.
Yet he behaves in ways that strike onlookers as remarkably virtuous. He is moderate in his appetites, courageous
in battle (he saves Alcibiades' life but lets the younger man
take the credit for bravery) and arguably a paragon of piety
(despite the charges levelled against him in his trial). Most
exceptionally, he places such a high value on justice that he
argues that it is better to suffer injustice than to commit
it. And when this argument is put to the test by what Plato
and Xenophon present as an unjust verdict against him, he
lives and dies by it, preferring to suffer an unjust sentence

of death than to escape it by acting unjustly himself. The sheer depth of Socrates' commitment to self-examination, his staunch rejection of the false gods of power and greed in favour of the value of knowledge and so of the continual search for it, shapes his outlook and disposition along virtuous lines. Even though he disavows full knowledge, Socrates' valuing of knowledge and virtue above all else leads him to act more virtuously than anyone else around him.[7]

Socrates and Democracy

In challenging the claims of generals, sophists and others of his contemporaries, Socrates does not let the reputations of the famous Athenian political figures of the past escape unscathed. So Themistocles had won naval battles – but what good was the empire that had resulted? So Pericles had built the long walls around the city, filled its treasury with gold and silver, and adorned the Parthenon temple with astonishing marble sculptures – but could he point to a single citizen who had become more virtuous because of him? These men and others like them had even been fined or ostracized by the very people whom they had advised – proof that, rather than making their followers more just, as a really good politician would do, they had only made them more unjust. Sure, Socrates acknowledges, these famous men of the past 'were cleverer than those of the present at providing ships and walls and dockyards and many other such things' (*Grg.* 517c) – but they satisfied the citizens' appetites merely, when they should have been forcing them to recognize that those appetites were not really worth satisfying.

This leads Socrates to a paradox. He himself had sought no fame through distinctive civic leadership. While he fought bravely in the Athenian army and took a turn in serving on the council, he made no speeches in the assembly, nor did he choose to frequent the law-courts. Instead he spent his time philosophizing, talking to people and asking them about virtue. It may not have been as recondite and pointless as measuring the jumps of fleas was made to appear in Aristophanes' parody, but to men like the arrogant Callicles it would have seemed an 'unmanly life' – a life of 'muttering in a corner with three or four boys, never saying anything worthy of a free man, important, or sufficient' (*Grg.* 485d–e). Indeed, as Callicles warns Socrates – a warning that Plato was penning after Socrates' death had already come to pass – if someone like him were to be accused 'on the charge that you're acting unjustly when you are doing nothing unjust' (*Grg.* 486a), such a skulking good-for-nothing would be useless, unable to protect himself, much less to win any renown in the city.

Socrates is presented by Plato as making a bold riposte, by means of a characteristic kind of redefinition: claiming that he himself is the only one among his fellows 'to pursue the true political art and to practise politics' (*Grg.* 521d) in Athens. If politics proper aims at caring for the souls of one's fellows, it is he alone who has done that. All the rest have sold their *psyches*, and their compatriots' *psyches*, in the selfish pursuit of gain or fame.

By offering this paradoxical definition of the political, Socrates turned Athenian democratic reasoning on its head. Democratic politics was, as we saw in Chapter 3, about the

power of persuasion turned to the end of majoritarian or communal profit and advantage. Socratic politics was about the power of argument in the form of rigorous questioning, turned to the end of individual virtue, which was the only genuine advantage, according to Socrates. As Plato's Socrates says in the *Laches*, 'It seems to me that to decide things well it is necessary to decide them on the basis of knowledge and not by the majority' (184e). A true political expert would not be dependent on selection by chance or acclaim. He would be qualified by his wisdom and known by his deeds, by his ability to make his fellows more just – an ability that Pericles and company had failed to manifest not just in the city but also in their homes, where they were unable to point even their own children towards virtue.

For Socrates, if we cannot be as sure of our political leaders' expertise as we are of our doctors or shoemakers in their own trades, we cannot hope to be well governed. Whereas democrats held that virtually any citizen was capable of judging correctly, Socrates insisted on a theoretical gulf between the expert and the non-expert – even while debunking all the putative experts and denying that he was one himself. To him, putting ignorant people in charge could not and would not achieve the highest aims of politics.

Socrates did not apply this stricture against rule by the ignorant to give a black mark to democracy alone. No regime – whether monarchy, oligarchy or tyranny – that was not ruled by people with knowledge able to direct their subjects to live well and to foster their virtue was truly admirable in his eyes. Virtue and knowledge are standards too high for any actual regime to meet very easily; by that very

token, they set valuable critical measures for every regime, democratic or not. Socrates himself never lived anywhere but Athens, except when on military service: the city, for all its faults in his eyes, let him speak freely for decades and may also have informed his commitment to doing so through its political value of frank speaking. Yet many of his followers portrayed the Spartan habits of discipline and self-denial as more congruent with Socratic strictures than the free-and-easy, pleasure-loving and novelty-hungry Athenian ways (though Athens was widely acknowledged to be more hospitable to philosophy than Sparta).[8] Many of those attracted to Socrates' charismatic, unsettling presence took his elevation of virtue and knowledge as reason to denigrate democracy, even though they might also see some worthwhile aspects in it or remain democratic citizens in practice.

Socrates on Trial

Writing a version of the defence speech – in Greek, an *apologia*, the source of English 'apology' – given by Socrates at his trial (along with its companion speech proposing a penalty once he had been convicted) became a competitive literary sport among his followers in the wake of his death. Only two versions have survived. One is by Xenophon, an Athenian who had led mercenary troops into and out of Persia, fought with the Spartans against the Athenians, was exiled for it, and lived the rest of his life outside Athens despite an eventual reconciliation. In Xenophon's version, each of the accusations made against Socrates – not acknowledging the city's gods; introducing new gods; and corrupting the

youth – is simply untrue. Socrates, for him, fits the existing model of an upright Athenian citizen perfectly, being distinctive only in his willingness to die so as to prevent his virtue from weakening in old age, and in his concomitant unwillingness to flatter the jury to avoid death.

In Plato's version, by contrast, Socrates defends himself with attitude, along lines that are deliberately and dramatically different from the ways that upright Athenians at the time would have been expected to behave. Rather than humbly pleading or flattering the jurors, he tells them in no uncertain terms that, far from posing a danger to the city, he is quite literally god's gift to it. He has been sent by the god to serve Athens by waking it up, acting as a good citizen not by the usual route of making speeches in the assembly or law-courts, but rather by questioning those he encounters about what they claim to know: 'I was attached to this city by the god ... as upon a great and noble horse which was somewhat sluggish because of its size and needed to be stirred up by a kind of gadfly. It is to fulfil some such function that I believe the god has placed me in the city' (*Apology of Socrates* 30e).[9]

Even once he has been convicted and is invited to propose a counter-penalty to the prosecutors' bid for death (Athenian law requiring the jury to impose either the penalty proposed by the prosecutor or that suggested by the defendant, with no compromise or alternative possible), Plato shows Socrates acting in a way that cannot fail to provoke the jury. His first response is that what he deserves is actually the same reward as that granted to Olympic victors: nothing less than free meals on the city for life (36d). Although he eventually proposes a fine as the official counter-penalty in an

amount hardly proportionate to the gravity of the charges, it is little surprise that substantially more jurors vote to put him to death than had initially voted to convict.

The point is that Socrates' values are antithetical to those of a typical Athenian jury. The jurors are accustomed to thinking of death as the worst possible penalty that might be proposed. But, since death affects only the body, not the *psyche*, which he insists is immortal, Socrates cannot possibly share that view. Indeed, putting his argument about virtue and wisdom into practice, he argues that, since he does not know whether or not death is to be feared, he does not fear it and nor should anyone else (offering a general and philosophical claim about death, in contrast with the reason for avoiding death that in Xenophon's version is kept purely personal). Since death is the worst that the prosecutors can ask the jury to impose, but death cannot harm his *psyche* and so cannot harm the real him, Socrates has no reason not to accept the jury's sentence.

The only possible exception is hypothetical, since it is not a penalty that any real Athenian jury would have inflicted: Socrates remarks in Plato's *Apology* (29c–d) that, had the jurors imposed a penalty on him of ceasing to philosophize, he would have disobeyed that penalty. Such a penalty would have set a human jury against Socrates' understanding of a statement by the divine oracle that no one is wiser than Socrates, one that Socrates has sought to prove valid by examining all the self-proclaimed wise men whom he encounters. It would be impious and unjust for him to disobey his interpretation of a divine claim. But, short of that hypothetical case, Socrates is content to suffer whatever

harm the Athenians believe they can do to him, secure in the conviction that physical blows, impoverishment, even death, insofar as they do not harm his *psyche*, do not actually harm him at all.[10]

Having been convicted and sentenced to death, Socrates is thrown into gaol to await a propitious day for his execution. Plato shows him rebuffing an entreaty by one of his close friends, Crito, to escape. Crito has set up the whole plan: he can bribe the gaoler and spirit Socrates into exile. It was not uncommon for Greek defendants to escape death by so exiling themselves, and, so long as they did not return to their homeland, they were likely to get away with it. But Socrates refuses. He will not be doing harm or injustice by accepting his punishment; therefore he has no affirmative reason to escape it.[11]

Socrates' philosophy does not direct him to defy the city. Indeed, it directs him to civil obedience, not to civil disobedience, though modern scholars preoccupied with justifying civil disobedience have often wished or imagined that it were otherwise. In his own political life, Socrates upheld the law (as he says, he resisted the putting of an unlawful proposal when presiding in the assembly as one of the councillors taking that role in turn);[12] refused personally to commit injustice and punish an innocent man (as he says he did when he refused to follow an order from the Thirty to round up an innocent man for execution); and chose to suffer injustice by staying in gaol to be executed, since that did not involve him in committing any injustice. Yet he did not find active democratic politics to be a forum for meaningful action. Insofar as everyday politics was insensitive or indifferent to the quest

for virtue as a critical and probing self-examination, it was not the arena for him. Indeed, his efforts were devoted to encouraging and prodding his fellows to pursue virtue and knowledge just as he did, trying to improve them individually rather than setting out to use political mechanisms to improve the city collectively. Perhaps he took it as a foregone conclusion that no one could succeed in using those mechanisms in a city where most individuals were motivated by greed, lust and power. If Socrates was going to change Athenian politics, he was going to do it one citizen at a time, by cross-examining one person in a way that might cause him to challenge himself, or that might bring an observer to engage in a self-examination of his own.

Enter Plato

Socrates spent his life speaking – not to the assembly or the courts, but to individuals and small groups, challenging and questioning them. He was neither an orator nor a teacher: he did his characteristic work outside formal institutions, individually and informally. Plato, by contrast, spent most of his adult life writing and teaching, as founder of an institute of higher education named the Academy, after the gymnasium where Plato and his followers had first gathered to talk about mathematics and philosophy. We know very little about how exactly the Academy functioned, though we do know that there were exercises in mathematics and logic, the practising of arguments and public lectures. At least one woman attended dressed as a man;[13] many other Athenians of varying social classes were drawn to study, alongside a

large group of foreign students like Aristotle. We have just tantalizing hints about the oral teaching offered there.

What we have in the main are the Platonic writings, and, in particular, his writing of dialogues – a form that seems to have been invented by him and others especially to convey the indelible power of conversations with Socrates. Socrates is the principal character in most of Plato's dialogues and a minor character in almost all the rest; only from a single dialogue, the *Laws*, is he absent altogether.[14] All these works were, we think, written after Socrates' death, an event that prompted Plato to abandon Athens for a time, spending years travelling abroad before an eventual return.

Here was a young man born to an influential family (related through his mother to the revered legislator Solon, and to Critias and Charmides, who would become infamous members of the Thirty Tyrants) in the city that was a hub of artistic and intellectual explorations and at the zenith of its imperial strength. For such a rich and well-bred Athenian boy, opportunities to win renown were manifold. He could have become a general like Pericles, a playwright like Euripides (indeed we know that the young Plato wrote tragedies, which he burned upon meeting Socrates), or an historian like Herodotus, reciting his histories for public adulation at festivals.

All of these would have been paths to glory readily recognizable to his parents and his friends. But Plato chose none of them. Instead he spent his formative years captivated by an ugly man bred to a trade rather than born to wealth and aristocratic standing: that is, by Socrates. Plato forswore democratic politics as well as immediate oligarchic

ambitions to spend his time watching and listening to his mentor's endless questioning of others. If we imagine his mother and stepfather distraught at the thought that their son had been brainwashed by a cult, leading him to abandon all plans and ambitions for a successful life by any traditional standard, we are probably not too far off.

When Socrates drank the hemlock in 399, Plato was about twenty-four years old;[15] after sixteen years or so abroad, he returned to Athens to found the Academy and wrote most and possibly all of his dialogues thereafter. Strikingly, he chose to set all of his writings not in the time he was writing but in the previous century, featuring leading characters who had lived when he himself was scarcely born. It is like an ambitious American writer and thinker in 2014 setting all his works – all of them, every single one – in the age of Johnson, Nixon and Ford, obsessively returning to the shadow of Watergate and larding his writings with premonitions of it in earlier years. It is a tribute to Plato, in a way, that readers tend to overlook this peculiarity: his works give us so much information about the 5th century, bring it so vividly to life, that we think of them almost as products *of* the 5th century rather than forty-odd years later. But, in writing these retrospectives when he did, Plato may well have been commenting on the politics of his own lifetime as well as of that bygone era, and we can gain by bringing that doubled vision – an eye on the 5th-century literary setting, and an eye on the 4th-century context of production – to bear on his works.

The years from 384 BCE (the year he probably turned forty) to 348/347 BCE (the year of his death) were turbulent.

The dominant position won by Sparta with its crushing of Athens in 404 soon evaporated in the face of constant jockeying for position and alliance between Athens, Sparta, Thebes and Persia, complicated by struggles for power within each of them. Then, eleven years before Plato's death, Philip II was appointed regent of Macedon – a borderland territory ruled by the Greek royal house to which he belonged. He was amassing power in neighbouring Thessaly, and Athenian politics from that point was dominated and divided by the question of how to respond. Should Athens make war against him to defend its independence, as Demosthenes urged, or make peace, as advocated by his opponents? (Plato's contemporary Isocrates would go so far as to see Philip as the potential saviour of a united Greece against Persia.) Platonic imagery and vocabulary have been shown to be prevalent in the later speeches of the peace party, suggesting that Plato's thought was received and perhaps also intended as a counsel against renewed war.[16]

This was a turbulent period of history. Each city and ruler seems to have been jockeying for power for the sake of power itself, rudderless in terms of larger political principles. Ironically, while Herodotus had contrasted the moral clarity of the Persian Wars with the troubling internecine warfare of Greeks against Greeks in the Peloponnesian War, for most 4th-century Athenians even the latter war would have seemed in retrospect morally unambiguous. Athens was fighting for freedom against Spartan oppression, Athenian democracy against Spartan oligarchy. (Compare the way that the Cold War, for all its problematic moral and political

aspects, sometimes nostalgically seems a simpler and morally clearer political era than those that have followed.) But the burden of Plato's work is to challenge that simplistic and nostalgic confidence. For his dialogues – most set during the Peloponnesian War – suggest that even when the Athenians thought they knew what they were fighting for, they did not. They liked to think of their war against Sparta as a war for independence, freedom and democracy. But in reality, Plato implies, it had been a war for imperial power and loot, trampling on any concern for virtue or justice.

Thucydides and Socrates (to the extent that we can reconstruct his thought independently from that of Plato) had already initiated that line of critique of the Peloponnesian War. Plato would take it one step further still. One might have concluded from reading Thucydides that the problem was only imperial tyranny abroad; get rid of that, in the way that J. A. Hobson would counsel Britain before the First World War, and then democracy at home could genuinely flourish. Plato, however, suggests that the rot went deeper. Democracy at home was itself incoherent, confused about what was really worth having and doing. That was the root of imperialism: not just a mistaken foreign policy, but one that was driven by greed and the desire for power. Socrates had not succeeded in extirpating that lust and greed from every Athenian's soul; indeed, he had scarcely succeeded in doing so from anyone's. By writing, Plato could potentially reach a wider audience, not just pressing them to challenge themselves but offering them a new portrait of what justice really requires, what success might look like, what it makes the most sense to desire and to pursue.

The *Republic*: A Deeper Case for Justice

These are the very questions explored in the dialogue of Plato that in English we call the *Republic*, famous as the first comprehensive analysis of how the best life of which humans are capable relates to the best constitution for a city, making it a model for subsequent reflection on psychology and politics from Cicero to Augustine to Rousseau and beyond. Its title in Greek is *Politeia* – the idea of a broad 'constitution' that we discussed in Chapter 2; in the edition of the 1st-century CE editor Thrasyllus, it has an associated subtitle, 'On Justice', the idea that we treated as central to Greek thought in Chapter 1. As the title and subtitle suggest, the dialogue raises a fundamental question arising from this book so far: can there be a constitution, a political organization that is also a way of life, that is just rather than exploitative? The question is addressed in the main body of the dialogue by Socrates, in conversation with two brothers of Plato, drawing a portrait of a city in which political rulers, who should be also philosophers, are the servants of the people, not their tyrannical or exploitative masters. Because they are philosophers, they will rule with knowledge of what is truly good; thus they are able to shape the city's actions as well as the citizens' characters in line with this standard of genuine value.

Here is an alternative view of the goals of power, coupled with a radically revised view of the appropriate means by which to attain those goals. Neither rhetoric nor lottery nor even election plays the role here that such mechanisms did in democratic Athens. Instead, in this 'beautiful city'

(Kallipolis), the rulers are decided on the basis of true merit of the kind that Socrates elsewhere envisions, reproducing themselves by eugenically prescribed couplings, followed by choosing and testing the most meritorious of the children to serve. All depends on knowledge and virtue, which – as we will see – come from the same root. Only in such a city can most individuals develop the self-control and discipline, shaped by knowledge, that will enable them to refrain from acting unjustly and so harming their souls. The beautiful city turns out to be the condition for all but an exceptionally philosophical few to be able to protect their souls.

The *Republic* begins with a traditional story about justice, told by a lucky old man named Cephalus. A metic who has founded a wealthy manufacturing business, but whose fortunes will be vulnerable in the oligarchic coups to come (one son will be murdered as a democratic partisan), Cephalus adheres to the traditional story about gods and virtue. That old story teaches that humans should be just on pain of punishment by the gods – 'just' meaning that they should pay their debts to gods and men. This story has worked for Cephalus. He has been lucky enough to be able to afford to pay his debts without hardship, and lucky, too, in not being visited by any Job-like misfortunes. He has cultivated the traditional virtues and been rewarded with a good reputation among gods and men. Meanwhile the physiology of age has weakened his bodily appetites to the point that they do not threaten to undermine his commitment to traditional piety and justice, linked in that paying one's debts to the gods through sacrifices is a form of both.

But, for many people in this milieu, Cephalus' story no longer works. We meet one of them early in the dialogue: Thrasymachus, a world-weary man from Chalcedon, in Athens on a diplomatic mission, who suggests that this form of conventional justice is really a con game.[17] There is no such thing as ethically valuable justice, because there is no such thing as political justice. Every city is ruled by men who exploit their subjects in their own interests, and do so by defining justice in the rulers' favour: 'Justice is what is advantageous to the stronger, while injustice is to one's own profit and advantage' (344c).[18] Thrasymachus means that if, for example, Cephalus pays his debts to men in Athens, he benefits the *demos* who are in power in that city. But the *demos* have set the rules to favour themselves (they may be exploiting aristocrats by denying the validity of debts owed to them, for example). So Cephalus, in paying his debts, is actually being exploited by the *demos*. More generally, in an exploitative world, being just and self-controlled is not the path to happiness. It is a form of self-abuse. Justice is not advantageous to the individual. It is, rather, a way in which the individual is taken advantage of, for the benefit of others.

Thrasymachus is uncompromising, and he is unmoved by the manoeuvres that Socrates goes through to try to persuade him otherwise. Socrates argues that rulers in the role of rulers must desire the good of their subjects; it is only in the role of money-makers that they may seek their own personal good. But, to someone who has painted such a bleak sociological picture, this kind of quibble is unlikely to be persuasive. Nor are the two brothers of Plato who are present in the discussion persuaded. But, they say, they want to be.

The upshot of their intervention is that Thrasymachus may be going too far when he says that the individual can have *no* reason to be just. Even under conditions of inequality, the poor might have reason to respect property claims, if only so that their own meagre property will be respected by others.

Justice, brother Glaucon says, can in some sense serve the individual's true advantage – but its service is only second-best. The best thing would be for the individual to be a tyrant: able to make the rules for others to the advantage of himself, exactly as the logic of Thrasymachus' position had implied. And brother Adeimantus adds that the promise of divine punishment that played enforcer in the old story is bankrupt. Either the gods do not care about humans at all, or they can be bought off by prayers and sacrifices – used not to pay a debt, but to pay a bribe. Looking around the world – and here Adeimantus' social vision does sound closer to that of someone akin to the biblical Job – he sees the unjust flourishing to the extent that he finds it hard to resist the conclusion that the gods allow themselves to be bought off, hence that there is no sanction for the old story on which one can rely. Both brothers, however, insist that they do not want to believe that the accounts they retail are true. These cynical arguments are what too many of the leading men of their city and visiting intellectuals have told them. They urge Socrates to defend justice by showing that it is actually advantageous to the individual – which, if it can be proved, must mean that Thrasymachus' story is wrong, since justice would not in every case, then, be tantamount to exploitation.

Socrates undertakes to defend justice by making a famous move: analogizing the individual's *psyche*,[19] where they are

trying to find justice, to a city. Let's look for justice in the city as a model for finding justice in the soul, he suggests, as it is easier to read characters written in large letters than in small letters. The city he has in mind will turn out to have three parts; so, too, will the soul. Among their interrelations he will claim to discover the role of each of four virtues: wisdom, courage, moderation and justice. What is political here is not only the city and its special Platonic three-part structure; the division of the soul is equally political. For both city and individual are shaped reciprocally by interactions between them. If people pretend to value honour but secretly crave gold, as in the unstable regime governed by honour that Socrates later describes, the regime itself is liable to topple, because ultimately the façade will crack. (Think of the last days of the Soviet Union: in country after country, people suddenly saw that no one believed in communism any more.) If people crave wealth and luxury, the inequalities spawned by their pursuit are liable ultimately to overturn the economic order, since the poor will eventually figure out that they are more populous and therefore more inherently powerful than the rich. Or, if people are resistant to education and cling to their varying whims, they are likely to swarm around a charismatic figure and thereby risk letting democracy mutate into tyranny.

Only in the case of a city where education shapes minds and characters in mutually supporting ways will a regime be sustainable in the long term. Kallipolis will turn out to be the first sustainable city and so the only genuine form of rule at all – since all others ultimately turn out to be counterfeits or impostors. Instead of relying on the old story about

divine reward and punishment, Socrates proposes that the rewards and punishment can be primarily understood as intrinsic to one's own psychology. Even when one considers the afterlife, it, too, can be understood as responding to the choices made by people to pursue justice or injustice during their lifetime: this is expressed by Socrates in the telling of a myth at the end of the dialogue in which, while the gods and the fates govern the structure of the afterlife, each individual soul has the opportunity to choose his or her own next life (within certain limits set by chance) and will in practice do so on the basis of how justly or unjustly they have lived during their last one. Thus justice in the afterlife depends overwhelmingly on its intrinsic value in mortal life, not on an external and so potentially arbitrary set of direct divine rewards or punishments.

Socrates begins his discussion by sketching the origins of a city that seems to have no reason to become unjust – it is a city that is naturally just, perhaps. This is a rudimentary city with a simple division of labour: shoemakers trade their wares for food from farmers, for example. As long as the needs they satisfy remain fairly basic, at a simple rustic level of cooking and clothing, there is no motive for injustice – because there are no engorged appetites that would lead anyone to act unjustly. Each person contributes his skills to the city without greed for more than the modest rewards (a simple rustic diet) they bring him.

Glaucon, however, is not satisfied with such a city. To a rich youth who has grown up in Athens, the most sophisticated, art-loving and cosmopolitan city of his day, such rustic simplicity looks primitive. To mollify him, Socrates proposes

to allow luxuries into their imagined city, feeding engorged appetites and prompting ever greater cycles of consumption. Those drive early city-dwellers to war, the pursuit of which requires warriors. Here Socrates makes an ideologically charged move. Whereas in democratic Athens the people themselves were also the warriors, he suggests that in the city they are founding a separate military class will be needed. These guards have the task of external defence, but they also have the role of internal overseers and protectors of the city's constitution. Thus it is the task of guarding that is treated as the fundamental political task: guarding the constitution and guarding the city against outsiders. The class of guards is then divided into two, in line with military divisions between officers and soldiers: an older and wiser group are to serve as rulers over a younger group, who serve as their military auxiliaries. Rule thus enters the dialogue first *within* the group of guards, and only then is it extended, with the wise group ruling over all the citizens.[20]

What, then, are the real virtues of a city? They arise within and among these groups. Two are straightforward: wisdom is the virtue of the rulers, courage of the military auxiliaries. Moderation and justice, however, are relational properties. Socrates defines moderation as the agreement of each group that the proper rulers should rule: it involves the willingness of the other two groups, the soldiers and the rustic producers, to limit their own desires in line with the direction of the rulers – and readers will find out eventually that the rulers will direct their desires and appetites in line with what is good. Socrates defines justice as each group doing its own task. In the primitive city, this was a matter of instinct; in a

luxurious city, constant vigilance is required to maintain this within the proper limits. Here Plato is indicting every regime in which people use rule to gratify their desires: tyrannies and aristocracies as well as democracies. Rule should not be seen as a tool to gratify desires, as the Athenian empire had used its power to do. Rule is to be harnessed to enable people to do what is just and right, by preventing them from conceiving and acting on the desires to do otherwise.

In a just regime, the virtues of the individual and the city fit together and mutually support each other. In an unjust one, the vices of the individual are constantly undermining social relations and threatening to worsen them, while social relations themselves offer incentives for further corruption. A virtuous circle or a vicious one: that is the political choice Socrates lays out. It is a choice that confronts modern polities as well. Does the society support sustainable choices and decisions by its members, or do the incentives for unsustainable behaviour shape destructive actions that thereby further undermine the value of the social contract?[21]

The *Republic*: Justice in the Soul

The Platonic ideal of politics is fundamentally different from the birth of actual politics as we have seen it emerge in Greece. In Greek history, politics was initially under aristocratic control, which was then challenged by the poor, seeking justice as protection against exploitation and slavery. In Plato's ideal city, politics would perform the function of guarding the city, providing justice to all within it, in the sense of offering protection against being overcome by one's

own greed and lust by providing a guardian to shape desires. For Athenian democrats, justice was essentially protection against the overweening rich and powerful, along with the enjoyment of equal civic powers. For Socrates in Plato's *Republic*, justice is essentially protection against developing one's own longing to become overweeningly rich and powerful – a longing that would result in making one miserable rather than happy. Power is nothing without justice; seeking conventional power is a recipe for injustice.

What about the individual? Having offered a radically unconventional account of the structure of Greek societies by dividing citizens from soldiers, Plato now offers a radically unconventional account of the structure of the *psyche* of each living, embodied person. That there is a division between the reasoning, calculating part of the soul and the bodily appetites is something that a Greek would readily grant – thus giving Socrates two of the three parts of the soul that he needs to posit to match the structure of the city. Identifying a third part is trickier. Socrates suggests that there is a spirited part, which seeks to feel pride and avoid contempt. The spirited part will ideally side with reason against appetite, but, if corrupted, it may do appetite's bidding instead.

Turning to how the virtues relate to the parts of the soul, Socrates suggests that wisdom and courage are, as in the city, easy to assign: wisdom belongs to the reasoning part of the soul, courage to the spirited part. Moderation is, once again, agreement by all three parts that reason should rule. But justice is, once again, elusive: for if all three parts agree that reason should rule, what does the justice of each part doing its own work add? What it adds is the relinquishing of

a desire by either of the lower parts to rule in reason's stead. Only if the lower parts pursue their proper objects within bounds, rather than seeking to usurp reason's role, will they avoid the injustice of seeking to gratify lust or greed beyond the bounds of what is acceptable to reason.

All this involves a picture of politics that would be radically unfamiliar to the Athenians who were Socrates' interlocutors, and to other Greeks at the time. Socrates indeed makes it clear that for this conception of politics to work, it would require a massive campaign of education – for the guards must not be corrupted by stories about injustice being rewarded by the gods (the stories Glaucon and Adeimantus recalled as all too familiar in Athenian culture in Books 2–3). Drama and epic poetry, and the musical modes in which they are presented, need to be strictly controlled so as not to incite inappropriate desires or attitudes. And this enculturation is ideally to be supported by a lie, one that the rulers themselves should come to believe, a lie about both the naturalness of the citizens' kinship as citizens, and the self-evidence of the (real) differences of merit among them. This 'noble lie' is less of an instrument of political manipulation than is often charged, since the rulers themselves are ideally supposed to believe it. But it is certainly an instrument of an unyielding commitment to meritocracy, rooted in supposedly discernible differences of aptitude tested further by character and achievement. And it is also a form of creating a shared sense of political identity in the guise of a myth of kinship.[22] Whether political regimes can altogether do without meritocratic divisions and myths of kinship is a question for readers of the dialogue to ponder. Certainly we find here

the connection between *politeia* as constitution and *politeia* as a way of life, with the latter as the means to achieving unity in the former.

This is the point reached by the end of Book 4, when it looks as if the argument is complete. The twist comes in Books 5–7, where it turns out that if the rulers are to protect the city, rather than exploit it, they will have to be far more different from ordinary rulers in who they are and how they live than might have first seemed to be the case. They cannot be any familiar breed of wise folk. Instead they have to be the strange kind of people exemplified by Socrates himself: philosophers who are inherently motivated to pursue knowledge of what really is, of what never changes, as opposed to mere beliefs about what seems to be the case.

These philosophers may be female as well as male: those women who are naturally capable are to be trained in philosophy and military service, and to take turns in ruling alongside their male counterparts. And precisely because all the philosophers, female and male, have to be wholly devoted to their roles in ruling and guarding, and protected from the temptation to exploit their rule, they must have peculiar living arrangements imposed on them (the women liberated from the constraints of the Athenian household): they are to copulate and bear children at the direction of the older rulers for the good of the city, to produce the best offspring, who will then be raised collectively. Like the Spartans, they are to have common meals and, going beyond Spartan requirements, to own no private property themselves. In this way, they can best defend the city, while aiming not at their own benefit but at the benefit of their subjects (unlike the

Spartans, who ruthlessly exploit their helot subjects for their own advantage).

The radical idea here is that a good society requires the abolition of property and family for the rulers. This deprives the rulers of any incentive for corruption, since they would not be able to accumulate any property without being found out, and, if they were to manage to accumulate it, they would have no one to whom to bequeath it. This is a paternalistic idea of politics that, for the time, goes further even than did Sparta in channelling reproduction and upbringing for the purposes of the community. Here eugenics is to be built into control of the very timing of conception among the military guardians, though it seems that no such restrictions are to be applied to the sexual relations of the agricultural and artisanal producers.

Without property or family, the ruling elite are to consider themselves brothers and sisters, transferring the power of familial ties to their affection for the city itself. The seeds of communism and feminism lie here in the *Republic* – as ideas of how radically one would have to remake society by pressing human nature into unconventional institutions, if the sources of greed and corruption are ever to be extirpated.[23] Some see the abolition of family and property for the guardians as a sign that Plato cannot be serious. I see it as a sign that he knew just how seriously all cities would have to change if they were to earn the right to call themselves just.

What is certainly meant to be funny in the dialogue, however, is that after introducing these bombshells imposing female equality, but no family or property, on the guardian class, Socrates says that his most 'ridiculous'-seeming

proposal is still to come: that the guardians are to be not just clever men in the conventional sense, but actual philosophers – those skulkers in corners whom Callicles in the *Gorgias* had derided as unmanly. And these philosophers are to be educated not just in poetry, music and military matters, but in mathematics, astronomy and higher philosophical studies. Far from being irrelevant to the city, as Callicles had painted them, or dangerously inimical to the city, as Socrates himself would be judged by a jury of his peers, philosophers who combine knowledge and moral character are potentially the city's saviours.

What are these higher philosophical studies? Plato calls them study of the Forms, and in particular the Form of the Good. But he gives only hints and pointers, most of them embodied in elaborate models and stories, as to what the Forms are, though we can say roughly that they are the universal, unchanging truths that explain crucial aspects of the particular, changing world around us, including such truths as equality, beauty, justice and, underlying them all, goodness. Goodness is the most fundamental Form, because it embodies the very essence of existing for a purpose, the quality that makes anything valuable.

The most dramatic story illustrating the role of the Forms is the story of the Cave, which Socrates tells as a parable of the education that cities provide and the dangers and difficulties of escaping it. In the parable, the life of humans in existing cities is compared with humans imprisoned their whole lives in a cave, fettered in such a way that they cannot see the opening of the cave or any of the natural light of the sun. All they can see are the shadows of the objects paraded

behind their backs in the dim space artificially lit by a fire. Honours and prizes come to those who can best reproduce or talk about the shadows that they see. None of them is willing to accept that there is any such thing as a reality beyond the shadows, let alone beyond the cave.

The story suggests the intuition that truth lies beyond the horizon of what most people, trapped in the city's fables of honour and value, can possibly conceive. The Forms are those truths about the essence and nature of reality. Just as the artificial cave-objects are seen only in the form of shadows cast by the man-made fire, so the Forms can be understood only in the light of the idea of the Good that is paralleled in the story by the sun. Philosophers are those who come, either by happenstance or by compulsion, to understand these truths. But trying to proclaim them to the inhabitants schooled in the ways of existing cities is a dangerous business. The cave-dwellers will not be inclined to follow anyone returning upward; they will rather say (Socrates suggests) that such an escapee has 'destroyed his eyes', concluding that 'it's not worth it even to try to go upwards' (in other words, to get out).[24]

Hence the abiding paradox of the *Republic*. Philosophers are potentially the city's saviours, but the citizens they would save are inherently disposed to resist and even to destroy those who offer such help. Any diagnosis of political unhappiness as profound as this one will face this kind of problem: if the rot goes so deep, whence – except from outside, or from someone who has been in a form of internal exile – can come salvation? The *Republic*'s way of squaring this circle is to posit that there might be necessities (whether human or

natural) that would compel people to accept a form of help that they would otherwise scorn. It is a slim and vague possibility, but Socrates insists that it is a possibility nonetheless.[25]

Even if philosophers could somehow come to rule, there is a further question: how would their knowledge of the Forms help them to be good rulers? Socrates' arguments in the dialogue never suggest that knowledge of the Forms alone is sufficient to make someone a good ruler. The identification of virtue and knowledge here, and elsewhere in Plato, goes both ways: if all virtue is ultimately knowledge, one cannot be knowledgeable without also being virtuous. In the *Republic*, Socrates tries to show how this might develop in someone with a philosophical disposition, suggesting that anyone with such a disposition will also be inclined towards asceticism in respect of bodily desires, and that this instinctive lack of interest in the bodily, compared with their love of knowledge, will incline them to developing good moral character and good intellectual achievements from the same root.[26] Yet he acknowledges that this process can go awry, especially if corrupted by temptations from outside. Hence a well-ordered city like Kallipolis would have to take pains to test the moral character, endurance, memory and other requisite qualities of its aspiring philosophers before deciding which of them would make good rulers.

Once a select group who are intellectually and morally qualified is chosen, the question remains: how would they rule better than others by virtue of having knowledge of the Forms? A natural objection would be that politics doesn't need highfalutin philosophical knowledge; it needs down-and-dirty abilities that knowledge of the Forms won't

provide, and might likely impede. But the Platonic answer is that deciding about particular cases – which is something the philosopher–rulers will emphatically have to do to manage the particularities of forming and educating a suitable next generation of themselves – is something that does require the illuminating perspective of the broadest possible understanding.

To know the Forms is to know what is real and unalterable and essential. The world can be understood and explained, can be intelligible, just insofar as it is understood in terms of the Forms (the rest is mere and inexplicable brute matter, which receives but also limits the shaping power of the Forms). Such knowledge of what is unalterable – the definitions of the virtues and the very idea of what makes any purpose or goal good – is to inform all the particular political decisions that the rulers make. They have to decide about particular cases. How should this child be raised? Is this aspiring philosopher intellectually up to snuff? These decisions are to be made in the light of an understanding of what is genuinely valuable.[27]

Here Plato completes the inversion of the usual view of politics that Thrasymachus had offered in such a dark and cynical tone. Conventional rulers rule for their own benefit; these newly fashioned Platonic rulers will rule for the benefit of those whom they govern. Their own benefit comes from the justice and other virtues that they enjoy owing to their own philosophical natures; the benefit to their subjects comes through the exercise of an art. Politics is not about one's own advantage, in Plato's view; it is not an exercise in self-interest, even if properly understood. Ruling others is

a form of *noblesse oblige*, serving the true interests of those who cannot identify or attain them for themselves. The influence of the *Republic* lies in its connection between the value of virtue for the individual and the need for a certain kind of constitution in which those naturally capable of (and subsequently trained in) full virtue and knowledge must rule the rest in conditions of harmonious acceptance. This has attracted reactionary followers who have emphasized the elitism and hierarchy in Plato's dialogue, but also progressive followers who have emphasized the ways in which the dialogue criticizes unmerited and socially divisive distinctions of gender and property.[28] The Platonic vision of harmony within the individual, and between the individual and society, achieved by philosophical rule that serves the benefit of the ruled rather than exploiting them, has been influential precisely in having unsettled its innumerable and diverse readers (ancient and modern, Jewish, Christian and Islamic, conservative and radical) to the same extent that it has inspired them.

Political Knowledge and the Rule of Law

The pride of place accorded philosophy in the *Republic* is a strength, and a weakness. Its strength is in showing how ruling must be directed to valuable purposes. But its weakness is in treating politics as essentially derivative of philosophy. Just understand the Forms, add some practical experience and military training, and stir. In pointing to the knowledge of the Forms as what defines the philosophers and girds them for rule, the dialogue does not ultimately

answer the question 'What is the political art?' with any insight that is specific to *politics*.

In another dialogue, the *Statesman*, in which Socrates is a bystander while the leading role is taken by an unnamed Visitor from another Greek city (Elea), Plato does define political knowledge head-on. He does so in tandem with an effort to define its counterfeit. He inquires first into the sophist, the person with the illusion of political knowledge, and then into the statesman, the expert political knower. But what is it that the expert political knower knows? He knows how to rule over other human beings – it's not as if he is a shepherd ruling over a speechless flock. As in the *Republic*, ruling over people is benefiting them – but how are people actually benefited? The statesman is not a doctor, able to heal people; not a baker, able to feed them; not a general, able to defend them. The closest arts to his are those of the general, who knows how to wage war; the orator, who knows how to persuade; and the jurist, who knows how to resolve disputes among citizens, oversee contracts and determine what is just. These three figures themselves may seem to embody and exhaust all important political roles: after all, when the Athenians spoke of their political leaders, they spoke of 'the generals and the orators' (*hoi rhetores kai hoi strategoi*). But to the Visitor from Elea, there is a special role for a statesman above and beyond the roles of the generals, orators and jurists (jurors and, in the context of dramatic competition, judges) who populate the Greek political scene. That role is the knowledge of timing. What the statesman knows is *when* to direct the generals to make war, when peace; *when* to instruct an orator to give a persuasive speech; *when* it is

appropriate for jurists to make a judgement. He does not determine *when* in a vacuum: he knows *when* to take these actions for the best, for the forming of a virtuous citizenry and for the true advantage of the city.

Another way to put this is that the *Statesman* introduces a new idea of what ruling means. For most Greeks, the rulers were the people who held the offices in the city: who were generals or treasurers or ephors; or, perhaps in a democracy, the councillors and by extension the jurors and assembly attendees. The Visitor from Elea, however, suggests that there is a function of ruling that is above all that. Yes, a city needs generals and orators and jurors and judges. But to weave together its citizens in virtue and enable them to achieve good aims, those offices and the corresponding arts are not sufficient. True politics requires a grasp of good timing that can direct the deployment of each of these subordinate arts. The true statesman transcends these given political roles and inhabits a new one: that of overarching coordination for the best.[29] Politics requires unity, as in the *Republic*; here we learn that unity, in turn, depends on the coordination of timing with an eye to what is best.

Such coordination works also on the temperaments and outlooks of the citizens. For political strife and damaging decisions arise from ingrained divisions of outlook. The dialogue contrasts the people who tend to be slow and steady with those who are more impetuous and daring. Think of the classic contrast between hawks and doves. Left to themselves, two such groups might routinely clash in ways that further widen the gap between them – for they are unlikely to intermarry or to interact, loath to associate with those whom

they find so temperamentally alien. The danger of citizens finding themselves alien rather than kin to one another – which can spur civil war – is perhaps the deepest political danger of all. The statesman's role as described at the end of the dialogue is precisely to set up the educational bonds and to encourage the intermarriages (we might think more broadly today of all kinds of social interaction and diversity policies) that can avert that danger. By enabling people to share evaluations and perspectives, they can develop common judgements that will make them more appreciative of each other and more likely to gauge the policies best suited to the changing times with accuracy.

A final contribution of the *Statesman* is on the role of law – and in particular written law – in politics. For if political knowledge is key, and if political knowledge is now understood to be knowledge of timing, knowledge changing with circumstances and involving personalized advice about what to do for the best (like the advice of a gym trainer or doctor), how can it make any sense at all for political life to be governed by *laws*? Laws are exactly the opposite of precise and personalized: they are 'stubborn and ignorant'. (Think of the three-strikes laws that force judges in many American jurisdictions today to impose harsh sentences on nonviolent defendants at great social cost.)

Ruling by law seems to be a prescription for unvarying and therefore imprecise policies, at least compared with what an expert statesman could advise were he or she to materialize. And law normally takes the form of written law – especially in democracies, proud of the accountability embodied in written laws, as we saw in Theseus' speech in Chapter 2. Yet, to the

Eleatic Visitor in the *Statesman*, writing down laws only exacerbates the dangers of rule by law. For, even though writing per se is not the problem – doctors might use writing to dash off a new prescription – the idea of permanently engraved laws on stone tablets and public walls makes writing part of the fixity problem. The *Statesman* shows that, while polities may inevitably need laws, in that even the best statesman, like the best doctor, will use written law as a tool, it is a mistake to define political rectitude in terms of law. Law is merely a possible tool for rule; only political knowledge embodies the reasons that can make rule good.

Despite these strictures against law as imprecise with regard to political knowledge, another one of Plato's dialogues makes law central to the life of another imagined polity. The *Laws* is the only dialogue in which Socrates does not appear at all, although aspects of his ideas in other works are repeatedly referenced. Here, three old men – a Visitor from Athens, a Cretan and a Spartan – are making a pilgrimage to the cave of King Minos on Crete when they begin to discuss the best laws by comparing those of their home cities. Crete and Sparta were famous as societies governed by ancient codes of law, sharing the Doric dialect of Greek and a common militarist outlook focused obsessively on training young men in courage and in the techniques of warfare, contrasted with the Athenian cultivation of rhetoric and the arts. The Cretan character eventually reveals himself to be a member of a group about to found a new colony, and invites his pilgrimage companions to turn their comparative and historical conversation to the project of founding laws as if for that new colony.

Thus the *Laws*, like the *Republic*, is a project of founding a city in speech – and, while the *Republic*'s interlocutors also proceed by drawing up laws, the *Laws* does so in far more detail.[30] Moreover it draws up laws for a regime in which philosophers do not seem to exist: the term 'philosophy' is used in varying grammatical forms only twice in the dialogue. This is a city that is self-avowedly second-best to the ideal city of the *Republic* in which private property was abolished for the rulers.[31] Instead, property here is allowed – resulting in four wealth classes of citizens, comparable with those that Solon established in Athens – but the citizens are directed towards using their property for civic ends. The main mechanism to direct them is the law. Instead of being a shorthand tool for a busy expert, law is here reconceived as an embodiment of divine reason. The citizens are to see the city as founded with the aid of the gods; those inclined towards atheism will be given reasoned persuasive arguments to believe in the gods. Piety, which was absent as a major virtue from the *Republic*, is the cornerstone of civic life in the *Laws*.

With that divine sanction, the citizens are to be conditioned to love and obey the laws from birth, and even before birth (the dialogue goes into detail about the best rules of music and exercise for pregnant women). The laws themselves shape a balanced constitution that is a mean between 'monarchy' and 'democracy' (693e).[32] The citizens are to accept rule 'voluntarily' – yet their doing so is shaped by the persuasion and compulsion exercised by the lawgivers. For those forces to work, the city must be relatively insulated and isolated, sited away from the temptations of the coast. Only a few citizens will be given permission to travel abroad,

and then mainly to learn whether there are any features of other societies that can be beneficially incorporated in their own. The *Laws* offers a picture of a modified Greek society, in which citizens govern themselves rather than being governed by godlike philosophical guardians, but are kept in line with virtue and goodness by strict obedience – even memorization – of a law code that is eventually to be made fixed and virtually unchanging, treated as if it enjoyed the status of the very divine law with which Antigone had contrasted human laws (Chapter 1).[33]

If the *Republic* offers a Platonic aspiration to philosophical rule, and the *Statesman* explains what makes ruling knowledge genuinely political, the *Laws* evinces a good city that lacks precise philosophical guidance, yet that can keep itself on the rails of virtue by strict obedience to its given laws. Some see the *Laws*' emphasis on the divine sanction for obedience as a contradiction of the Socrates who would not have obeyed a verdict telling him to stop philosophizing. But that same Socrates obeyed the verdict that imposed his death. If the *Republic* imagines a city in which someone like Socrates could use philosophy to benefit his fellows (rather than be seen by them as a danger), the *Laws* gives us a city in which a decent life can be lived without the direct rule of philosophers – since they are so hard to find and to entrust with power without the danger of corruption. Notwithstanding the establishment of an elite council to meet at dawn, charged with amending the laws if necessary and with overseeing influences from outside the city in doing so, the *Laws* most significantly embodies wisdom not in individual philosophers, but rather in the content and authority of law.

Plato at Sea

Alongside Plato's dialogues is a tantalizing but problematic source: a series of thirteen letters said to be by him, but almost certainly written by others – the writing of letters attributed to famous personages being a favourite literary pastime of antiquity. Yet scholars are still divided over whether the 'Seventh Letter' might be genuine.[34] It would be an amazing source if it were, and, while I think its genuineness is unlikely, the letter is still instructive as to the views of Plato held by his followers. For it purports to present Plato in his own voice recounting his disillusionment with politics after the death of Socrates, and then telling the tale of three journeys that he made to Sicily in later life, trying to convert to philosophy a young man born to inherit tyrannical power: first to educate the young man, in partnership with his adviser and close Platonic friend Dion in 388; then to treat with him as ruler (Dionysius II) in trying to protect the banished Dion in 366; then again in 361–360, when the suspicious Dionysius II kept him in close confinement while Plato tried unsuccessfully to persuade him to let Dion return from banishment.

All three visits ended ignominiously. Plato was sent home the first time on a Spartan ship whose captain was bribed by Dionysius I to sell him into slavery; he was imprisoned the second time before being released; and he was threatened by Dionysius II's mercenaries on the third voyage. (The mercenaries hated him because 'they believed that he was trying to persuade Dionysius to give up the tyranny and

live without a bodyguard' (*Dion* 19.5).[35]) We must take these details with a large pinch of salt, since later Greek historians and biographers disagree about many of the details of the travels, including even the number of trips that Plato made to Sicily.[36] Nevertheless, it is fascinating to imagine Plato trying to cultivate a philosopher–ruler in person.

In the *Republic*, two paths to establish philosopher–rulers are proposed: either turning an existing ruler into a philosopher, or positioning a philosopher to take power. Plato perhaps tried the first with Dionysius II, the second with Dion. In his life of Dion, Plutarch says that Plato insisted that tyrants were wretched because they were unjust, whereas just men were the ones who lived blessed lives (*Dion* 5.1). Persuading a tyrant to give up injustice for philosophy would have been a striking proof of his philosophical contentions. In a happy moment of the second voyage, the palace floors were supposedly covered with sand as the philosopher and tyrant did geometry together.

Perhaps the lure of Syracuse enticed Plato to imagine a stage where his philosophy could be put directly into practice. Yet the Academy and his dialogues would prove the more powerful stages for propounding Plato's ideas in the long run. For in teaching, he established a model that was all the more attractive for being evanescent: the mystique of oral arguments and oral teaching is powerful in many cultures. And in writing, he forged a new genre of written works that staged emotions, interactions and ideas in such a way that the reader had to include himself in the effective audience of the work.[37] By creating images to encapsulate

and convey his arguments, and by inviting his readers into the dialogues, Plato made his writing effective at changing hearts as well as minds. He made philosophy into a performance piece of dramatic confrontation, one in which each reader is invited to play a part in coming to understand himself afresh. And in the realm of politics, he created a vision of rule by knowledge for the sake of a virtue that is the only genuine advantage and benefit, contrasting it with the prevailing visions in all existing regimes of rule by rhetoric or force for the sake of personal advantage defined as power and greed. The radical challenge to the basic goals that politicians everywhere pursue, and the very idea of politics as a fit subject for philosophy, rather than merely a realm of power contestation, have been learned from Plato above all.

Citizenship

Plato created an idea of political philosophy focused on the need for those with knowledge and virtue to serve others less able to understand or to attain them. In his vision, politics was a rare expertise, one that only an expert statesman or a small group of philosopher–kings and philosopher–queens could most safely and beneficially practise (it was second-best to have a large group of people governing themselves, as in the *Laws*). The highest and best form of politics was a service that an elite could provide to the many, saving them from sordid power struggles and directing them for their own best interests. Such an elevated political art could be possessed by only one or a few, who must use it to guide the ordinary humans incapable for the most part of doing so for themselves.

The Academy that Plato founded came to nurture an important transformation of this vision in the ideas of Plato's student Aristotle. Studying and researching under Plato from the ages of seventeen to thirty-seven, later founding his own school in Athens (the Lyceum), Aristotle – who will be introduced in more detail below – would eventually develop a view of politics that was at once profoundly shaped by Plato's and profoundly distinct from it. We might say that for Plato (again

setting aside his *Laws*) doing politics is in essence an hierarchical relation: in most of his writings, it is a power that one or a few people can and should wield to shape those who cannot sufficiently shape themselves. For Aristotle, by contrast, to do politics is in essence a cooperative relationship. Politics is something that human beings, *qua* human beings, do together. It is an expression of our most distinctively human capacities. While the Platonic view of the proper goal of power – using knowledge to achieve virtue – remains fundamental to Aristotle's vision of politics, Aristotle sees that goal as generally best achieved when virtuous citizens are able to share in carrying it out for themselves.

That fundamental idea of citizenship has a complicated relationship to the other ideas that we have so far discussed in this book (beyond the point noted in Chapter 2, that *politeia* originally means 'condition of citizenship', so that the relationship between constitution and citizenship is extremely close). For, in implying a relationship of equality among citizens who share together in a community (a *koinonia*), citizenship may seem to be also proto-democratic or at least to have an elective affinity with democracy. But, as we have seen, there were many other kinds of constitution in Greece; Aristotle was aware that he must also account for the citizenship shared in oligarchies and under monarchies. Moreover, he had learned from Plato to recognize that no existing constitutions actually aimed at virtue in the way that their theories of politics ideally prescribed. They may aim at freedom, wealth or honour, but not at virtue; in pursuing their chosen aim, they will develop their own self-serving theories of equality, justice and liberty.

To think about citizenship is, therefore, to think about who is ideally and actually 'inside' a given constitution as a citizen, who is 'outside', and why. This makes it a Janus-faced ideal. It seems to articulate a universal potential, and also to close it down, defining a community that is smaller than humanity and directing its members to serve each other and themselves preferentially over others. (Chapter 6 will consider the genesis of the alternative ideal of 'Cosmopolitanism', or, literally, the conception of being a citizen of the entire cosmos rather than one *polis*.) When Aristotle reproduces the exclusion of slaves and the partial exclusion of women from politics, positing a category of natural slaves, those exclusions contrast for modern readers with his affirmation of humans as political animals. Likewise, his exclusion of the poor from citizenship in his version of an ideal *polis* ('the *polis* of our prayers', *Politics*, Books 7–8) disturbingly crosses the normative and empirical lines, holding that their lack of education and leisure debars the poor from the pursuit of virtue that a normatively good *polis* demands.

For readers today interested in Aristotle's ideas of citizenship, this tension takes a further special form in the case of the idea of democracy. Modern democrats characteristically celebrate the innate and equal potential in all citizens to contribute to self-rule. That makes democracy sound like the ultimately rational form of constitution, expressing the basic meaning of citizenship, and so leads many modern democrats to seek in Aristotle a theoretical justification for democracy despite his specific criticisms of it as a non-ideal regime form.[1] In sorting out why Aristotle was critical of

democracy and also how his thought has been appropriated by democratic theorists, we will be able to understand the complexities of his theory of citizenship. The identity and goals of a citizen will be fundamentally shaped by the *politeia* of each regime, in both the narrower and the broader senses. Thus the value of citizenship in any particular regime ultimately depends on the values that regime pursues, embodies and instils in its citizens, indeed in all of its inhabitants. To celebrate citizenship is also to raise the possibility of a radical critique of those regimes that fail to direct it to the most worthwhile ends.

Human nature for Aristotle was fully realized only when its potential for citizenship flowered fully (and so, too, its potential for understanding the world, a higher capacity still). But that capacity was not one that ordinary people, who would have to work for a living and who lacked education, would necessarily be able to develop and exercise well. Aristotle's vision of an ideal polity was indeed deeply interactive: those who were equal to one another should exercise their capacities for virtue and practical wisdom in determining political affairs together. Yet, ideally, those exercising self-rule would be limited to those with the opportunity actually to exercise and cultivate the ethical and political virtues. Virtue for him, as for Plato, remained the ultimate aim and test of political life. If some or most people were unable – whether for innate or circumstantial reasons – to achieve it, they were not fit participants in politics. In taking inspiration from his work, we need to attend to the sources and limits of his own vision as well as to the ways in which it can be developed further in our own age.

Who was Aristotle?

Aristotle's life (384–322 BCE) is marked by a paradox. The great exponent of citizenship and political participation lived abroad for the whole of his adult life and so did not participate in politics among his compatriots. He left his homeland of Stagira when he went away to university in Athens at the age of seventeen, never to return, spending most of his life (with the exception of two interludes described below) in Athens, first as Plato's pupil in the Academy and later as the founder of his own school, the Lyceum.

Aristotle's lifetime in the 4th century BCE coincided with the rise of a new threat to the independence of the Greek *poleis* (the plural of *polis*), in the form of the kings of Macedon, who came from northern Greece near Aristotle's own birthplace. Following in the footsteps of his father, who had been physician to the Macedonian court, Aristotle served these rulers for a brief time, tutoring the young prince who would come to power in 336 BCE upon the assassination of his father Philip and become known as 'Alexander the Great' for conquering most of Greece and much of Asia as far as Afghanistan. When Alexander died suddenly in 323 BCE, the furore in Athens (which was chafing under the domination of Alexander's general Antipater) gave rise to an accusation of impiety against the resident non-citizen and Macedonian-aligned Aristotle, who was living and teaching there. Unlike his teacher's mentor Socrates, who had also been charged with impiety, Aristotle fled Athens to avoid a trial – so as, he supposedly said, to prevent Athens from sinning a second time against philosophy. He died of natural

causes within a year, leaving as executor of his will the very general Antipater whose rule was bitterly resented by many Athenians.

Thus, unlike Socrates and Plato, who were citizens of Athens, Aristotle was enmeshed in the complex rise of Macedonian power that threatened the independence of the city in which he lived and taught and of other Greek cities more generally. The dramatic and unprecedented reach of Alexander's conquests, extending from Greece far into Asia and incorporating Persia and a number of other eastern kingdoms, would forge a new model of imperial monarchy, fusing Greek and more eastern political ideals, languages and styles (even though cities and realms retained varying forms of relative autonomy within it). It was at some point while such global political reconfiguration was looming or under way in the hands of Philip or Alexander that Aristotle penned his paeans to citizenship and the *polis* – probably during his second stay in Athens (335–323 BCE) when he founded the Lyceum. Living in Athens as a metic who celebrated the civic self-rule in which he could not there take part, aware of the attractions and ambitions of imperial kingship, while praising the self-contained ideal of the *polis* – these are the tensions that marked Aristotle's staggeringly productive intellectual life.

There is one more tension that we need to examine. I have stressed so far that Aristotle praised politics as a distinctively human excellence. Only humans, he argued, have the capacity for speaking and for reasoning individually and collectively about how to act – practical knowledge or

wisdom (*phronesis*) – that makes politics both possible and necessary. But at the same time, he held that humans are not merely human. Mortal human animals share some capacities with the gods. In particular, we share the capacity for reasoning about the nature of things and for understanding and appreciating ('contemplating') the permanent truths of reality, which Aristotle called theoretical knowledge (*theoria*). Paradoxical as it sounds to us, such contemplation is in fact for Aristotle the highest possible form of activity, since in contemplating the natures of things we are actively understanding them (*Pol.* 1325b).

This leaves humans in Aristotle's account of nature in an unusual position. He identifies the distinctive nature of most creatures as also constituting their highest capacity. For example, what makes a cow's life distinctively cow-like are the capacities that sum up the highest possibilities of cowhood. For humans, however, the most distinctively human capacity that we have, which is political participation, is not the same as the highest capacity that we have, which is contemplation. We might say that the life of politics is the *most* human life, but it is not the *best* human life. Yet the best human life, the life shared with the gods of contemplation, is not a fully possible human life at all – because, being human, we can only contemplate in intervals, having to interrupt to look after our other needs and functions in ways that the gods have no need to do. Humans are perched between beasts and gods, ideally aspiring to live as much like gods as we can, while knowing that we cannot do so all the time.

An Aristotelian Approach to the Universe

Opening his *Metaphysics* with the confident assertion that 'All men by nature reach out to know' (980a), Aristotle throws himself into the search for knowledge with unparalleled energy and erudition, directing his associates in research on topics from the soul to colour to plants to metaphysics to poetics. And these are only the works that survive (some thirty out of about 500 recorded titles), most of them in the form of lecture notes by Aristotle or his students, as opposed to the treatises and dialogues that were irretrievably lost in the centuries between Aristotle's lifetime and our own.

All his inquiries are governed by a special method. He begins from existing beliefs or opinions (the *endoxa*, sometimes also called the 'appearances' or *phainomena*). These include, on the one hand, the beliefs of ordinary people ('the many') and, on the other hand, the theories of the especially learned ('the wise'). In Aristotle's view, all these are sources of potential truth and understanding, though they might need some correction and refinement: for different reasons, the many, and the wise, may get things wrong or make mistakes that have to be corrected. Still, fundamentally, the way that people see the world is a good guide to understanding its true nature. Unlike Plato, who was inclined to treat ordinary people's beliefs as misleading and deceptive, Aristotle saw humans as by nature well suited to understanding the world.[2]

With this method in hand, Aristotle launches into understanding the eternal truths of nature as well as the special

qualities of human nature. Nature, for him, is populated by 'substances': distinct individual beings, whether animals, plants or artefacts, that embody a particular kind of nature (a form) within matter. The form of each kind of nature is best defined by its *telos*, its goal or end, which in turn determines the characteristic way that each being functions (its *ergon*, or function). This is easiest to understand in the case of artefacts, shaped by their makers to carry out specific functions for a given purpose or end: for example, a bowl that is given a concave shape in order to serve the purpose of holding fruit. Aristotle applies the same kind of analysis to the species of living beings, which he sees as eternally existing, embodying functions and serving ends. For example the *telos* of a cow is to live the full life of a cow, carrying out its distinctive function so as to reproduce another generation of cows. For living beings, the full development and exercise of one's capacities for appropriate action, the life of characteristic activity, is what counts as happiness.

What about humans? Humans share with other living beings, especially with other animals, a set of common functions: nutrition, reproduction, movement, perception, emotion. And humans share with the gods the function of being able to contemplate eternal truths. Yet humans also have a sphere of action that pertains to them alone: the sphere of deciding how to act in the case of things that could be otherwise, deciding by using language and deliberation, rather than acting (like ants or bees) from instinctually guided forms of communication. In reaching out to explore the world, we form an intention (*prohairesis*), which is at once a grasp and a yearning. That intention structures our

reflections as we decide how to act – shaped by our habitual dispositions to act either appropriately or excessively.

What is unique in human nature is this capacity for practical reasoning, a capacity that we perfect when we develop 'practical wisdom' accompanied by the dispositions to act rightly in the diverse respects that constitute the ethical virtues. Aristotle thinks of virtue as lying in a mean between two excesses: for example, courage is the mean between rashness and cowardice. Because happiness comes from activity, we can't really be happy if we remain as couch potatoes or live isolated, bored lives. We are doers, happy only when exercising capacities that include the sublime, divine activity of thinking and contemplating along with the characteristically human activity of deliberating and deciding, in the proper degree, moment and context.

Where does politics belong in this story? Human action is not a precise domain of study, as is the study of the changeless truths about the universe. But it is a special domain of study, pursued not merely to understand but in order to act well. In his major treatise on ethics, the *Nicomachean Ethics*, addressed to his son Nicomachus, Aristotle writes that 'The goal is not knowing but doing' (*EN* 1095a), specifically, the doing of virtuous action. In the domain of human action, 'we are inquiring not in order to know what virtue is, but in order to become good.'[3] So the fundamental goal of human action is to act well in relation to things that could be done otherwise, that is, in relation to the choices that humans face. Moreover, there is no sharp divide between individual and collective action, between ethics and politics. Ethics and politics alike aim at what is good as the goal (*telos*) of action,

understanding this highest good as happiness; both use practical reasoning and knowledge in order to do so.

Politics is the domain of collective choices and decisions. And those, in turn, make possible virtuous individual decisions, because the laws and customs of a political community provide the context in which individuals can learn to exercise their capacities for virtue well. Humans are capable of developing bad and vicious habits just as they are capable of developing good and virtuous ones. The laws established in a polity help to make the difference, providing the context for habituation to form a virtuous 'second nature' out of the potential of our inborn first nature – and giving an extra incentive to obedience by imposing the fear of punishment. Once again, we see how the narrowly political *politeia* shapes the broader *politeia*, how political organization and structure shape the way of life and the character of a polity's citizens.

In bad or imperfect polities, people don't learn to aim at virtue. Too often they are seduced instead by the goals of pleasure, wealth or honour divorced from genuine goodness. People who devote themselves to feasting at the expense of health or family; plutocrats who ignore civic duties in the quest to amass wealth; generals who violate the ethical duties of war in order to retain the honour of command – each such person destroys his prospects for genuine happiness by letting some subordinate goal distort his understanding of a wider good. But this is not to say that pleasure, wealth and honour have to be abandoned altogether. Aristotle is not an ascetic. Far from it. For the capacities to enjoy pleasure, wealth and honour are also genuine human capacities. His view is rather that we should be educated in such a way as

to bring these motivations together with the goal of seeking the genuine good.[4] A child who is habituated to take pleasure in treating others well; to earn money by completing worthwhile tasks; and to find honour in playing by the rules – such a child will develop the kind of disposition that will allow him to be truly happy. He will enjoy pleasure, wealth and honour, but will do so only when and by exercising his capacity for virtue.

The 'he' here is deliberate; as we will see, Aristotle, unlike Plato, treats females as generally and significantly less capable of reliably developing and exercising reason in virtue of their sex. Women supposedly have a less secure capacity for exercising their reason, and are therefore said to benefit from being ruled by their husbands. Yet Aristotle ties himself in knots on this point, calling the rule of husbands over wives 'constitutional' rule (*politikos*, the adverb), but having to acknowledge that, unlike most forms of constitutional rule, the natures of the citizens here are not equal and so they are not to rule and be ruled in turn. Another such form of constitutional relationship that does not involve reciprocal equality in ruling will be found when Aristotle comes to consider monarchy. These two problematic cases reveal the faultline in defining constitutional rule as in some way involving equals, yet also allowing certain forms of it to permanently inscribe relations of hierarchy and inequality.

There is a further sting in the tail of this prescription. For if someone is not well brought up on these lines – if the adults around him are thieves or liars, who train him to put on a virtuous front but profit from unjust action behind the scenes – reading a book like Aristotle's *Ethics* or *Politics* will

be of no help in getting him to act correctly. Studying ethics can lead to action, as it ideally should, only if the ground is prepared with well-directed habits that dispose people to recognize and pursue what is good. The study of ethics can't convert the immoral; its role is to further educate and to help perfect the well brought up (*EN* 1103b).

That again points to the sense in which ethics requires politics, in which citizenship traverses the public and the private formation of character, to use categories with a more modern valence. Habituation is not a matter merely of home life, but of the laws and customs by which children learn how to behave; we saw this in Chapter 2 in discussing Sparta, where boys and girls were subjected to such stringent training that many preferred to die rather than submit to military defeat or live as slaves. But, again, politics is not conceived here as a matter of some kind of external imposition. Rather, participation in politics is itself part of the excellence and fulfilment of adult human nature – and doing so provides the proper context in which younger people can be raised to enjoy such excellence and fulfilment in their turn. Citizenship is a condition for the good life as well as a constitutive part of it.

Inclusion and Exclusion

This puts us in a position to appreciate one of Aristotle's most important sentences. We can begin by asking in more detail how it is that humans come to live in polities at all. In Book 1 of his *Politics*, Aristotle traces the origins of human communities as they originate in natural inclinations to

associate. One natural association – the sexual attachment between female and male, resulting for the most part in pro-creation – is like the reproduction of other animals: it happens by nature in the sense of the reproductive functions, not as a result of specifically human deliberative choice. A household is composed of one such pair and their offspring; and a village is composed of an agglomeration of households, perhaps originally bound by kinship ties, as the brothers of a family establish households of their own. This is where Aristotle specifies that in a household pair, one person will be better able to govern the common life than the other, and he expects the superior in practical reasoning capacity will normally be the man (he does not consider here same-sex pairings): 'the male is by nature fitter for command than the female' (1259b, though he also admits there that some cases may violate this general natural principle; as he cautions repeatedly in his *Physics*, natural tendencies only ever hold 'for the most part').

All these communities arise originally for the sake of survival and fulfilling basic animal needs and functions. But, because humans inevitably use as much of their full range of capacities in associating together as much as possible, in families and beyond, this means that the family is already a locus for people to pursue the good life (the happy life, which is the virtuous life), not mere survival alone (what Aristotle calls 'mere life').[5] Yet there are limits to the extent to which the good life can be pursued in an isolated household or village. For the capacity for practical reasoning together as equals, using speech to decide collectively how to act in relation to 'the good and the evil, the just and the unjust',

is one that can be fully expressed only in a *polis*, which is the community that arises from the union of a set of villages (1253a–b).

A *polis* is not just a larger scale village. In having 'reached the limit of complete self-sufficiency', it forms a framework for the exercise of all human capacities. And so, while 'coming into being for the sake of life', the *polis* exists 'for the sake of the good life' (1252b). It constitutes the *telos*, the final end, of human association.

This is the conclusion that Aristotle draws in his famous sentence: 'Hence it is clear that it is by nature that the *polis* exists, and that the human being by nature is a political animal' (1252a). This does not mean that we find states popping up in forests like mushrooms. Quite the opposite. 'By nature', for Aristotle, does not mean that something is inevitably or spontaneously realized to the exclusion of human intervention. Indeed, he immediately acknowledges that not all humans do live in *poleis*. Political communities are built by humans, and humans may sometimes fail to build them, or be expelled from them. But what he means by saying that the *polis* exists by nature and that 'the human being by nature is a political animal' is that it is an innate capacity of human nature to associate with others to decide, using speech, how to act in relation to what is good and bad, just and unjust.

Humans have that capacity, and can live a fully human life, only if they realize it and are able to act upon it in the unique and peculiar state form of the *polis*. Some are simply unlucky in not getting to do so; a handful of others may be freakish solitaries, condemned by this defect in their nature to be 'a lover of war'. So, for Aristotle, what is natural is not a

'war of all against all', as would be the case for the 17th-century English philosopher Thomas Hobbes in his work *Leviathan*. On the contrary, Aristotle would say that it is unnatural to be naturally at war with other humans. Human nature (not universally or inevitably but characteristically) is to be sociable, and specifically to be political: to live in a political community, one in which people associate and speak together, making decisions for the sake of the good life and ruling themselves in accordance with justice. Only someone alienated from such a common life is 'eager for war', and only because he is by nature freakish in being solitary and 'unyoked' (1253a). The normal and natural human condition is not one of readiness for war but of readiness for politics.

This brings us to another controversial aspect of Aristotle's analysis of human nature. This is his category of natural slaves. In a theory in which equal rule depends on equal capacity for practical reason, any significant failing of practical reason would logically require a corresponding inequality in rule.[6] Aristotle thinks that he has found one such failing in women, whose practical reason, he says, is characteristically less authoritative than that of men. He thinks that he has found another in the case of natural slaves, who (on this logic) would be people who are wholly incapable of governing their own behaviour. Such people would not be independent agents at all. They would instead be living tools for their master, and would benefit the master's purposes as well as receive benefits from a life under such despotic rule, being stipulatively unable to rule themselves.

But did Aristotle think that there were really any such people? He acknowledges that many of those who are

captured in war and forced into slavery – the typical mode of acquiring slaves in Greece and neighbouring realms at the time – are not natural slaves at all. (Consider the noble women of Troy sold into slavery after their city was destroyed, for example.) And he remarks on claims having been made that all slavery is merely conventional, a matter of happenstance, with no basis in nature (alas, he names no names, so we don't know the identities of the critics he had in mind). Nevertheless he insists on the possibility of a justified category of natural slavery: that, in principle, there could be humans who lack the capacity to direct their own actions and so are available to serve others as human tools – for the good of their masters and, as a consequence, their own.

Yet his discussion of this possibility is riven by tensions. For how can a slave be utterly lacking in rational capacity, if he is a human being, and if he has to be able to understand and follow his master's instructions in order to serve his interests? The idea of a human being who is able to communicate and to reason sufficiently to act effectively, yet who lacks all grasp of the ends of action and all capacity for self-discipline, seems an unstable theoretical category, rather than a real possibility. (This has not stopped numerous defenders of slavery from appealing to Aristotelian natural slavery, for example, in writing of the Spanish American conquest and in defending the practices of the antebellum American South.[7]) And if there are, in actuality, no such natural slaves – even though Aristotle insisted that it was possible that there might be; and if women are not less capable of self-rule than men – even though Aristotle had believed they were – his theory of human nature would point not

to domination and patriarchy but in the direction of equal citizenship. This is why many theorists of equal citizenship have been able to find inspiration in Aristotle, even though he himself accepted and justified forms of civic domination.

Contesting Equality

Equality is the essence of politics properly understood. As Aristotle says: 'constitutional rule is of those who are free and equal' (1255b). Conceptually, there should be no rule (no relation of subordination) among equals, because there is no logical basis to subordinate one equal to another. But, since rule is necessary in practice – a vital concession by Aristotle to experience – free and equal citizens take it in turns. Hence Aristotle's famous account of the good citizen as one who knows how to rule and be ruled, though his definition proper of the citizen has come earlier: 'he who shares in judging and in office' (1277a, 1275a). Yet this definition does not automatically imply democracy (nor does it imply that all citizens must be eligible to hold all offices); nor does it deny the possibility of monarchy, since citizens may share in some functions of government even under a monarch. To have a share – to be equal in having *a* share – is not necessarily to have *an exactly equal* share. It leaves room for those functions, and for others, to be shared unequally on the basis of other relevant characteristics.

The fundamental question of 'who is an equal' is for Aristotle a question that has to be parsed logically into different possible meanings of 'equal'. To give equality meaning, one modern scholar notes that we must always ask, 'Equality

of what?"[8] Aristotle had already taught that 'equality of what' is always also tantamount to 'equality for whom'. Depending on what counts as the basis for equality, some people will be included into citizenship or excluded from it.

In the ongoing conflicts between oligarchies and democracies, together with the spectre of oligarchy sharpened into monarchical empire, Aristotle acknowledges two fundamentally different ideas of equality at work. One of them is 'arithmetical equality': each person simply counts for one, as in majoritarian voting – which is more friendly to democracy. The other is 'geometrical equality': only those people are equal who are of equal merit or worth – whether that be measured in terms of virtue or more prosaically in terms of wealth – a definition more friendly to oligarchy. That is, these two logically open interpretations of equality give rise to two opposed political positions. In reality, democracies and oligarchies can both count as forms of constitutional rule. For they are each premised on equality, even though they identify 'equals' on different grounds. But each side will view the other's interpretation as flawed: democrats viewing themselves as 'being equal, claim to be worthy of sharing equally in all things', while oligarchs, viewing themselves as 'being unequal [to the many], seek to get more for themselves' (1301a).

The violent tussles between partisans of oligarchy and democracy that marked the Greek world in the 5th and 4th centuries BCE were real-life illustrations of Aristotle's point: that treating politics as a matter for equal citizens does not yet settle which citizens are to be considered equal. (The same is true of the struggles for the franchise for workers,

one-time slaves and women in modern times.) Indeed, Aristotle sees the conflict over equality as lying at the bottom of virtually all political and factional unrest: 'everywhere civil conflict arises because of inequality' (1301b), though that desire may characterize oligarchs who resent their perceived equality with the poor as much as democrats asserting their equality with the rich. More generally: 'Inferiors engage in civil conflict in order to be equal, and equals in order to be superior [to their inferiors, but equal among themselves: which they see as true equality]'(1302a).

It is the role of the statesman to take measures to prevent revolution, following advice that Aristotle gives in a broad spirit: for example, never to 'treat those seeking honour unjustly in an affair of disrespect, or the many in an affair of profit' (1308a). 'The most important thing in every constitution and in all the laws and other administration is that they be so arranged that no one can profit from holding public office' (1308b). Here, Aristotle recalls Plato's conception of politics as service, versus self-enrichment and self-aggrandizement. For Plato, only reluctant rulers should rule, and they must do so for the benefit of the people, not for their own benefit; for Aristotle, even if officials may legitimately seek to hold office as a form of honour, they must be prevented from using it to make themselves rich.

As his discussion of political conflict shows, Aristotle's understanding of the fundamental nature of politics is accompanied by a sensitive grasp of the vagaries and varieties of its actual practice. He is caustic about the way that 'what is not said by people to be just or advantageous for themselves, they are not ashamed of doing to others; they seek just rule

for themselves, but in relation to rule for others they care nothing for what is just' (1324b). Yet he is not above using his knowledge to describe what a tyrant should do to hold on to power: either sow distrust, take away power from his subjects and humble and frighten them, or else try to act more like a king, guarding public revenues and protecting the city in case of war. He holds that each kind of regime will fall into difficulty if it pursues its innate goals too far in an untempered way, just as, in his ethical theory, virtue is always found in the mean between two extremes. Should the rich oligarchs busy themselves only with extracting more privileges for themselves, their regime will be less likely to survive than if they mollify the common people by treating them moderately. This was a live issue. Aristotle observed an oath sworn by some extreme oligarchs in his day, oligarchs who understood their own interests as opposite to the interests of their opponents: 'I will be evil to the people [meaning, the poor or the common people who in these regimes might not even be citizens] and will seek out ways in which I may harm them.' On this Aristotle comments tartly that oligarchic self-protection would be better served if they were to swear the exact opposite: 'I will do the people no injustice' (1310a).

Ruling in the Common Interest

Mediating between his fundamental account of the nature of politics as expressing the human capacity for practical reason, and these shrewd remarks about incautious tyrants and revolutionary oligarchs, is Aristotle's classification of political regimes with respect to one crucial question. For

deciding who is to hold power as a citizen is only half the battle: the other half is determining what those citizens should use their power to do. Should they selfishly pursue their own interests at the expense of others? If so, they would be deviant forms of government by the one, the few or the many defined by ruling in their self-interest only. Aristotle systematizes the definition of the good and bad kinds of the basic three Herodotean constitutions by means of a test of ruling in the common interest or in one's own interest. On the bad side, he puts 'tyranny' (rule by one person in his own interest), but also the familiar Greek categories of 'oligarchy' (rule by a few people in their own interest) and 'democracy' (rule by the many in their own interest – as against that of the few), all three of these featuring as pervasive but perverse mistaken regimes. In contrast, he identifies the 'correct forms of government' as 'those in which the one, or the few, or the many, rule for the sake of the common advantage' (1279a), naming these 'monarchy', 'aristocracy' (a more self-consciously virtue-laden name than 'oligarchy') and 'polity' (in Greek, *politeia*, here appropriating the general name of 'constitution' for this one regime form in particular, and using this in place of the now pejorative 'democracy' for an approved form of rule by the multitude).

The correct or true forms of government are rule of the citizens and for their benefit, even if not by all of them at all times; the deviations are rule of the citizens for the benefit of the rulers alone. But it might not be easy to set up the correct forms of government, especially polity, which Aristotle says at one point will succeed in its aim of ruling for the common interest only if populated by those

who are virtuous or excellent in some way. In practice, he says, these are not all the citizens but rather specifically the hoplite class, those citizens able to afford to train and fight with armour (1279b). The polity as an example of rule by the many is actually an example of their exclusion: the poor many, who cannot afford hoplite armour, will not be citizens in this constitution.

But even this kind of sociological correction may be inadequate to ensure a correct form of government, in Aristotle's view: because the one, few or many were likely to have nominated themselves for rule on the basis of sheer wealth or power, not of genuine virtue. (So he sets apart from all six regimes just mentioned the 'best regime', in which all and only those who are virtuous are citizens: we will discuss this further below.) And that self-nomination opens the door to instability in the correct forms of the three regimes as well. For example, the poor many will resent the paternalist rule of a self-appointed few. This leads Aristotle to consider how regimes might in practice stabilize themselves by balancing between opposed forms.

One way to do so is for a regime to take a leaf out of an opponent's book of policy prescriptions, as for example when in modern times a conservative government extends unemployment benefits. This requires the ruling group to look beyond its partisan blinkers and concern itself not with pure party principle, but rather with its own longevity. 'He [the legislator] must not think that what is popular or oligarchic is that which will give the city the most democratic or oligarchic way of life, but rather that which will make it last for the longest time' (1302a).

Another way is to establish a regime that in some way fuses two principles normally opposed, as for example by giving some rights to the free and poor many and others to the rich few. Just as Aristotle describes how tyrants might save themselves by moderating their behaviour, so here he describes how democracies might moderate themselves and become more viable long term by incorporating some measures that are oligarchical in their tendency (such as a lowish property qualification: many Greek democracies imposed a low property qualification for at least some civic purposes). This is one of the origins of what later writers would call a 'mixed regime'.

Yet Aristotle's favourite idea of this kind is not that of a mixed regime, but of a middling or middle regime. Unlike the mixed regime, a middling regime will not combine democratic and oligarchical policies, but will rather have its political centre of gravity and identity in a group of citizens 'in the middle' (as *mesoi*) between the few rich and the many poor (1295b). Such citizens are most likely to be 'equals and similars' and so to constitute a secure base for political life. In practice in m ost cities there were very few such *mesoi* to be found, though Aristotle would want there to be more for this kind of regime to work. He says that this kind of middling regime is 'the best constitution for most *poleis* and the best life for most human beings' (1295a) – for those living in the ordinary circumstances of life, as opposed to the absolutely best regime that he had much less expectation of finding realized.

How far does the 'common interest' extend – that is, how demanding should it be? Aristotle views the *polis* as 'a community' in which the citizens share: it is a community of

common activities, embracing the activities of ordinary life in the family and household, and encompassing them with the political decision-making of citizen equals.[9] The question is which common activities are necessary and sufficient for the *polis* to thrive. Should property, for example, be owned in common? That tenet of communism is one that Aristotle thinks has been actually proposed in Plato's *Republic* for the state as a whole (*Pol.* 1261a; but, as noted earlier, the *Republic* proposes that only the rulers be deprived of property, which is a different thing).

Aristotle, for his part, rejects common ownership, on the grounds that it is generally inefficient (he thinks it will diminish responsibility and encourage factiousness) and that it goes too far in unifying the state, as if it were one giant family instead of a plurality of distinct citizens each with his own household. Yet he favours an ideal of viewing property as providing public benefit and sometimes public use. This is to be put into practice, for example, by allowing others to hunt over private land, and by providing common meals: either by tithing from the produce of private lands, or by the establishment of *polis* property that could be farmed to feed the community together. Common meals, as practised in Crete and Sparta, and more ceremonially and restrictedly in Athens, are both a symbol and an incarnation of the ideal of sharing in common activity by which a *polis* community is defined.

The Case for Democracy – and Its Limits

So far we have stressed that Aristotle's analysis of political equality and citizenship is far from a simple endorsement

of democracy. He treats the regime he calls 'democracy' as a deviation from a superior form of 'polity' that would actually exclude the many poor from citizenship. He acknowledges ways of thinking about equality that support oligarchy rather than democracy. He takes virtuous flourishing as the ideal goal and ground for political participation. And he also shares elite views of his time (and for many generations to come) that assume that the poor who have to work for a living would be unable to cultivate virtue: at the very least because they lack the leisure and education to do so. Nevertheless, at one point in the *Politics*, he pauses to consider in what way the poor multitude might be incorporated into politics. Is there some truth in the democratic dictum that the people (including the poorest citizens) should be sovereign in government – and, if so, what should that sovereignty mean?

That question frames a famous chapter of the *Politics* (3.11) that considers the claim of the whole body of the *demos* – as opposed to, say, only the better sort of people – to be *kurios* in deciding what is left open by the laws (the laws, he insists, are to be *kurios* overall). A good case can be made for translating *kurios* as 'sovereign' (for starters, it is the same word used for the slave master and the husband or other male guardian of a woman, just like *dominus* in Latin).[10] With *kurios* translated in this way, the chapter squarely raises the question of democratic or popular sovereignty. It answers that question by developing an account of how the *demos* are sovereign in selecting and scrutinizing the highest office-holders. That is a real form of popular sovereignty. But it is not an indiscriminate or wholesale endorsement of any and every form of democratic participation (as

it is often taken to be). Aristotle is concerned to demarcate the proper claims of the democratic multitude. In so doing, he is as concerned to rebut broader claims that they might make as he is to refute objections to their participation at all. Once again, however, the ideas that he proposes for ways of thinking about the value and capacity of mass participation in judgement have inspired later adherents to take them further, to develop them in institutional settings very different from the ones to which Aristotle restricted his own case.

His own starting point is that the highest individual offices of a political regime should be allocated only to those who could be more reasonably expected to have developed their individual political capacities. In practice, that means a property requirement on office-holding for the highest individual offices, though he acknowledges elsewhere in a Platonic spirit that wealth is only a crude proxy for virtue (there were plenty of wealthy Greek men who failed to use their means to avail themselves of virtue). Yet this in turn raises a problem. For in the constitutionalist milieu of 4th-century Greek thought, those holding the highest offices (*tas archas*) were easily understood as those who were ruling (*archein*). But, in that case, it would seem that the poor multitude excluded from the highest offices were not actually 'ruling and being ruled in turn' – and so were not being treated as equal citizens.

Aristotle solves the problem by expanding the linked ideas of ruling and of sovereignty in one of his character-istic on-the-one-hand-but-on-the other-hand moves. In one sense, certainly, it is the highest office-holders who rule. But at the same time, it is those who *choose* the office-holders

(and decide by scrutiny on their eligibility to serve) and who *judge* their performance in office who are sovereign – not by holding high office themselves, but by controlling (in these ways) those who do. The sovereign powers of the democratic multitude are the powers to decide (who should rule) and to judge (how well they have ruled). And he gives reasons to think that even a poor multitude will be able to exercise those functions well: 'For the many, who are not as individuals excellent men, nevertheless can, when they have come together, be better than the few best people, not individually but collectively, just as feasts to which many contribute are better than feasts provided at one person's expense.'[11]

Aristotle's image of 'feasts to which many contribute' is as alluring as it is elusive. The usual reading of the 'democratic feast', as this passage is often called, is that he is referring to the greater diversity that the many can provide, though he may rather be stressing the greater aggregated quantities that they can offer (and the same ambiguity applies to other images that he provides as examples in this discussion).[12] Whatever the precise sources of better collective judgement, the role of the many in exercising such judgement is tailored, in its political application in the chapter, to their role in controlling the high office-holders. There, it is turned to the purposes of explaining how the exercise of popular sovereignty can control office-holders even if the people are, in specific institutional contexts, excluded from serving in those offices themselves.

All officials, including the highest ones, are to be subordinate to the law.[13] Here Aristotle again goes beyond the practice of Athenian democracy, which alternated between

declaring men the judges of what the law was and paying obeisance to the laws as greater than men. Aristotle fully entrenches law as the ideal ruler in the community, above the magistrates, insofar as it is passionless and impartial: the magistrates or officials are to be sovereign only over those matters on which 'the laws cannot pronounce with precision'.[14] Laws themselves, however, will be relative to a given regime. The same laws will not suit an oligarchy and a democracy. The best regime will have laws that may differ from both.

The Best Regime

At the end of the *Politics*, Aristotle turns to discuss the best regime in general, the '*polis* of our prayers', as opposed to the best regime for most men and most societies. This is a topic requiring recapitulation of what is the best life. The happy man must have all of the three different kinds of goods – 'those that are external, those of the body, and those of the soul' – but ultimately all these are chosen for the sake of the soul, so that 'each one is accorded just so much happiness as he has of virtue and practical wisdom and of action with regard to both.'[15] Being happy is not wholly a matter of luck. While one's happiness might well be marred or undermined by lack of education to develop one's capacities, or by the blows of fortune (losing one's family or home), it is rooted in one's own activity. The *polis* is happy when it makes possible the realization of the happiness – the virtuous activity, theoretical as well as practical – of its citizens. And the best

polis is the one that makes possible, and is populated by, such fully virtuous citizens.

Aristotle has various things to say about how such a regime might be set up in practice. Perhaps because in his time political and military assemblages depended on the human voice for their ordering – generals shouting orders, heralds convoking assemblies – he thought that the *polis* had to have a natural limit in size: 'For who will be the general of a multitude grown exceedingly large, and who the herald, if not a Stentor [someone with a famously loud voice]?' (1326b). The best *polis* would need enough territory to be self-sufficient, but, unlike Plato in the *Laws*, Aristotle is not against the city's having a port to engage in external trade (though he applauds cities that demarcate a political gathering space from the commercial functions of the marketplace). And we see in his discussion of this best *polis* the tensions that mark his consideration of politics throughout. For, on the one hand, he insists that none of the citizens must lead the life of artisans or tradesmen, 'for such a life is ignoble and opposed to virtue', nor the life of a farmer, since farmers have no leisure to cultivate virtue (1328b–1329a). Yet these are presented as disabilities due to habits and practices, not necessarily to inherent capacities. It is the lives they (are forced to) lead, not the kind of people they inherently are, that debar the workers and farmers from citizenship in this best *polis*.[16] Like the 'Old Oligarch', who attributed the poor's ignorance to their lack of education, rather than to their inherent capacities, so Aristotle here ascribes the political incapacity that he would enforce on the poor to their circumstances rather than to their natures.

This suggests that their exclusion is not inherent in Aristotle's ideal regime, but rather a consequence of the way he assumes that societies must be economically constituted. In a regime where some are excluded from citizenship, a virtuous regime consists of the virtuous few governing themselves. But where economic and social conditions make it possible for the many also to enjoy the education and leisure to develop virtue, the logic of Aristotle's argument would expand the circle of self-governing citizens to include them. We see here once again how Aristotle's logic resists an over-idealization of democracy in his terms and in ours, yet also how it can potentially be expanded in a democratic direction.

Aristotle concludes the *Politics* by stressing that education should be suited for each particular constitution (1337a), in order to imbue habits appropriate to its perpetuation. Indeed, every form of regime will endeavour – some more successfully than others – to mould their citizens to suit their own political aims. This is why legislating for a good regime is of such enormous human importance. For it is only in the best regime that the good human being and the good citizen will fully coincide. In each different kind of imperfect regime, the citizens' capacities and dispositions will be distorted to suit the particular or perverse interests of the ruling group – even if that should include all the citizens themselves exercising a kind of tyranny of majority opinion. We must endeavour to make politics in the image of what is best in our nature, lest it shape us in the image of what is worse.

While in exercising theoretical reason humans share a capacity with the gods, they can best exercise and perfect their practical reason in concert with fellow citizens.

Citizenship is ideally the condition and the pinnacle of exercise of a deep capacity in human nature, a capacity that may be celebrated in its potentially equal distribution, but that may also be distributed unequally in ways taken to be consequential for the distribution of citizenship itself. The equality of citizens to one another leaves open many questions about the political arrangements obtaining among them, and also about the basis on which citizenship itself is shared.

While Aristotle's thought encompasses much beyond citizenship, his explorations of the nature of the citizen and his relation to a regime articulate an ideal while exploring the many possible variations of, and deviations from, that ideal in real-world political practice. Different constitutional regimes may misconstrue what virtue requires or allocate political power based on inadequate proxies for virtue such as wealth or number alone. Citizens living in those regimes, internalizing and upholding their values, are vulnerable to replicating their weaknesses, while only citizens of the best regime would be able to develop the full panoply of civic virtues and strengths. For Aristotle, as for Plato, the political regime in which one lives has profound consequences for the kind of person one will become. In the next chapter, we will find that some of their successors in teaching philosophy in Athens would explore a range of ways in which the political regime might be even more encompassing, while others challenged the classical link between the best political regime and the person seeking to live the best human life.

Cosmopolitanism

Aristotle's political ideal was citizenship in a single *polis*, a city-state that would normally govern itself by its own laws and protect itself by its own walls.[1] Subsequent generations of Greek and later Roman philosophers would begin to question the boundary and definition of a political community. From differing perspectives and within divergent schools, they began to ask whether the best such community might perhaps not be coterminous with city laws and city walls. Perhaps it might include only a select group of friends within a city's precincts; perhaps, alternatively, it might extend outwards to include all rational beings, wherever they might geographically be found.

These and other possibilities began to be explored already in Aristotle's lifetime, and especially within some twenty-five years of his death, when two new leading schools of philosophy established themselves in Athens. These two schools would give shape to important challenges to city laws and city walls as political ideals. Zeno of Citium, founder of the Stoic school, wrote a *Politeia* (*Constitution*) in which he is said to have argued against demarcating cities or localities by individual systems of justice (Plutarch, *De Alex. Fort.* 329A–B).[2] Meanwhile, Epicurus of Samos, the founder of the

Epicurean school that would become the Stoics' chief rival in philosophical debates, would inspire an enthusiastic follower centuries later to inscribe in stone a vision of an age when 'there will come to be no need of city-walls or laws.'[3] These two schools, as we will see in this chapter, offered fundamentally divergent understandings of politics. Yet they shared a belief in philosophical and political ideals that were not ultimately defined by the boundaries of city laws and city walls.

The best known of these new ideals was developed in Stoic terms as the ideal of Cosmopolitanism. Cosmopolitanism is actually only the most important of a wide set of challenges to the boundaries, value and definition of political community developed in this period. In these new challenges, debates over the source of justice in either nature or convention, the definition of equality and its relationship to citizenship – to name key themes from earlier chapters – came into focus afresh. The radical challenge of whether there can be a politics beyond the boundaries of a given polity's laws or walls calls into question what the nature of politics itself might be.

The first vision of Cosmopolitanism had been articulated within Aristotle's lifetime by the proponent of another new philosophical movement. This was a man called Diogenes, who replied to a questioner asking where he was from by answering that he was a *kosmopolites*: a citizen of the cosmos, not of any one *polis* or political form. 'Cosmopolitanism' for Diogenes (who came to be known as a Cynic, from the Greek for 'dog', because of his commitment to living according to his nature as an animal) meant that he was rejecting the claims of any political community on him altogether. Taking the word over from Diogenes and his followers, the Stoics

developed it in a subtly but crucially different direction, to include a positive vision of cosmic citizenship in which local forms of citizenship are subsumed but not abolished. They mounted this vision against the Epicureans, who had already begun to articulate a vision of the ideal community as limited to a community of friends, situated within a political order that would simply provide security and justice. Finally the 'Sceptics' or 'Inquirers', who arose in two lineages (one of them more moderate 'Academic' Sceptics within the post-Platonic Academy, the other later tracing a more radical model of doubt to a forebear who had been a contemporary of Zeno and Epicurus), treated all political claims as merely apparent conventions, withholding judgement about whether they are rooted in reason or in nature.

With the exception of Diogenes, all these thinkers and ideas belong to what is called the 'Hellenistic' era in Greek history: the period of Greek history from Alexander the Great's death in 323 BCE to the surrender of Ptolemaic Egypt (the last part of his erstwhile empire to be ruled by descendants of his generals) to Rome in 30 BCE.[4] The variations on, and alternatives to, Cosmopolitanism debated during and just prior to this period broke new ground in thinking about politics: its origins, value, location and extent. Alongside the new schools and movements founded in this period (the earlier Cynics, and the Stoics, Epicureans and Sceptics), we also find a continued development of Plato's ideas in his Academy, and of Aristotle's in his Lyceum, his followers now called Peripatetics. Most of these schools considered these questions of politics in the framework of larger theories of physics, logic and ethics. I will refer to these only as needed

to make sense of their political views that formed one part of the subject of ethics.

Debates about nature and convention between Socrates and the sophists were revived and continued in these new philosophical frameworks, while the new questions about Cosmopolitanism and its meaning were raised alongside. Key questions in Hellenistic philosophical debates included: are humans really naturally sociable in ways leading directly to some political realization, as Aristotle and the Stoics in different ways propounded? If so, is that political realization naturally or ideally bounded by the walls of a single *polis*, or is it 'cosmopolitan' in some wider sense? Or is politics, on the contrary, merely a set of useful conventions that are independent of the deeper sources of human fulfilment – as the Epicureans contended, and the Sceptics acknowledged as an undecided possibility? Or are those conventions actually inimical to human flourishing, as the Cynics had denounced them for being? The origins and loci of communities, the nature of law, the question of whether virtue or pleasure is the source of the good life, and the value of justice all became battlegrounds in these debates.

Cosmopolitanism, Take 1: Cynic Anti-politics

When the Cynic Diogenes was asked where he was from, he did not give the expected answer of naming the *polis* in which he had been born (Sinope, a Greek settlement on the Black Sea that would later furnish the red clay used in outlines of Renaissance frescoes). When he replied instead that he was

a *kosmopolites*, meaning literally a citizen of the cosmos (DL 6.2.63), he seems to have meant that he was not by nature a citizen of any particular *polis* at all. He was not envisioning universe-wide civic duties. Instead, Diogenes was renouncing and attacking the claims that any ordinary human *polis* might make on him.

Because he acknowledged none of the ways of life enforced or expected by any *polis* as having a claim on him, Diogenes did not live as a citizen would conventionally be expected to do. Instead he lived a life that those around him saw as the life of a dog (*kuon*, from which comes the term 'Cynic': Diogenes embraced the term of abuse with pride). Since dogs have no active political ambitions or identity, no more did Diogenes.[5] His living as a dog was an attempt to live purely as an animal, to whom all laws and conventions are alien and unnatural. Thus he urinated, defecated and fornicated in public as dogs do, uninhibited by any shame at doing so. He took to living in a large terracotta storage jar (a *pithos*, loosely translated as a barrel) as the kind of shelter that a dog might seek, as opposed to building the kind of habitation that humans have come to think appropriate for them. He defied every stricture of politeness and shame, or, rather, rejected them as having no claim on him. He had nothing to gain and nothing to fear from political favour or from circumstance. Even when Alexander the Great supposedly approached him one day to offer him some boon, the Cynic – basking naked outside – asked only that the prince stop blocking the sun.

Diogenes did not live this life because he had no knowledge of human affairs – he was no mere primitive. On the contrary, he lived it as a philosophical commitment. Harking

back to the *nomos/phusis* (law versus nature) debates of the 5th century, he rejected *nomos* as mere arbitrary human convention, while radicalizing the understanding of what *phusis* or nature means. Whereas Socrates, Plato and Aristotle had criticized some conventions but ultimately insisted that there was a form of true justice consonant with nature, Diogenes saw justice as nothing more than a mere convention to which nature was unalterably opposed. Living according to nature was the path of reason and the path to happiness, freedom and self-sufficiency. Even when sold into slavery for a time, Diogenes remained independent and master of himself, being recognized by his purchaser as more fit to master the household than anyone else within it (DL 6.2.74). The Cynic form of living, according to nature, prescribed not a founding of laws in accordance with natural justice, but rather a rejection of all purported requirements of law and justice altogether. Diogenes declared himself a *kosmopolites* as a way of declaring himself to be no *polites*, no citizen, at all: 'The only correct *politeia* is that according to the cosmos' (DL 6.2.72).

That declaration did not stop other Cynics, modelling themselves on Diogenes (who of course founded no formal school), from teaching and even making themselves part of various royal courts.[6] Instead of establishing a full philosophical system or a single location for their school, the Cynics embodied a counter-cultural way of life that repeatedly captured the imagination of new adherents. As a result, Cynicism enjoyed recurrent waves of popularity in the last centuries BCE, incorporated into itinerant preaching and embodied by beggar–philosophers, first at the turn of 300

BCE, just as other new Hellenistic schools were getting going, and especially again among Romans in the 1st century CE – at the same time as the rise of Christianity.[7] Somewhat like later medieval jesters, but more uncompromisingly, Cynics turned ordinary expectations of court flattery and favour-seeking on their heads. They flaunted physical embodiments of the independence and self-sufficiency that they, like all Greek philosophers, professed to value. Alexander himself was said to have recognized the parallel between the freedom and self-sufficiency that Diogenes gained by rejecting all convention, and the mastery that he himself sought through conquest. There is an ancient tradition of his having said: 'if I were not Alexander, I would be [that is, would want to be] Diogenes.'[8]

Cosmopolitanism, Take 2: Stoic Trans-politics

Zeno, the founder of Stoicism, had studied with the Cynic Crates, who in turn had sat at the feet of Diogenes. This encouraged Zeno in a vein of anti-political thinking, which we must first examine, before seeing how he fundamentally reshaped the Cosmopolitan ideal. In doing so he would transform what had been part of the Cynic attack on the naturalness of any local political order into a view affirming the naturalness of a political order among certain inhabitants of the cosmos as a whole.

Zeno imbibed the Cynics' suspicion of existing everyday institutions, believing that most had no part to play in an ideal polity. Even ideas taken by Greeks to be as fundamental

to civilized order as the bans on incest and cannibalism were challenged by his student Chrysippus, who argued that 'sexual intercourse with mothers or daughters or sisters' had been 'discredited without reason', and that cannibalism, even of deceased parents, was not unnatural if it could be useful, for dead bodies were simply materials to be consumed or abandoned as the beasts do.[9]

In contrast to these unjustified taboos, Zeno and Chrysippus each wrote a text called *Politeia* (constitution), proposing ideal new institutions that offered more thoroughgoing and rigorous radicalizations of the *politeia* delineated by Socrates in Plato's *Republic*. To appreciate the Stoic innovations, we must briefly recall the model of the ideal city in Plato's work. This involved philosopher–kings and philosopher–queens who would be deprived of private property and of private families, instead being fed and housed by the city, and procreating children to be raised in common. In the Socratic–Platonic scheme, those restrictions applied only to the ruling elite; the ordinary citizens would enjoy their own wealth and children. Moreover, only the ruling elite in the Socratic–Platonic city would be fully virtuous, because only they would possess the knowledge that virtue requires. Other citizens would be as virtuous as possible, governed by the surrogate reason of the rulers, but not fully so.

Zeno puts his finger on this tension in the Platonic *Politeia*: it would not be a wholly virtuous city if not all its citizens were wholly virtuous. Hence, in his version, all and only the virtuous will be 'citizens, friends, relations and free'. In contrast, all those who are not virtuous 'are foes, enemies, slaves and estranged from one another' (DL 7.32–3, as trans.

in LS 67B). The virtue of such genuine citizens, however, needs special social and political institutions to support it.[10]

It was here that the Stoics diverged from the Cynics. Instead of rejecting all laws and conventions, they developed – as Plato had done – their own account of the laws and conventions that could characterize a genuine *politeia* and accordingly command the allegiance of its citizens. While Zeno and his followers criticized some existing laws and customs as harshly as Diogenes had done (Zeno's ideal city would also prohibit temples, law-courts, gymnasia and money),[11] they proposed replacing them with laws and customs that were genuinely in accordance with nature – a feat that Diogenes would have held to be as impossible as unnecessary. The institutions proposed by Zeno included sexual sharing among all citizens (restricted to the regime for the guardians alone in Plato's *Republic*) and also unisex clothing allowing near-nudity for both men and women, both of which were intended in Zeno's *Politeia* to encourage love and harmony as the bonds of unity among the citizens.

As this shows, living according to nature for Zeno and his school was not the simple dog-life that it had been for Diogenes. Rather, living according to nature requires reshaping one's responses to accord with reason and so to perfect virtue. Nature is normative. Not everything one might feel like doing counts as natural. Genuinely natural are only those actions that express and connect our nature to the reason that pervades the cosmos. It is a moral achievement to learn to do, and to desire to do, all and only what is most fully natural.

Learning to reason develops in young humans out of a

natural impulse that is shared with other animals. That impulse is to seek out that to which a young animal has a natural affinity: first in its own life, in which it seeks what is 'congenial' to it while avoiding what is harmful (DL 7.85.4); and then in beginning to associate with others.[12] This natural impulse of affiliation, described as *oikeiosis*, ripples outwards from self to family to community and eventually, following the guidance of reason, to the cosmos as a whole. Thus humans are naturally sociable: there is no sharp or natural divide between one's own good and the good of others. This is important because it suggests that ethics and politics are, correctly understood, equally natural. Living virtuously and living as a citizen are rooted in the impulses that are natural to humans and the development that we are naturally able to make of them.

Yet, if living as a citizen (*polites*) is seen by Stoics as a natural outgrowth of *oikeiosis*, going on to identify also as a *kosmopolites* is its ultimate natural extent. In a summary of Stoicism, we find the view that 'the world is like a city consisting of gods and men' who 'are members of a community because of their participation in reason, which is natural law'.[13] The idea of natural law is elaborated in the opening of Chrysippus' treatise *On Law*: 'Law is king of all things human and divine. Law must preside over what is honourable and base, as ruler and as guide, and thus be the standard of right and wrong, prescribing to animals whose nature is political what they should do, and prohibiting them from what they should not do' (Marcian I, as translated in LS 67R). Especially in the later Stoics, the idea that natural law could give its content to human laws became a key way to

reconcile ordinary politics with Cosmopolitanism. The later Stoic Epictetus (a Greek ex-slave, who wrote in Greek under Roman rule) would spell out that you must fulfil the actions appropriate to every social relationship in which you stand (as a son, brother, councillor or whatever it might be).[14] But you must also remember that 'you are a citizen of the cosmos' (*polites ei tou kosmou*).[15] In that capacity, your role is to deliberate about all things not as if you were an isolated part cut off from the whole, but, rather, thinking and acting always with reference to the whole. Here we see the new ideal of citizenship as a *kosmopolites* used as a critical standard for action, even while ordinary political affiliations are also maintained. The Stoics never abandoned the stance that Cosmopolitanism could include local political allegiances also, a stance that has been defended in recent political philosophy as an ideal of 'rooted cosmopolitanism'.[16]

Community of Friends: Epicurean Infra-politics

In viewing humans and gods as part of the same cosmic city, the Stoics affirmed that they shared access to a common natural standard of reason and law. They had to defend that connection between the human and the divine against the followers of their philosophical rival Epicurus, who had brought his young philosophical school to Athens and planted it in a garden there in 307 BCE. According to Epicurus, the gods were to be understood as having no role in or relationship to the human, sublunary world. Human life unfolds independently of divine sanction or punishment.

It also unfolds in purely mortal timespans; Epicurus argues that 'death is nothing to us', since with the cessation of sense experience, everything that can affect humans – pain and pleasure – also ceases. Thus the task for humans is simply to contrive as best they can to seek secure enjoyment of pleasures while avoiding pain.

In this task, there is no such thing as a natural law of reason to provide direction, as for the Stoics, nor even a natural standard of justice, as for Socrates, who remained a model for Cynics, Stoics and, later, Sceptics alike, but who was firmly rejected as a model by the Epicureans. For the associates within the Garden of Epicurus, laws are simply what some of the 5th-century sophists had considered them: humanly made conventions, to be judged coolly on the basis of their utility for promoting secure pleasure and avoiding unnecessary pain. Politics may be helpful in helping humans to survive, but it is not the result of a natural impulse to sociability privileging either a local or cosmic *politeia*. It is merely an artificial contrivance, and one that should be designed not to inspire virtuous self-sacrifice, but rather to promote quotidian pleasures (though Epicurus takes an unusual view of pleasure, arguing that it is best achieved by minimizing desires so that they may be reliably satisfied; his pleasures are bread and water rather than truffles and champagne). Nevertheless, politics may well be useful in achieving a secure tranquillity.

In pursuit of security and tranquillity, the Epicurean does not flout social conventions, as does the Cynic (nor did the Epicureans occupy themselves with devising more rational bodies of laws, as did Zeno and Chrysippus). The Epicurean

leads an outwardly ordinary life: he marries and follows laws about sexuality, feels grief at losses, may even 'bring lawsuits, and leave writings when he dies'.[17] In the same account we are told that 'he will not engage in politics' – though he 'will on occasion pay court to a king'. But, while not pursuing politics for the sake of honour or out of a duty of virtue, Epicureans are enjoined to carry out ordinary civic functions: Epicurus insists that any follower of his should be willing to 'serve as a juror'.[18] Nevertheless, Epicureans tended to wax notably less lyrical about conventional forms of political participation than did the Stoics, calling rhetoric for example 'a vile technique'.[19]

Thus political ties are for the Epicureans primarily functional in their role, to be assessed and supported in the light of a cool-headed judgement of their usefulness, rather than in terms of any intrinsic merit. Law, for its part, is merely an instrument of human coercion, not a pillar of divine reason. As the Epicurean Hermarchus teaches: 'the only remedy against the ignorance of utility' is 'fear of the punishment fixed by the law'.[20] Justice is not rooted in nature, as the Platonists and Stoics held. Rather it is a convention serving mutual utility: 'the justice of nature' is not fixed, writes Epicurus, but is 'a pledge of reciprocal usefulness, neither to harm one another nor to be harmed'.[21] An unjust action is not inherently wrong. It is no violation of nature. Rather it is wrong only insofar as it will produce fear in the doer that his unjust act may be requited with harm or punishment, so undermining his or her confidence, security and tranquillity.

With neither the political community nor any posited Cosmopolitan community being central to Epicurean

analysis, their attention focused instead on a particular form of community that we may call *infra-political* (that is, within or below the level of the political). That community was defined by the relationship of friendship.[22] It was a community of friends who populated the simple life in the Epicurean garden. Friendship was central to constituting the sense of security and peace of mind that the Epicureans sought.[23] Indeed, it was said to constitute the greatest and most lasting of pleasures, true joy.[24] Although friendship, like justice, must have originated in utility, the true tranquillity to be found in friendship requires one to love one's friend like oneself. Hence the Epicurean commitment to friendship could be absolute rather than conditional, to the point that the Epicurean wise man 'will on occasion die for a friend'.[25]

Whereas the Cynics sought to live like other animals, Epicurus condemned the situation of 'feeding without a friend' as 'the life of a lion and a wolf'.[26] And, in contrast to the Stoics, it is friendship, not law, that the Epicureans celebrated as a model of community. Yet friendship could potentially grow beyond a garden, to embrace a wider community, one in which the ordinary forms of politics might wither away. Some Epicureans were accordingly enthusiastic philanthropists. Notable on this score is the source of the Epicurean vision of a world without city walls or laws, which was (ironically enough) carved into the city walls of Oenoanda, in the Lycian mountains, by an Epicurean philosopher sometime around 200 CE: 'there will come to be no need of city walls or laws'.[27] Now identified as Diogenes of Oenoanda, this philosophical benefactor introduces his inscription by explaining that 'it is right and proper to help

those who live after us', to help prevent them from suffering from the 'epidemic of false opinions'.[28] An Epicurean world without divisive walls and laws would be a community united by utility and friendship, rather than subject to a natural and divinely originating law.

However broadly philanthropic they might have been, Epicureans generally accepted the terms of justice established in their particular society, and defended their acceptance in terms of their philosophy of seeking secure tranquillity. While their Stoic and Platonist opponents were not satisfied, seeing their attitude to justice as calculating and self-serving, the Epicureans at least treated justice as secured in shared utility. Moreover, for all their differences, the Stoics and Epicureans agreed that the good life could be lived only as a result of correct philosophical argument and understanding.

The final Hellenistic school to emerge, that of Scepticism (in two branches), would offer a more excoriating critique in theory, even though accepting in practice a rather similar 'quietist' adherence to existing political demands. Once one understands why and how to live according to nature, one can become wise, virtuous and so happy and free as a Stoic; once one understands the nature of the gods, of death and of pleasure as the one good, one can become wise, secure and so tranquil as an Epicurean. It is attaining truthful understanding of the world that bestows these goods. (In the haunting words of Epicurus in his *Vatican Sayings* 31, whereas humans can obtain security against most other things, 'when it comes to death we human beings all live in an unwalled city' (LS 24B).) By contrast, the latest-blooming

Hellenistic philosophical movement – Scepticism – held that the very effort to understand the world was what, in practice, undermined tranquillity. Suspending that effort – suspending judgement – was paradoxically the best path to the tranquillity that all the Hellenistic schools took to be essential to happiness.

Scepti-politanism

Taking their name from the Greek word for inquiry (*skepsis*), the Sceptics began from the very disagreements among Stoics and Epicureans (and other groups) that plagued the Hellenistic schools. How could either side present its instruction as a path to tranquillity, if believing one side only exposed its hapless adherents to a barrage of counter-fire from the other? The Sceptics argued that there was no rational basis on which to decide these counter-claims. The only reasonable response was to suspend judgement about the truth and falsity of all of them. One might rationally decide that one side was more probable and persuasive than the other, and so follow it in practice, or one might simply follow the conventions of one's community without holding them to be justified at all, as would a later lineage of more radical Sceptics, flourishing especially from the 1st century BCE to the 1st century CE and styling themselves as followers of one Pyrrho, hence as 'Pyrrhonists'. Their exciting sceptical discovery was that the very tranquillity that had been sought through philosophical arguments would come once one had withdrawn full assent from all of them.

The implications for politics were profound in theory – though we will see shortly that they may have been less momentous in practice. In theory, Scepticism laid waste to the very beliefs that the Stoics and Epicureans held to be crucial to attaining the good life. Nowhere do we see this more clearly than in the embassy of three philosophers – a Peripatetic, a Stoic and a Sceptic – sent from Athens to negotiate with Rome in 155 BCE. The demonstrations that each made of his philosophical style of argument mesmerized the Roman elite and were a spur to their sending their sons to Greece to study philosophy, and to their welcoming travelling Greek philosophers into their households and circles in Rome.

None of the demonstrations was more powerful or disturbing than that made by the Sceptic Carneades, who represented the moderate Sceptical turn that Plato's Academy had taken by that date. He famously delivered a public speech praising justice as essential to political life one day, only to follow it with a public speech praising injustice as essential for the same purposes the next. This opposing of arguments for and against a philosophical proposition was the core of the Sceptical method. By seeing that neither argument could overcome the other, the Sceptic would be led to withhold judgement about the proposition rather than claiming a dogmatic knowledge of its truth or falsity. But, while the method could be adopted in a more modest way, even by Carneades himself, to conclude that one side was more probable than the other, in the case of the praise of injustice it was the content of his argument that positioned Scepticism as the philosophy most potentially corrosive to the justification of political ties.

Our best account of Carneades' speeches is given in Cicero's *De Re Publica*, where Cicero portrays two Roman citizens at a gathering in 129 BCE (hence within living memory of Carneades' visit to Rome) re-creating in reverse order the speeches that the Athenian Sceptic had given. While Cicero will be discussed at length in the next chapter, we focus here on the evidence that his writings provide for the ideas of Hellenistic philosophy, which he studied and recorded as well as developing. In particular, his literary presentation of Carneades' speeches – put into the mouths of later Roman citizens – is the most extensive surviving source suggesting what those speeches contained. Cicero has Lucius Furius Philus give the speech praising injustice first, followed by Gaius Laelius giving the speech praising justice. Laelius' response survives in an even more fragmentary state than the rest of the work. But we can tell that it offered a resounding restatement of the Stoic position: 'True law is right reason, consonant with nature, spread through all people ... There will not be one law at Rome and another at Athens, one now and another later; but all nations at all times will be bound by this one eternal and unchangeable law, and the god will be the one common master and general (so to speak) of all people.'[29] Our main interest, however, is in the praise of injustice that Cicero made Philus give, channelling Carneades.

Carneades is reported to have argued, in direct opposition to the Stoics, that 'there is no such thing as natural law.' Re-creating this argument against the Stoics, Philus advances the Epicurean thesis 'that men ordain laws for themselves in accordance with utility'. But he takes this in a more radically

sophistic direction. Whereas Epicurus had argued that there are grounds to respect laws and justice as useful, the Sceptical gauntlet is that 'either there is no justice at all, or if there is any, it is the highest stupidity' – because the just person would sacrifice his own good in respecting the good of others.[30]

Philus first develops the claim that justice does not exist, or, rather, that it exists only as human convention and not as something natural (reprising a sophistic theme). For 'if it [justice] were natural', he argues, 'then – like hot and cold and bitter and sweet – just and unjust things would be the same for everyone'.[31] Yet, as we saw Herodotus bring out in his historical accounts (in Chapter 2 of this book), human societies disagree dramatically as to what they consider just and unjust. Philus offers a multitude of examiples to show that justice and law cannot be natural, since they are so drastically shaped from moment to moment by conventions.[32] (Among his examples is a change in Roman law to the effect that wealthy men could no longer name most women as their heirs, a law that Philus describes as 'highly injurious to women': he asks, 'Why should a woman not have money?'[33]) And he argues that, given the conventionality of justice, to pursue it – especially in the domain of foreign affairs – is to sacrifice what wisdom instructs one to do: 'to rule over as many people as possible, to enjoy pleasures, to be powerful, to rule, to be a lord'.[34]

The continuity between the challenges to justice that we surveyed in Chapters 1 and 4 – arguments that we saw Plato's Callicles making, and that Glaucon and Adeimantus were eager to hear refuted in Plato's *Republic* – is clearly being referenced here. At the heart of the Sceptical challenge

launched by Carneades and rehearsed by Philus is the sophistic attack on the naturalness of justice, allied to the sophistic and later Epicurean view of justice as (at best) utility. But Philus diverges from the Epicureans too, by offering cases in which justice and utility clearly come apart. Surely the natural and smart thing to do *in extremis* is to save one's own life, even at the cost of seizing a plank from another shipwreckee? If so, then wisdom and justice do not go together – *contra* Socrates, Plato and the Stoics. But neither do utility and justice always coincide – *contra* the Epicureans. The Sceptic cannot assent wholeheartedly to either the Stoic or the Epicurean case.

The implications of Carneades' reported speech in praise of injustice, for personal and political life alike, are stark. If his praise of injustice stands, it goes beyond the Epicurean analysis of justice as utility, to enjoin an active pursuit of advantage and power irrespective of the injustice of the means used to pursue them: whether evading the law in one's private financial affairs or treating conquered nations unjustly in imperial expansion. It was the Epicurean and sophistic strains that made the content of the speech so disturbing, even as the Sceptical method posited that such arguments could not be satisfactorily refuted. But the Sceptical method also said that the arguments for justice could not be satisfactorily refuted either. This is why Scepticism proved less disturbing for politics in practice than in theory. For the opposing of the case for justice with the case for injustice was designed to lead, not to a hellbent pursuit of injustice, but rather to a suspension of judgement of the truth or falsity of both claims. The Sceptic does not draw Epicurean

or sophistic conclusions, or Stoic conclusions either; he or she is rather brought to withhold full assent from all sets of opposing philosophical claims.

How, then, would a Sceptic live? With no doctrinaire reason to flout convention, the Sceptic will live in accordance with the customs of the land in which he finds himself, a practice that may be further bolstered if he adopts the criterion of following the most probable and persuasive arguments. Still, even if following what seems probably to be the best course, he will withhold judgement as to whether these customs and laws are *truly* right or wrong.[35] Thus the path of a Sceptic will look outwardly like those of their ordinary unphilosophical neighbours. Live without full commitment to any claim about how things are by nature, and you can live in peace and quiet. The Sceptic will be no provocateur or provocatrice; if we imagine a female Sceptic, she will have no doctrinal reason for doing anything to provoke her neighbours or the authorities. She will not sign up unreservedly to a philosophical creed, but by that very token she will have no reason to flout convention. She will follow a form of what we may dub *scepti-politanism*, hollowing out her commitment to the *polis* from within, rather than taking up any form of Cosmopolitan identity to eviscerate it from without (as did the Cynics) or to relativize its demands to those of the cosmic community of rational beings (as did the Stoics).

Hellenistic Philosophies *in extremis*

The choice among these philosophies was no trivial matter. For Greeks and Romans who had to choose which

philosophical path to follow, the choice of which philosophical life to live – which school to join – was urgent and immensely consequential. One's worldly ambitions, decisions about whether to seek public office or live retired from the world, as well as one's psychological profile – how one responded to the death of a spouse or child – depended on which philosophy one followed and how thoroughly one internalized it. In the case of the Epicureans and Stoics in particular, to choose a way of life was also to commit to a course of pursuing more or less complete and arduous philosophical understanding. One's ethical and political decisions were interwoven with a choice of outlooks about the nature of the universe. Deterministic, pervaded by mind and reason, and with gods intending cosmic benefit, as for the Stoics? Or random, material, and with gods benignly detached from human affairs, as for the Epicureans? Or, as for the Sceptics, should one refuse to make any of those choices at all?

Of these various philosophical outlooks, it is striking that Stoicism most naturally supported ordinary political participation and leadership, notwithstanding its embedding of local political claims in a Cosmopolitan understanding. The favourite student of Zeno, the founder of the Stoic school, had been born a slave: this man, Persaeus, studied with Zeno, went to the Macedonian court, and was eventually made archon (ruling official) of the Greek city of Corinth. Another Stoic may have advised the Spartan king Cleomenes III in his radical reforms in the 3rd century BCE, purportedly restoring the ancestral Lycurgan order. The Stoics were not alone in promoting political activity among their students; they were joined especially by Aristotle's school, perhaps

understandably, given their parallel commitments to the naturalness of human sociability. The Lyceum, which continued to operate throughout the Hellenistic period (as did Plato's Academy), educated the man who would be installed as caretaker and general of Athens by the Macedonian power-brokers after Alexander's death. Another Lyceum student would be sent by Athens as an emissary to a foreign monarch and be set by him to write a constitution for the new city of Megalopolis (Polyb. 5.93). Another still would be tutor to the son of the first Hellenistic monarch in Egypt.

Hence a paradox. Even as ideas of Cosmopolitanism were being born, philosophers in the Hellenistic era played the classical roles of advisers and tutors to rulers even more successfully than their classical predecessors had done. The context of the *polis* did not immediately vanish, either in practice or in theory, well into the Hellenistic period. If some Greek cities lost their independence early on, others were able to establish federations and maintain independence and liberty for some centuries more. Meanwhile, in theorizing, the founders of Stoicism outlined ideal *politeiai* or constitutions, just as their classical predecessors (a mere fifteen-odd years earlier, in the case of Aristotle) had done. And even those of their rivals who were more dubious about the claims of the political community – the Epicureans exalting the claims of friendship, the Sceptics withholding judgement about the reality of political allegiance – still served that political community when needed. (One of Julius Caesar's assassins in Rome in the 1st century BCE would be the Roman politician Cassius, who subscribed to Epicureanism: Epicureans could act to rid their political community of a tyrant posing

a dramatic threat to security and tranquillity, as Cassius and his confederates believed that Caesar did.)

Cosmopolitanism in particular, in the hands of the Stoics, came to offer new ways of thinking about a *politeia* extending beyond the traditional boundaries of the *polis*, even while its Stoic adherents and their rivals continued to take the boundaries of existing political communities seriously in theory and in practice. Cosmopolitanism could serve to put the demands and value of ordinary politics in a certain perspective, by comparing it with one's standing and duties as a rational being linked to other rational beings in the cosmos as a whole. This, we will find, is one of the roles that it played for Roman republican thinkers, who were shaped by these very Hellenistic philosophical debates at the same time that they sought to serve their own distinctive political community. We turn next to explore how the Romans, and the Greeks under their sway, would articulate the distinctive nature of the Roman republican constitution, and would draw on, develop and reshape classical and Hellenistic Greek ideals in doing so.

Republic

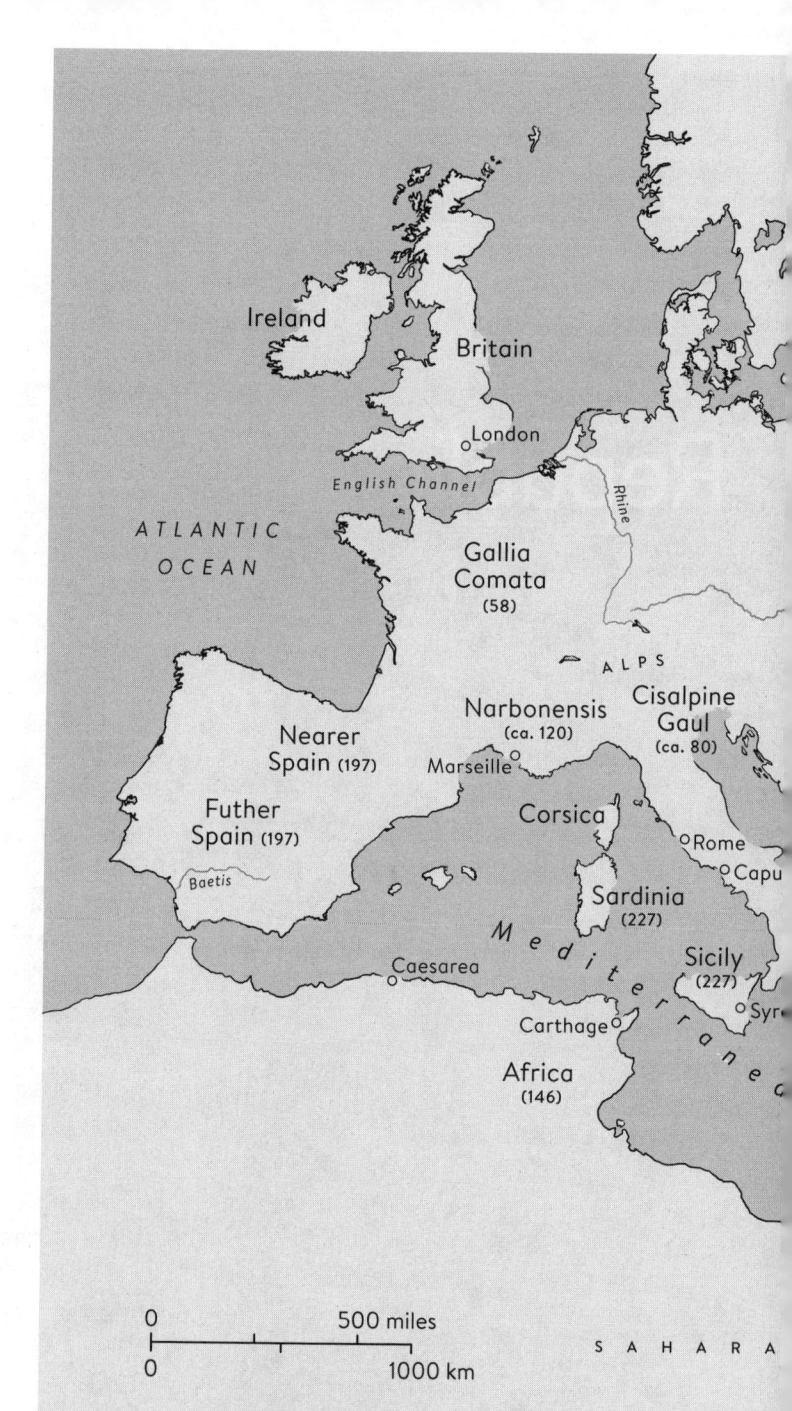

Roman Expansion (to 30 BCE)

Caspian Sea

Don

Black Sea

Danube

donia
(6)

Byzantium

Asia
(133)

Bithynia and Pontus
(64)

Ephesus

Cilicia (ca. 102)

Maeander

Athens

Antioch

Syria (64)

Damascus

Cyprus
(annexed to
Cilicia, 57)

Crete (67)

a

Jerusalem

Alexandria

Cyrenaica
(ca. 74)

Egypt
(30)

S E R T

Nile

Red Sea

In the archaic and classical periods, Greek and Roman histories broadly paralleled each other. According to legend, the city of Rome was founded in 753 BCE (about the same time as Sparta), as a kingship; the last of seven kings was reputed to have been overthrown in 509 BCE (almost exactly the same time as Cleisthenes was transforming the Athenian constitution). Following that overthrow, the Romans established the foundations of a regime better able to protect the *res publica* (in Latin, the 'people's thing', in the sense of their affair or concern). The idea of the *res publica* has given its name in English to the Roman republic understood as a normative ideal, as the best constitution to protect and advance that common concern.[1] In Roman thought, the common concern of the people included an emphasis on the concrete and material: what was *publicum* paradigmatically included collectively owned lands, revenues and provisions, generating the useful English translation of *res publica* as 'commonwealth'.

As initially established, the Roman republic replaced the king with two consuls, who exercised executive powers and military powers alongside a deliberative and advisory Senate (dominated initially by patrician aristocrats, eventually

selected from the aristocrats and wealthy plebeians who had held high elected office) and a set of popular assemblies that variously elected officials, passed laws and carried out other functions as their convening magistrates set them to do. Over the next centuries, Roman history developed along two intersecting directions of change, which this chapter will explore. On the one hand, the constitutional arrangements of the republic continued to evolve, often prompted by social and political struggles between the nobility and the poor. On the other hand, the republic embarked on a remarkable series of military conquests, first within the peninsula of Italy, then Sicily and Sardinia, Spain, southern Gaul, Illyria and the Balkans and the Greek world more generally, and then further afield still. Concentrating their overseas conquests between 264, when the First Punic War with Carthage for control of Sicily began, and 146, when they destroyed the Carthaginian capital (now Tunis) and the Greek city of Corinth, the Romans would dominate the wider Mediterranean world for centuries to come. Their hegemony over Greek polities, in particular, brought Greek ideas flowing into Rome, and stimulated Roman thinkers to engage with the whole gamut of Greek history, literature and philosophy.

For all of its distinctiveness, the Roman constitution could be defined as a complex combination of the three basic Greek constitutional categories that we discussed in Chapter 2 and have found at work, often elaborated, in many analyses of Greek politics so far. More generally, all of the ideas that we have studied so far primarily in Greek societies and thought have counterparts in Rome, as a brief review of the

relevance of each chapter so far to Roman thought will confirm. In Latin, the basic Greek question of whether justice and advantage could be reconciled or must remain at odds (Chapter 1) would be appropriated as a debate as to whether what it is *honestas*, or 'honourable', to do is ever at odds with what is *utilitas*, or 'useful', to the individual. The nature of equality – who counts as an equal citizen, and what political arrangements that entails – was for its part fundamental to understanding Roman politics. So, too, was the complementary value of liberty, which played a large role in Chapter 2.

Both Greek and Roman ideas of freedom, epitomized in the words *eleutheria* (Greek) and *libertas* (Latin), pivoted around the conceptual and legal opposition between freedom and slavery. These ideas of freedom could be applied to individuals and to the polity alike, expressing an ideal of independence from the arbitrary will of another individual, group or outside polity, and so related to the ideal of self-rule discussed in the form of Athenian democracy in Chapter 3.[2] Virtue was conceived in Rome as a vital attribute of republican citizenship, as it was of citizenship for Socrates, Plato and Aristotle (Chapters 4 and 5). And the Roman constitution could be defended as resting on the Stoic law of nature, as it expanded to include so great a proportion of the known peoples of the time that it could be compared almost with the cosmopolitan ideal of certain Hellenistic philosophers discussed in Chapter 6 (a theme to be picked up in Chapter 8). Like Greek polities of the time, Rome cultivated civic shrines, rites and festivals, though citizens could honour other gods so long as they acknowledged and carried out the common rites.

Yet Rome was also in many important ways different from the Greek cities that we have so far discussed, even as its orbit expanded through negotiation and conquest to include those Greek cities themselves, and its political ideas included subtle innovations as well as variations on Greek models. Given the elaborate formulation of Roman law in practice and in the writings of the jurists who would chronicle and systematize it, legal vocabularies and forms of argument came to furnish especially influential ways of thinking of politics. Romans thought of the political unit as a *civitas* or a *societas*. Rather than battling over different kinds of regime for that community, they focused their political struggles (after the inception of the republican constitution) on what the law and the distribution of power should be within it. In other words, political struggles remained within the boundaries of a broadly accepted non-monarchical constitution, even as they effected in practice significant changes in its workings. Sometimes these struggles resulted in major institutional changes: above all, the establishment in 494 BCE of annually elected tribunes (originally two, later expanded to ten), who were able to defend ordinary citizens against violence to their persons and to seek to advance their collective interests. By contrast, attempts over several generations to redistribute, to the poor, public lands that had been appropriated, often corruptly, by the rich, were ultimately unsuccessful.

Despite the legal protections that they won over time, the political voice of the non-elite Romans was in significant ways far more restricted than at Athens, especially in the

powers of initiative and accountability. The Roman idea of the republic stands as a model of a constitution that gives an entrenched political authority to a meritocratically chosen elite, alongside an important but partly defensive role for the poor. From a Greek perspective, Rome embedded an oligarchy into the heart of a democracy, even while it protected certain roles of self-assertion and moments of political decisiveness for the poor. The result is a distinctive regime. On the one hand, it may suggest new institutional mechanisms by which modern 'democratic' regimes can protect and even empower their poorest citizens;[3] on the other hand, it raises uncomfortable questions about the extent to which those modern 'democracies' may similarly harbour oligarchical tendencies.

The politics of inclusion and exclusion in relation to citizenship were different in important ways as well. Roman slaves were property, as in Greece, but if they were freed by means of publicly registered procedures, they became citizens with only a few remaining civil disabilities, if also a lingering social stigma. Roman citizenship was gradually extended to pacify newly conquered or allied cities (sometimes originally without the right to vote, but that was gradually extended too), to the extent of there being some 900,000 adult male voters in the last decades before the advent of the principate (to be explained in Chapter 8). A Roman head of household (the *paterfamilias*) had extensive legal powers over slaves as well as women and children, including even adult sons. But it was possible for women in some circumstances to be emancipated from the need for

male tutelage and to own property in their own names, and many women in practice played lively roles in commerce as well as in religious rites and social gatherings.

Observers at the time saw the Roman constitution as distinctive in being a special combination of the three simple Greek constitutional types (one/few/many) introduced in Chapter 2. Rome was seen to be like Sparta in not fitting neatly into any one of these categories, drawing its strength instead from its balancing of elements of each. And what strength it was! Rome had risen to an unparalleled dominance by the middle of the 2nd century BCE, the point at which the first major observer and analyst of its political life whom we will consider (Polybius) encountered it. After looking at his account of the Roman constitution, we will turn to an analyst and participant in Roman life a century later: Cicero. While Polybius will introduce us to Rome through the eyes of an observant Greek marvelling at its rise to geographical hegemony, Cicero will provide a distinctive account of the nature of the *res publica* from within the tumultuous history of the 1st century BCE, in which the republican allocation of power was repeatedly threatened and ultimately permanently transformed.

Meet Polybius

The question that Polybius thought must, and should, be preoccupying his readers was simple: 'How, and with what kind of constitution, almost the whole inhabited world was subjected and brought under a single rule, that of the Romans, in less than fifty-three years?'[4] He was referring to

HIGHLIGHTS OF ROMAN HISTORY DISCUSSED IN THIS CHAPTER

753 BCE	Legendary founding of Rome by Romulus
509 BCE	Founding of the republic: overthrow of last king, replaced by two annually elected consuls

5ᵀᴴ CENTURY BCE

494 BCE	Tribunes of the plebeians established
451–449 BCE	Twelve Tables – basis of Roman law

3ᴿᴰ– 2ᴺᴰ CENTURIES BCE

c. 200–c. 118 BCE	Lifespan of Polybius
146 BCE	Roman conquests of Carthage and of Corinth
133 BCE	Tribune Tiberius Gracchus attempts land reform
123, 122 BCE	Tribune Gaius Gracchus attempts similar reforms

2ND–1ST CENTURIES BCE

106–43 BCE	Lifespan of Cicero
63 BCE	Cicero becomes consul; exposes Catilina
44 BCE	Julius Caesar assassinated ('Ides of March')
43 BCE	Cicero assassinated
27 BCE	Octavian made Augustus Caesar

the 'less than fifty-three years' from 220, when the Romans had annexed the Po region of Italy in the course of their rivalry with Carthage (today Tunis, in Tunisia), to Rome's smashing of the kingdom of Macedon in 168 BCE. That was the timespan that he originally set out to document in his *Histories*; he would eventually carry the narrative on through 146, the year in which Roman armies sacked both Carthage and Corinth, doing away in a single year with its greatest rival (the Carthaginian general Hannibal had inflicted a shocking defeat on Rome in 216 at Cannae) and with the independence of the cities of mainland Greece. The expansion of Rome had actually begun well before, with the conquest of the other inhabitants of the Italian peninsula below the Po valley; the

occupation of Sicily, Sardinia and Corsica in the teeth of Carthage; and power plays that led to Roman domination and influence, expressed in varying ways, over most of the Mediterranean world and beyond.

Polybius appointed himself the task of answering that question, by writing a history not of Italy or Greece or Egypt alone, but a 'universal history' (5.31, 5.33) befitting the rise of Rome through combat or negotiation with virtually all the other powers known to it at the time. He was extraordinarily well qualified by his remarkable life circumstances to do so. He was born around 200 BCE in the relatively recently founded city of Megalopolis (for which a Peripatetic had written the constitution, as we saw in Chapter 6), to a leading family in the Achaean League, a federation of Greek cities in the Peloponnese.[5] At the time of his birth, the league had succeeded for some decades in managing its relations with the rising Roman power with sufficient finesse to enjoy a good measure of meaningful political independence. The constituent cities of the league called themselves 'democracies', meaning that they were not tyrannies or oligarchies, and that all citizens were entitled to attend the ordinary and extraordinary assemblies that made league policy. But they were moderate regimes very different from classical Athens, say, in affording a larger role in practice to their elites, while empowering their poor to a much lesser extent. They did not pay poor citizens for attending the rotating assemblies of the league, for example, meaning that in practice relatively few would participate. In accordance with this political culture, and like his predecessor as an historian, Thucydides, Polybius was critical not only of tyranny (e.g., 5.11, contrasting tyrant

with king), but also of unbridled democracy (which he called an *ochlokratia*, or 'mob-rule', 6.57).

Son of a statesman active in the league, belonging to a family privy to the high councils of diplomacy and frequently playing host to Roman and other foreign guests, Polybius rose to the high office of 'hipparch' (cavalry leader) for the federation. But in 167 he was among some 1,000 Achaean citizens whom the Romans seized and held in Italy in the course of a dispute about alliance politics, on the pretext of needing to investigate their denunciation by a pro-Roman fellow citizen. Most of his fellows were kept in provincial peninsular towns where they could not cause trouble. But, perhaps due to family connections, Polybius managed to move to the very heart of Roman urban society and to spend most of what would turn out to be his seventeen years as a hostage there. He became attached as a tutor to the family of Scipio Aemilianus, who would rise to become a successful consul and general, leading the final assault on Carthage in 146 BCE. Polybius watched as those inhabitants who survived his friend's siege were sold into slavery and the conquered city was set alight and left to burn. Afterwards he took a boat and explored up and down the west coast of Africa (he was an intrepid traveller, having already retraced Hannibal's journey through the Alps). Meanwhile, in the same year, other Roman troops destroyed the Greek city of Corinth, dissolving the Achaean League and the democratic constitutions of its member cities, including the city in which Polybius had grown up and served as an official as a young man. Polybius, brought in to mediate a political settlement with Rome, was rewarded by both sides, with heroic statues of him erected

across the Peloponnese. He would undertake further travels with Scipio Aemilianus and the Roman armies, for example probably witnessing and certainly writing an account of the destruction of Numantia in Spain in 134–133 BCE, which was an important moment in the Roman expansion to the west.[6]

Polybius had already started to write his *Histories* while still a hostage. What was perhaps initially designed as a guide to inform his fellow Greek political leaders as they sparred with Rome would become a chronicle and analysis of Rome's ultimate triumph and its ways of exercising power. As an outsider with unparalleled access to the inside of Roman senatorial politics, steeped in Greek history and philosophy but living long among Greece's Latin-speaking conquerors, he was in an excellent position to provide an account that tells us a great deal about Rome through the lens of Greek constitutional analysis. We will pay attention to what this lens led him to downplay or exclude, as well as to what he so richly included.

'In less than fifty-three years': Explaining Rome's Rise

Polybius, who was conversant with the works of Thucydides and Plato, held that states succeeded or failed most fundamentally due to their constitution, or *politeia*. Thucydides had contrasted Spartan stability with Athenian expansionism. According to the Athenian historian, the uniquely austere laws framed by Lycurgus had made Sparta's domestic constitution stable, but the boldness cultivated by Athens led to its imperial aggrandizement, which was, for a time,

more successful. Plato, for his part, had told a story of constitutional change in the *Republic*, Book 8, which depicts an ideal regime degenerating into a 'timocracy', literally, a regime prizing honour and military victory, associated by Plato with Sparta; then into an oligarchy prizing wealth; then into a democracy prizing freedom; and finally into a tyranny prizing the satisfaction of the tyrant's basest appetites. Later historians and philosophers had offered less stylized accounts of constitutional changes, exploring how oligarchic luxury and arrogance might generate democratic envy and resentment. Aristotle, for example, as we saw in Chapter 5, traced sequences of constitutional change generated by various types of motivation among different groups. To these variations on the classical themes of constitutions governed by one, few or many, either well or badly, the post-classical Epicurean school explored in Chapter 6 had added an emphasis on the original desire for security, which they saw as having prompted the development of laws and constitutions.[7]

Drawing on the classical schema of one/few/many and the Platonic idea of a characteristic sequence of constitutions, Polybius integrated these with his own vivid dramatization of polities as living organisms that are bound eventually to die. The result was his famous account of a natural cycle of constitutional change that is bound to recur. Humans in a primitive state – a state not confined to prehistory, but one that natural catastrophes like floods or earthquakes may repeatedly produce – will, like animals, follow the strongest leader, the condition of despotism. But in associating together, their natural powers of reason will begin

to produce ideas of gratitude, honour and justice, and, most fundamentally, utility (Polybius, on this point, was influenced by the Epicureans), so that they start to conceive of their leader as a king who benefits them rather than simply as a despot of whom they are afraid. Hereditary kings, however, inevitably become corrupt, turning into tyrants, who are then deposed by leading nobles, who establish aristocracies. But the aristocrats become corrupt in their turn, degenerating (as in Plato) into avaricious oligarchs, and it is the common people this time who revolt and establish democracies. Yet corruption will inevitably set in once again, in the person of greedy and ambitious nobles who bribe the common people, until eventually the democracy will be convulsed by massacres and destruction – and despotism will reign again.

So far, so Greek, indeed in many ways so Platonic, though Polybius emphasizes the idea of a natural order of growth and decay more than Plato had done (and the orders of their sequences somewhat differ). But what makes his work most innovative is what happens when he turns to the case of Rome, comparing it with Sparta. For he argues that the instability of each regime in the natural cycle is exacerbated by its unmixed, simple character. A simple oligarchy, for example, has obvious vices, such as the greed of its leading men, and these put it on a straight path to decline, like the rust that naturally corrupts iron (6.10, discussing Lycurgus' avoidance of this fate for Sparta). But there is a way to sidestep the inevitability of such flaws. This is to establish an equilibrating constitution that can balance the virtues of each kind of constitution, correcting its characteristic vices with the virtues of another kind. Lycurgus did this for Sparta through his

legislative wisdom; the Romans did it for themselves through experiment and conflict. An equilibrating constitution can stave off decline, at least for a very considerable period – long enough to explain Rome's remarkable political ascendancy. It can perch outside the cycle of constitutions, stable and flourishing – perhaps for decades, perhaps for centuries, though ultimately all cities, like natural beings, must die.

To be sure, Polybius found some precedent for the idea of a 'mixed constitution' (as this idea in his work is often described)[8] in brief discussions in Thucydides, Plato and Aristotle. Thucydides describes the rule of the Five Thousand in Athens – a short-lived successor to the oligarchic coup of 411 BCE – as a 'moderated mixing' of the few and the many.[9] In Plato's Laws, Sparta is presented as curbing the arrogance and potential corruption of power partly by Lycurgus' having 'blended' the kings with a council of elders, followed by the establishment of the board of five annually selected ephors to put a 'bridle' on the government (the language of 'bridling' suggesting an external check rather than an internal blending).[10] The unnamed elderly Athenian man who leads the discussion in the Laws offers a more general lesson: that in legislating one must mix together the two 'mother-constitutions' of monarchy and democracy for a constitution to be good and stable.[11] Aristotle in his Politics focuses rather on the mixing together of oligarchy and democracy as a practical recipe for political stability (as we saw in Chapter 5).[12] All of these classical-period writers treat a 'mixed' constitution or regime primarily as one in which two constitutional forms – either in the sense of their characteristic institutions or their dominant social groups – are blended together.

While picking up on this classical idea of combining simple constitutional forms, Polybius was more interested in balancing than in blending. In his analysis (perhaps following that hint about the ephors as a 'bridle' in the *Laws*), the mixed constitutions of both Sparta and Rome work by playing off monarchical, aristocratic and democratic elements of the constitution in an ongoing dynamic balance – even a struggle – in which each is responsible for checking the others. This is the most influential source of the idea of checks and balances that would fascinate later republicanism and political theory, as taken up especially by 18th-century French political thinker Montesquieu and by the American founders.[13] Polybius describes it succinctly in the case of Sparta, crediting Lycurgus with designing the constitution so that 'each power being counter-balanced by the others, none of them should determine the inclination or do so for the whole, but being equally balanced and equilibrated according to the principle of opposition, the governing body will continue in permanence forever' (6.10).

Such delicate balancing might seem necessarily to result from artifice, from deliberate human invention. Yet the Romans, Polybius claims, have attained a mixed constitution 'not ... through reasoned argument [in contrast with Lycurgus], but through many struggles and experiences, constantly drawing the best solution from the learning gained from these trials' (6.10). Just as the Greek constitutional analysts scratched their heads over Sparta – did its two kings make it a kingship, or its council of elders (the *gerousia*, literally 'body of the elderly', who were elected for life) make it an aristocracy, or its strictly limited citizenship make it a

democracy? – so, too, Rome cannot be easily pigeonholed into the simple forms of Greek constitutions: 'no one, not even those of that land themselves, would be able to say with certainty whether the governing body as a whole is aristocratic or democratic or monarchical' (6.11). Polybius' fellow Greeks might be inclined to hold up their noses at Rome, a constitution without the benefit of a founding legislator, but that would be a mistake. The Romans have by experience and struggle attained an acme of constitutional excellence comparable with that bestowed by the most revered legislator of Greece.

The Three Parts of the Roman Constitution

How did Polybius come to view Rome as an equilibrating constitution? He identifies each of three elements in turn as candidates for being the 'greatest part' of the constitutional governing body, only to show how each is dependent in practice upon the others. Since none of them can act so unambiguously as to be said to be unqualifiedly dominant, none of them can rightly give its name to the overall constitutional form (as a dominance of the *demos* would make a regime a democracy). Instead, it is in the balancing of their different roles and powers that the constitution as a whole takes shape. Polybius demonstrates this by examining the elements of the Roman constitution embodying kingship, aristocracy and democracy in turn. He shows that none of these can account for the complex balancing of different sources of power that Rome actually evinced (as he saw it: his observations themselves reflect his particularly Greek

theoretical outlook). Each might try, but none in practice could succeed in overbalancing the others so thoroughly as to merit calling the regime exclusively by its name. In other words, Polybius shows that Rome cannot fairly be described as kingship, aristocracy or democracy; it is instead a complex constitution consisting of the balanced competition of all three.

Consider first, as Polybius does, the consuls. These are the candidates who would constitute a monarchical or despotic principle in Rome. The question is whether their power is so great as to warrant considering the constitution a kingship (it can't literally be a 'monarchy', as two consuls served in office simultaneously and collegially). Polybius' evidence for considering the consuls in the light of kings is the fact that they were believed to have inherited their powers of *imperium*, which meant strictly their military command, though the term was sometimes used in a wider sense for general power.[14] To make the provisional case for the consuls' making Rome count as a kingship, Polybius says that they give orders to the other magistrates. (In reality, each magistrate had his own sphere of duties, so this hierarchical ordering was less clearly a relation of command than its portrayal in Polybius.) He also claims that the consuls organize all military preparations and command the armies in the field; and they play a role in setting the agenda for the Senate and (some of) the popular assemblies, and execute their decisions (6.12). And they could order the expenditure of public monies for the purposes that are theirs to carry out.

Nevertheless, it is hard to see annually elected officials who were subject to accountability procedures at the end

of their term as plausible embodiments of the principle of kingship. And, indeed, Polybius concludes that the existing form of the *res publica* should not be described as a kingship. He points out that each consul's exercise of power will be subject to a financial audit at the end of his term and to an oath swearing to have obeyed the laws in general, which can be challenged by prosecution in popular courts (albeit not organized in the same way as the lottery-selected courts of Athens). Moreover, while each consul enjoyed full *imperium* over his own troops while in the field, drawing money to feed them had to be authorized by the Senate. Indeed, a consul's very sphere of military activity was decided by the Senate, which set each one in charge of a particular province or military campaign. And while outside the city on campaign, he could not at the same time exercise his consular powers at home. In short, despite the elements of kingly power that had been transferred to the consuls, Rome could not, in Polybius' view, be plausibly described as a kingship.

Apart from the purposes of exercising their Greek constitutionalist muscles, no Roman would have been inclined to describe the *res publica* as a kingship. The Romans presented their public actions as the work of the 'Senate and People of Rome' (*Senatus Populusque Romanus*), and it is S.P.Q.R. that is engraved on the monuments of republican rule. No Greek council had been nearly as significant, with the possible exception of the Spartan *gerousia* – whose members served, like the Roman senators, for life (in the middle republic, the senators were selected from among those who had held the higher magistracies). Was Rome, then, best described as an aristocracy, in virtue of the Senate's important role within it?

The Senate had originally been the preserve of elite kinship groups. But, over time, wealthy plebeians joined the elite, and together with the original patricians they comprised the nobility. Meanwhile, the Senate's membership became restricted to the ranks of those who held or had held the higher magistracies. Still, it was that aura of elite status that gave the Senate much of its sway. For, as Polybius points out (and contrary to later theories of the balance and division of powers), the Roman Senate had no power to legislate, all power to do so belonging to the people. Instead its powers were deliberative, investigative, managerial and advisory. The Senate used its powers of deliberation in managing public funds (apart from those specifically assigned to particular magistracies); investigating public crimes; and handling foreign relations. Probably after Polybius had finished his history, the Senate began occasionally to issue a kind of decree called (albeit only twice in surviving sources) *senatus consultum ultimum*, advising certain magistrates 'to see to it that no detriment befall the commonwealth', a decree that put the Senate's weight behind those magistrates to encourage them to do what they might judge necessary – even if not wholly according to law – to preserve the republic.[15] Before and beyond such decrees also, the Senate carried an important gravity and weight. Yet, for all the deference and authority that it enjoyed, the Senate, too, could be checked, in ways demonstrating that the *res publica* could not well be judged to be a simple aristocracy. As Polybius notes, the tribunes of the plebs (elected by the non-noble plebeians only) could block any senatorial decree and could even bar the Senate from meeting altogether. The people, in their lawmaking

capacity, could also more broadly reshape the Senate's prerogatives.

Given the importance of the popular assemblies' unique capacity to pass and repeal laws, asks Polybius finally, should Rome be termed a democracy? This is a question that has recently been revived by scholars, with some coming close to saying yes by emphasizing the importance of the democratic element in the constitution.[16] Polybius, like these recent scholars, notes that the power to legislate remained solely in the hands of the people throughout the republican period (indeed long into the imperial era). Only the people could pass or repeal laws. The power to make laws also extends into a power of setting other fundamental parameters for the existence of the republic: the people have the sole power of making peace or war, and of ratifying treaties and alliances, issues that would be put to them upon recommendation from the Senate. Polybius links this further to a more general role of what he calls the Roman *demos* (in Latin, this would be the *populus*) as being 'sovereign [*kurios*] in the *politeia* over honours and penalties' (6.14). By 'honours', he means primarily the elections of magistrates, and the conferring of every grant of *imperium* by means of a *lex de imperio*; by 'penalties', he means judicial cases involving the death penalty and heavy fines. (Polybius said relatively little about the powers of the tribunes, who had no exact equivalent in Greek constitutional theories.)

Should these substantial popular powers be enough to classify the state as a 'democracy'? Against that suggestion, supported by some later scholars, others have noted that the power to pass laws was not the power to frame them. No one

had the right to propose a law to a popular assembly except a magistrate or a tribune, and no one had the right to speak in a voting assembly at all; even in those assemblies called for discussion without decision (*contiones*), no one had the right to speak unless called upon by the presiding magistrate or tribune. (Contrast Athens, for example, where the council setting the agenda for the assembly was selected by lot, and where anyone who wished could speak up in an assembly.) Roman popular assemblies themselves took several different forms, but in all of them votes were cast as a member of a group, whose position was itself determined by majority vote. In one kind of assembly, the groups were called forward in sets determined by status and wealth (they originally correlated to military rank), meaning that some of the later groups would never even get to vote before the question had already been decided. In another, citizens were allocated to another set of groups in ways that made some more highly populated than others, so diminishing the relative influence of individuals within the larger groups.

Polybius' own answer likewise denies that Rome was best described as a democracy, despite the significant role of the people within its constitution. But he draws on different features of the constitution to make his case. He balances the people's sovereignty over honours and penalties, laws, war and peace, with their dependence on the Senate for financing public works; the judicial role in civil suits played by senators; and the subjection of individual soldiers (who, until 107 BCE, were conscripted only from those above a certain property threshold) to the *imperium* of their generals.

Thus Polybius concludes that Rome should no more be

classified as a democracy than as an aristocracy or a kingship. Instead, it should be construed as an equilibrating constitution among the three parts that incorporate those tendencies, one that protects the liberty of all of its citizens through the very process of overreaching and adjustment:

> For when any of the three parts swells up, becoming intoxicated with winning and with exercising power beyond what is appropriate, it is clear that – none of them being self-determining as the argument so far has shown – each has the power deliberately to counter-balance and catch hold of the others, so that none of the parts is able to swell up or to become overly disdainful (6.18).

Yet the historian believed that even Rome would eventually become unable to ward off corruption, bitter rivalry for power and popular ambition (6.57). He describes that degeneration in deeply Platonic terms, envisaging that Rome would eventually become a constitution called a democracy (*demokratia*), a name hiding its actual nature as a form of 'mob-rule' (*ochlokratia*, 6.57), one that would ultimately fall prey to despotism in the next turn of the cycle of constitutions.

For Polybius, it is primarily these features – what we might call the checks and balances – of the Roman constitution that answer the question he originally asked: how has Rome been so unprecedentedly and overwhelmingly successful in its imperial expansion? While Polybius classified the Roman constitution in Greek terms with this equilibrating twist, the most influential Roman analyst of the constitution would go further in investigating the internal connections

within that constitution between liberty, property, justice and natural law. If Polybius was our guide to the Roman republic's rise to its zenith, we turn now to Cicero, writing in the later part of the republic's tumultuous history.

For almost the whole of the 1st century BCE, Rome was shaken by repeated waves of threat and civil war, as individual generals used their armies abroad to manoeuvre for greater forms of power at home, transforming the scope of the various political roles that they and others held either by passing new laws or by bestowing new powers on themselves by bending or breaking the laws. A first wave of civil war in the 80s resulted in Sulla making himself dictator; the patrician Catilina conspired against the republic in 63; the breakdown of an erstwhile alliance of three strongmen in the 50s resulted in Julius Caesar's invasion of Italy in 49 and a renewed bout of civil war; Caesar was assassinated in 44, but his aides and heir were able to seize power, with an eventual final struggle between Mark Antony and Octavian (Caesar's heir) being decided in the latter's favour at the battle of Actium in 31, after which he was able to consolidate power while restoring republican forms, as we will see in Chapter 8. Cicero's lifetime encompassed the bulk of this traumatic period of Roman history, and he was a political player in many of these events as well as a philosophical interpreter of what the republican constitution meant.

Meet Cicero

As a young man, Cicero left the city of his birth (in 106 BCE) in the south of Italy – where his family were among the lesser

landowners in a town that had received full civic rights only relatively recently – to pursue philosophical studies in Rome and Athens, before returning to Rome to embark upon a political career. Despite a 'harsh and unmodulated' voice,[17] he made his name as a lawyer, beginning with the prosecution of a corrupt governor of Sicily in 70 BCE, and also serving as a defence attorney even as he rose up the *cursus honorum* (the scale of honours as a magistrate) through sheer brilliance and ambition. His triumph in being elected one of the two consuls for 63 BCE, despite his less than exalted birth and at the youngest legally possible age of forty-two, would prove a fine and yet also a fateful hour for his career.

As consul he exposed a conspiracy led by the patrician Catilina against the republic, but then suppressed it brutally and arguably illegally by putting the ringleaders to death without trial. That act would shadow the immediate glory he had been accorded as 'Parent of His Country',[18] driving him into exile for a time, even though he himself touted his acts for saving the republic: 'when I held the helm of the republic, did not arms then yield to the toga? ... What military triumph can stand comparison?'[19]

Having returned from exile, Cicero found himself still gallingly excluded from public affairs. He licked his wounds in philosophical composition from 55 to 51 BCE, producing three of his most important works of political philosophy: the *De Oratore* (*On the Orator*), *De Re Publica* (*On the Commonwealth/Republic*) and *De Legibus* (*On the Laws*) – all modelled stylistically and thematically on Platonic dialogues. He was then given the governorship of a province for a year, in which he could again put some of his theories and ideas

into practice. As the republic began to tear itself apart, with powerful men jockeying for power in vertiginously shifting alliances, his position became awkward with the triumph of Julius Caesar in the civil war and his being proclaimed Caesar 'dictator' in 49 BCE. (The dictatorship was an office that Roman history and constitutional practice recognized and occasionally conferred, bestowing emergency powers upon one man that allowed him to abrogate other offices and laws for a limited period.) Cicero and Caesar had a complicated relationship compounded of mutual admiration for philosophical and rhetorical abilities, and mutual opposition for most of the time in their political aims. Cicero spent the two years after Caesar's victory in strategic retirement at his country villa, during which he engaged in his second bout of concentrated philosophical production.

Cicero was not invited to participate in the conspiracy to assassinate Julius Caesar in 44 BCE; the conspirators 'feared both his nature, as lacking in daring, and his age' (*Cic.* 42.2).[20] But after the assassination took place, Cicero defended it in a coded form in his *De Officiis* (*On Duties*), written some months later in just a few weeks, just as he was also penning the *Philippics* castigating Caesar's aide Mark Antony, who was seeking to capture public opinion and power in the wake of Caesar's death. On account of his hostility to Antony and his miscalculations about the loyalty of others, Cicero himself was murdered in 43 BCE on the orders of the Second Triumvirate (Antony, Lepidus and Octavian: the last of these would sixteen years later become Augustus). His head and his hands were cut off for public display – a warning to other enemies of the new order who harkened back too longingly to the old.[21]

Unlike the more fragmentary remains of the Hellenistic philosophers, which he had studied (being strongly influenced by the Sceptics and Stoics, and also by Plato, while opposing Epicurean claims), Cicero's speeches, letters and other writings have been passed down in abundance, though not all are intact and others are lost. We know a good deal about his personal life (he divorced two wives, and was devastated by the death in childbirth of his beloved daughter Tullia),[22] and about his work as a lawyer and a politician (his exchange of letters with his brother includes the latter's instructions on how to win Roman elections).[23] His political identity was above all that of an orator, one who allied philosophy to rhetoric in his practice, and who also wrote philosophical dialogues and studies, especially at times when he found himself unable to devote himself to public affairs.

The Romanness of Cicero is nowhere more evident than in his understanding of oratory. Defending his own profession in *De Oratore*, he insists, in bald opposition to Plato's *Gorgias*, that rhetoric is a genuine art, a branch of knowledge, and indeed the supreme art, above even philosophy.[24] The rhetorician is no trickster or shyster; he is the fount of good *mores* (customs and habits), who is uniquely able to instil virtue in his fellow citizens. Cicero assigns expertise in oratory the highest role in enabling him to fulfil his sacred duties to the republic. While philosophy was valuable and important, any man who failed to respond to his country's call because of its blandishments, or who disdained to use rhetoric when it was called for in place of pure logic, would be a failure as a man because he was a failure as a citizen.

Cicero would write in his own voice that experienced

statesmen are wiser than 'philosophers who have no experience at all of public life', and celebrate the value of political life: 'there is nothing in which human virtue approaches the divine more closely than in the founding of new states or the preservation of existing ones.'[25] Writing philosophy, and contributing to the forging of a Latin vocabulary and discourse grappling with Greek philosophical ideas, was a way to contribute to the republic when more direct political ways were barred, as well as a personal consolation and source of satisfaction.[26] Cicero's corpus of philosophical texts, together with his speeches and letters, reveal the world of a man concerned to inform and justify his actions in the terms he and others had developed in their engagement with Greek philosophy, while acting at the highest levels of Roman politics.

Cicero on the Roman Constitution

Polybius had provided an analysis of the Roman constitution written in the course of his friendship with the 2nd-century consul Scipio Aemilianus (the conqueror of Carthage whom we met earlier), an analysis that Cicero and his contemporaries studied closely. Perhaps in homage to Polybius, Cicero puts his own account of that same constitution – embedded not in a history of Rome's rise, but in a Platonic-like dialogue – in the mouths of Scipio Aemilianus and his circle, in the year 129 BCE, a turning point in the history of the republic roughly two decades before Cicero's own birth. Four years before the dialogue's dramatic date of 129, Tiberius Gracchus had been elected tribune and had proposed a law to redistribute a body of public lands (lands that had been acquired

by the republic by conquest or bequest, and that had been appropriated largely by nobles, often corruptly, for the payment or sometimes non-payment of a low tax) to the landless poor. In the process, he had illegally demoted a fellow tribune who had vetoed the measure. A group of senators, who identified themselves as standing for the interests of the *optimates*, or 'best men', strongly opposed that demotion together with the land redistribution itself. Led by Scipio Nasica, a cousin and associate of Scipio Aemilianus, that opposition group carried out the murder of Tiberius Gracchus and the subsequent undoing of the laws he had championed.

By making Scipio one of the main characters in his dialogue, charged with presenting the arguments in favour of each of the simple forms of constitution and then defending the 'mixed' constitution of Rome as best, Cicero exhibits his solidarity with the *optimates*, who identified Roman liberty overall as resting crucially on the prerogatives of the Senate and on a view of property that dictated a rejection of land redistribution. The historical Scipio, who is presented as Cicero's spokesman for this part of the dialogue, had died a few days after the dialogue's dramatic date. Thus the dialogue (surviving only in fragments) is cast as an elegy for a man who might have helped to avoid the further tumults that convulsed the city in subsequent years, including a second attempt at land redistribution by Tiberius' brother Caius Gracchus, who would be driven to ask a slave to kill him in the midst of an outbreak of violence against this attempted reform.

Whereas Polybius had presented his analysis of the Roman constitution by asking which of the simple forms

of Greek constitution it might resemble, Cicero sets his in the more Platonic context of a question about the *optimum statum civitatis* (1.33): the best condition, or form, of the commonwealth. Scipio is asked to recall his former discussions of this topic with Polybius and another Greek philosopher, in order to explain his view that the constitution inherited by the Romans of their day is actually that best condition. He begins by explaining just who the 'people' are who figure in the definition of a *res publica* as the people's thing or affair. A people is not just any group or gathering of human beings whatsoever, but 'a collection of a mass which forms a society by virtue of agreement with respect to justice and sharing in advantage' (1.39).[27]

The question is then under what kinds of constitution a *res publica* – understood in the legal terminology that permeated Roman philosophical argument to be a thing over which the people enjoy certain rights that they may choose to entrust to others – may be enjoyed and protected. Scipio allows that this is possible under all three non-corrupt Greek models. Even in a monarchy, it is possible for there to be sufficient concern for the people's interests and for what they are owed (we may use 'rights' to describe this, though Cicero tends to use the singular), though he concedes that this does not give enough credit to the general understanding of what the people want to possess in possessing the *res publica*. Scipio then sets out the Polybian-type claim that even where each of the three basic types of constitution is well governed, each has a characteristic flaw, lacking due provision for the characteristic goods provided by the others (1.43). In a monarchy, no one but the king enjoys a share in justice and

deliberation; even under a wise and just king, it is hard to argue that a simple monarchy is a very desirable *res publica*, or 'people's thing', at all. In an aristocracy, by contrast, the people have scarcely any participation in 'liberty'. And in a democracy, even when the people rule justly and moderately, the equality enjoyed is actually 'unequal', since it fails to recognize different degrees of dignity (he is doubtless implying the kind of dignity rightly, in his view, enjoyed by the Roman senators, for example).

Having surveyed these three types, Scipio then presents his own opinion that the best condition of a commonwealth consists of a fourth type: one that is measured and mixed from the original three (1.45; see also 1.69).[28] Like his real-life tutor Polybius, he argues that this, happily, is the very condition into which Rome has evolved through the practical experience and statecraft of many generations – indeed, he goes further by claiming that only Rome, not even Sparta or Carthage, has achieved such a mixed constitution, a point he illustrates by offering his own version of the Polybian cycle of regimes. Scipio is said by Augustine to have summed up his argument at the end of the first day of reported dialogue with this claim: 'What the musicians call harmony with regard to song is concord in the state, the tightest and the best bond of safety in every republic; and that concord can never exist without justice' (2.69a).[29]

Property, Justice and Law

While Scipio's endorsement of justice as the basis of civic concord is deeply Platonic, when he and his friend

Gaius Laelius come to discuss the institutions, *mores* and laws that can foster a true commonwealth, they chastise Plato's *Republic* and Spartan customs alike. This is because they see the Platonic and Spartan constitutions as involving a flawed and dangerous understanding of political community: to wit, as based on property held in common rather than privately. The discussion of these topics in *De Re Publica* hardly survives, however, and so we must turn to Cicero's other writings to reconstruct his defence of private property and its political implications at the time. Looking at his speeches, we find that he engaged in a reprise of the debates over the land reforms of the Gracchi that form so stark a background to the *De Re Publica* that he would later write. In 63, one of the newly elected tribunes proposed a new form of agrarian law, which would use an unusual and partial electoral procedure to establish an independent commission with powers to sell, tax, and use various categories of public lands so as to distribute land in Italy among the Roman poor.[30] Cicero, as consul in 63, made three speeches against this proposal, one before the Senate and the other two before popular assemblies, which he chose to publish three years later as another effort of land reform was under way.

Cicero attacks primarily the form rather than the substance of the agrarian law proposed in 63: that is, he says less about the benefits and disadvantages of distributing land per se, and more about the arbitrary and tyrannical authority by which it was (he argued) proposed to be done. It is arbitrary insofar as the commissioners would be immunized against any legal challenge: he claims that they will be able to name

any property they choose as public property and then to sell it as they wish. This, he urges his fellow senators, will be a threat to their own safety and liberty and dignity. And he argues to the people that the law would also undermine the peace, liberty and leisure that they enjoy, depriving them of their 'right of voting' (because of the irregular voting procedure, allowing only a randomly selected subset of voting units to elect the commissioners), and by doing so would deprive them of their 'liberty' (2.17, 2.16).[31]

To fill out Cicero's views on the importance of law and of property respectively, we can turn to still other writings. He presents his fullest account of law in the dialogue *De Legibus*, a dialogue that, although he began to write it in the same year that *De Re Publica* was published (the year in which he himself was serving as governor of the province of Cilicia, 51 BCE), is set in a very different dramatic context. Its protagonists are not admirable ancestors but he himself (as 'Marcus'), his brother Quintus and his closest friend, Atticus, depicted as talking together at his country estate in Arpinum and discussing the nature of the civil law. This brings them to imagine an ideal law code suitable for the mixed commonwealth of Rome that had been defended in the earlier dialogue.[32]

Caustic about the petty details ('party walls and gutters')[33] on which Roman jurists concentrate when they should be considering the fundamental nature of the laws, Marcus insists that law is the embodiment of reason. To understand this, one must move beyond particular written laws to 'seek the roots of justice in nature'.[34] This approach exhibits the Stoic inclinations that Cicero often expressed

in his writings about ethics and politics, inclinations to be understood in the context of his moderate Scepticism, which allows him to find certain views more probable than others. Because humans share reason and so this fundamental law with the gods, 'this whole world must be considered to be a common political community [*civitas*] of gods and humans'[35] – a statement invoking the Stoic Cosmopolitan ideal discussed in Chapter 6.

Marcus makes the fundamental law of nature a critical tool to be wielded against the unjust laws made by either tyrants or certain democrats (using Athenian history for his examples). Nevertheless, most of the laws he proposes are quite close to existing Roman institutions, reflecting a similar view to Scipio's: that the Roman constitution is actually the best possible condition of a commonwealth. Defending the tribunate but criticizing secret ballots (he proposes instead that the people's votes be open to the aristocracy to scrutinize), Marcus here demonstrates a reverence for the law as more than the sum of its parts. Particular laws may be changed or improved, but their reference point and justification should always relate to the cosmic reason that is embodied in natural law.

While natural law structures the cosmic order, private property comes about through a more tortuous route. Indeed, Cicero argues in another work, the *De Officiis*, that 'by nature there is no private [property]'.[36] Land becomes private as it is appropriated by groups of people in settlement, war, agreement or by lottery; so, too, individuals come into private property. Cicero concludes without further ado that 'each man should hold on to whatever he has obtained',

and that to do otherwise is to violate 'the law of human association'. This defines justice (respecting what is common as common and what is private as private).

When Cicero later returns to the topic of property, he criticizes a tribune who had, in 104 BCE, proposed an agrarian law tending to an equal distribution of material goods. In doing so, the philosopher adds a particular twist to the Stoic account of natural sociability: 'Although nature has led men to congregate together, nevertheless they sought to live in cities in the hope of protecting their material things.'[37] The life of the advanced political community is based on the motive of protecting private property, and this is a baseline requirement – though not perhaps the highest aspiration – for its justified existence. He goes on to attack those elite politicians (such as Julius Caesar) advocating land reform, known as *populares* for their policies favourable to the plebeians, for undermining the concord and equity that are the foundations of the political community.

By basing justice firmly on the rights of private property, Cicero advanced a tradition of Roman thought about justice and property that was unabashedly elitist in its context, in at least two ways. He worked to entrench certain entitlements of the political elite, and he rejected any redistribution of certain public lands. These political (and social and economic positions) underpinned his broader ethics of republican probity. As a result, those ethics were influential, though far from universal. In the rivalrous politics of his day, his understanding of justice and property was undeniably partisan. His ideas have, nonetheless, resonated beyond the confines of the debates of his own day.

Duties to Self, to Others and to the Commonwealth

Defending the nature and value of the commonwealth in abstract terms was one thing; determining one's duty in defending it in practice, when its fundamental provisions for allocating and restraining power were threatened, was something else – though for Cicero the two were intimately related. We find him reflecting on these dilemmas especially in the *De Officiis*, his last philosophical work, written while he was also composing the series of speeches in which he risked his reflection on them at high stakes: the fourteen *Philippics* in which he attempted to muster opposition to Mark Antony. In the *De Officiis* he sought to prove that the duty or obligation (*officium*) that it was always honourable to perform (*honestas*) could never contradict one's advantage or benefit (*utilitas*). In the *Philippics*, he pursued a course that he believed honourable, even though it posed the gravest threat to his life, relying on his view that one's duty as a citizen is the highest and most honourable duty that one has. As he wrote in the *Second Philippic* (the only one not delivered as a speech at the time), 'I will freely put my own body on the line, if by my death the liberty of the city may be made present' (2.119).[38]

Written in the autumn of 44 BCE, *De Officiis* was addressed as a work of ethical instruction and exhortation to Cicero's 21-year-old son, advising him on the duties of a virtuous Roman citizen and upright human being, at a moment when the future prospects for fulfilling those duties within the traditional republican constitution were in grave doubt.[39]

Nevertheless, he lays out a handbook to honourable political success in the hope that somehow the political world
he is describing may not come to an end. He harks back
to the *mos maiorum*, the customs and practices of the ancestral Romans, idealizing their instinctive adherence to the
virtues and duties. Even in the case of ten Romans who
were captured by Hannibal after Cannae and sent to Rome,
bound by an oath that they would return if their mission
were unsuccessful, but refused to return to captivity – still
Cicero commends the Senate of that time for having stripped
them of their citizenship privileges in punishment for having
broken their oath (1.40).

The heart of the argument comes in setting out the
Roman *officia*, or duties, that subtly reshape the Greek virtues.
The Romans include wisdom and justice, as did the Greeks,
but also greatness of spirit and decorum. These latter virtues
had featured in Greek writing in various ways, but neither
was ever as central in Greek ethics as Cicero makes them for
the Roman elite, whom he enjoins to aim for a greatness of
spirit that nevertheless disdains human affairs as minor in
comparison with the universe (1.72) and to manifest seemly
conformity with expected conduct, or *decorum*, even while
striving for renown. His injunctions here are specific. You
should not hurry about huffing and puffing; neither should
you stroll too languidly (1.131). You should converse wittily
(1.134), not build a house beyond your means (1.139), nor
elevate learning and study above ordinary social interaction
(1.157). All of these ethical duties can be called *honestas* (virtuous, with the connotation of honourable).

The question, then, is how what is *honestas* comports with

what is *utilitas*, the seemingly useful or advantageous. In this way, Cicero tackles in his *De Officiis* the same challenge as had Plato in the central arc of his *Republic*: is it really to my advantage as an individual to be just? And he gives essentially the same answer: when properly understood, justice (or duty) and advantage can never conflict. An action like stealing 'destroys the common life and fellowship of men', as does violence (3.21, 3.26): in acting unnaturally, one violates one's own nature, in line with the Stoic ideas of natural sociability and natural law that we met in Chapter 6. Treating others unjustly cannot be to anyone's real advantage, because it breaches the natural ties of solidarity that bind all humans.[40]

This claim can have a political edge. Cicero does not hesitate to condemn some Roman actions. The Romans' sacking of Corinth in 146 BCE was, he says, not truly advantageous, for 'nothing cruel is in fact beneficial' (3.46). But, whereas Plato had delved into psychology to make his case, focusing on the psychic misery and strife that injustice constitutes, Cicero makes his as a practising lawyer. He confronts specific cases of apparent conflict – many of which had become stock tropes in the Stoic literature and that of their critics – head on.

Does the seller of a house have the duty to disclose all details about its condition, if doing so might lower the price and so his profit? (Yes.) Should one resist temptation to profit at the margins in administering the estate of an orphan (a task that often fell to the lot of prominent Roman men)? (Yes: though Cicero himself divorced his wife to marry an orphan whose estate he was administering, doing so – so thought observers – to get hold of her money.[41]) Would a

good man who has temporary advantage in the corn market tell his buyers that more corn from other sources is on the way – '[O]r would he keep silent and sell his own produce at as high a price as possible?' (3.50). (No: this is concealment in the interests of profit, which will make one appear to be 'crafty, roguish and sly' – a reputation that cannot be beneficial to possess.) Here Cicero appeals to the recent innovation in Roman legal practice of *formulae* banning malicious fraud (3.60): such *formulae* are exactly the kind of resolution of a legal dispute that he wants to effect in his philosophical analysis. Must one resist all temptation to act unjustly, even if doing so seems necessary in the pursuit of political success and glory – even if one believes that one can best serve the republic by attaining those heights? (Emphatically, yes.)

This pattern of analysis was put to work in a cloaked analogy for the tyrannicide of Julius Caesar, which had occurred not even a year before. 'What if a good man were to be able to rob of his clothes Phalaris, a cruel and monstrous tyrant, to prevent himself from dying of cold? Might he not do it?' (3.29). Cicero's answer is telling. On the one hand, simply trying to stay alive for your own benefit by robbing someone else is against the law of nature. But, on the other hand, if by staying alive you can benefit the political community and human fellowship, you should do so. Similarly, 'if a man who has deposited money with you were to make war on your country', you should not return the deposit: 'for you would be acting contrary to the republic, which ought to be the dearest thing to you' (3.95). And, even more bitingly, in the case of Phalaris and other tyrants, 'there can be no fellowship between us and tyrants ... and it is not contrary to nature to

rob a man ... whom it is honourable to kill' (3.32). This coded justification for tyrannicide would be enormously influential with medieval philosophers, although Cicero's injunctions to political leaders to demonstrate liberality and good faith in *De Officiis* would become specific targets in Machiavelli's *The Prince* (1513).[42]

Nevertheless, apart from these extreme cases, the moral duties of universal human fellowship identified by Cicero are limited and largely negative. 'One should not keep others from fresh water, should allow them to take fire from your fire, should give trustworthy counsel to someone who is seeking advice' (1.52) – but one has no duty to be generous except insofar as this is compatible with one's own light shining no less (in the poetic phrase he quotes, 1.51). This is because everyone has special duties of liberality to those close, and also duties of civil law to respect private property once established by law and custom of use. These closer ties arise first from the animal drive to procreate, producing marriage, children, and then family and the bonds of marriage that unite people by blood and by their religious duties to the ancestors. The Cosmopolitan ideas that Cicero entertains find their limits and, for the most part, their practical realization in the attitude one adopts towards one's ties to more local communities.

While familial bonds are closer and more intimate, Cicero insists that 'of all fellowships none is more serious, and none dearer, than that of each of us with the republic' (1.57). Able men have the duty to serve it by engaging in public life and so therefore can achieve and display greatness of spirit (1.72). The Roman republic is the best possible constitution – the

argument he had given to Scipio, now in his own voice; and the best human life, perfecting the sociability that animates humans to live together and the justice that they thereby seek to protect, is the life lived in such a regime in which power, deliberation and liberty are allied together.

Cicero had a particular vision of what that required. His hostility to land reform and insistence on deference to the Senate was not shared by all republicans of his time or before or since. In the kind of regime he praised (and even in the most radical populist thinking of his opponents), the Roman poor were accorded none of the powers of initiative or lottery selection, and fewer of the powers of accountability and control that had been exercised by their Athenian counterparts. The particulars of Cicero's anti-populist stances, as well as his broader vision of popular liberty as secure only when balanced by more informed counsel and by decisive executive powers, have been recurrently adopted in later thought. Most profoundly absorbed by later ages was his model of a citizen's duties, and his idea of how citizenship and a healthy constitution for the *res publica* mutually reinforce one another.

Sovereignty

Within decades of Cicero's death, the exercise of power in Rome was being fundamentally reshaped. The struggle for power between the heir and aides of the murdered Julius Caesar, first against the forces of his assassins and then among themselves, led ultimately to the consolidation of military power in the hands of Octavian (the adopted son of Julius Caesar), who soon began to call himself 'Imperator Caesar divi filius' ('General Caesar, son of the god').[1] That combination of military power and religious–personal authority connected to Julius Caesar allowed the younger Caesar to accrue new forms of political power, for example, summoning the Senate without any official authority to do so in 32 BCE, and then getting each of the municipalities in Italy to demand that he lead them in a last wave of battle against his erstwhile ally now allied with the queen of Egypt.[2]

Octavian did not abolish the republican magistracies. On the contrary, he presented himself as the restorer and defender of the republican constitution. But he demanded and received from the Senate new combinations of roles and powers for himself. He was in 27 BCE elected to a consulship in which he would serve continuously for several years (violating the republican requirement of yearly election),

after which in 23 BCE he was accorded the powers of a tribune to preside over the Senate and veto the actions of any magistrate; he accrued other powers, positions and titles as well. Alongside this unprecedented assemblage of powers in a single set of hands, Augustus was given titles of *princeps* ('first man' or leader) in the Senate and *civitas* that had some republican pedigree. Although the Senate granted those titles and itself continued to exist throughout the imperial period, as did the idea that the people were the ultimate source of imperial legal authority, the independence of the Senate's deliberations and the meaningfulness of the people's role would become so compromised as to become largely hollow.

The titles of *princeps senatus* and *princeps civitatis* suggested that Octavian was simply the first among equals. But the title of Caesar Augustus that had been conferred on him by the Senate in 27 BCE, ironically in gratitude for his having given up his powers with the end of the war (only to have new powers conferred upon him), confirmed what events had already made true: that he was now an unequal, with no true peers among his fellow citizens.[3] Any remaining attempt to cling to a fiction of continued equality would eventually be abandoned when the Senate inaugurated the reign of Vespasian in 69 CE with what is called the *lex de imperio Vespasiani*, empowering the new emperor to act according to his discretion to do what he judged best, irrespective of the existing laws. This would break openly with the republican commitment to the principle of *aequa libertas*, or equality with respect to the laws.[4] Still, the title of *princeps* gives its name to the whole period that historians call the 'principate', or the first phase of rule by emperors in Rome

(27 BCE–284 CE). After that time begins the 'dominate', so called from the formal imperial title of *dominus* – master or lord – adopted in the reign of Diocletian.

As the varied titles adopted by Augustus and his successors suggest, there is no single word or concept that alone captures the emergence of new ideas of what may be called 'sovereignty' in imperial Rome. ('Imperial Rome' means in this chapter the Rome ruled by the emperors, as opposed to the territorial empire possessed by the Roman people, which had begun to be acquired centuries earlier under the republic as shown in the previous chapter.) Perhaps the closest is the word *imperium*, with the root sense of giving orders and being able to enforce obedience to them, describing powers that had been ascribed to a range of magistrates in the course of the republic. *Imperium* was accorded in an augmented form to Augustus in 23 BCE when (and despite the fact that) he formally resigned the consulship, and it would be granted to each successive emperor by a vote of the Senate. Yet the specific power of *imperium* (originally in the provinces, then for Augustus from within the city of Rome and over the whole of Italy, which was treated as a province) was only one of the powers that the emperors would enjoy. The proliferation of new titles for the emperors suggests that Romans struggled to articulate the sense in which the continuing roles of the people and the Senate were altered by confrontation with these individual rulers who, if they were made by the people in theory, ruled over them in unaccountable ways in practice. This chapter discusses 'sovereignty' not as the translation of any one particular Latin word, but rather as the emperors' evolving set of powers, which combined, augmented or

superseded the highest powers of the republican magistracies. To an even greater extent, it explores 'sovereignty' in terms of the control of one's self, an interest that preoccupied many of the writers of this period – whether because they felt their ability to shape political events ebbing away, or because without such internal control even the powers of the emperor were of little value. To consider these dual themes of outer and inner sovereignty, we will examine aspects of the lives and writings of Tacitus, Seneca, Epictetus, Marcus Aurelius and Plutarch.

While the Romans were well aware of models of kingship in the world around them and in Greek history and theory, they could not simply adopt these models wholesale. Instead they had to evolve ways of thinking about the ideals and realities that the new sovereigns embodied, and about the ethical and political predicaments of those subject to them. The idea of Sovereignty marks the point at which the powers that still in Roman law theoretically emanated from the people were put, in practice, largely beyond the reach of their control. As with the idea of the Republic, this notion is radical for us today largely in its uncomfortable closeness to predicaments of our own. Whether such powers can somehow be guided without popular control and accountability, and how ordinary people should live under the powers that now dominate their lives, are questions that speak to the experiences of many today.

At the same time that these new sovereign figures were asserting themselves at the heart of Rome, the regime's borders and the place of subject peoples within them were also undergoing transformation. We have been tracing the

role of city walls and laws throughout this book, observing in Chapter 6 certain Stoic and Epicurean visions of a world not divided by the walls or laws of distinct cities. Those visions of the *kosmos* as demarcating the reach of natural fellowship took a new turn as Rome expanded. Now it became possible to see Rome itself as tantamount to a single cosmopolitan community. So a Greek orator would proclaim before Antoninus Pius in 155 CE, declaring that Rome had made of the whole world a single *polis* (Aelius Aristides, *Or.* 26.36). Instead of a vision of no walls, he likened the armies guarding Rome's borders to the walls of a single giant city (however fancifully, given the shifting and contested frontiers of the time) (*Or.* 26.80–81).[5] A few decades later, in 212 CE, the idea of a single set of laws for the whole empire would also be taken to a new level, when the emperor Caracalla promulgated the *Constitutio Antoniniana*, making all the free inhabitants of the empire into full citizens (and so conveniently subject to his increasingly punishing taxation demands).

In the course of these transformations, historians and philosophers debated the value and values of the emerging forms of sovereign rule, and the role that citizens should play under them. Deprived of the possibility of real political self-rule, many of the philosophers living under the empire were inclined instead to cultivate a form of self-rule, of personal sovereignty, to maintain a kind of immunity to the public depredations. Republican political ideals and Stoic philosophical ideals (as well as other schools of philosophical thought) were mined to provide critiques of sovereignty in addition to new conceptions of, or alternatives to, it.

A Republican Critique of Sovereignty

Despite the efforts of the early principate's rulers to con-
serve the appearance of republican forms, many observers saw this as a figleaf for a fundamental abandonment
of republican values. No one was more excoriating in this
analysis than the historian Tacitus (P. Cornelius Tacitus,
c. 55–118 CE). In his writings, he looked back to the history
of Rome from the death of Augustus in 14 CE, all the way
to 96 CE, when Domitian was assassinated.[6] And in other
writings, especially in his *Dialogus de Oratoribus* (*Dialogue
on Oratory*), written in a much more Ciceronian style of
Latin than his other works, he reflected bitterly on the distance between republican *mores* and the attitudes possible
under the new dispensation.[7] Just as we found political
ideas embedded in the *Histories* of Polybius, so emphatically
do we find them in Tacitus (and so would other readers,
especially in the 16th and 17th centuries, when those jaun-
diced by the *hubris* and folly of early modern rulers found
confirmation for the bleakness of their political outlook in
his work).

Looking back to the years before his birth and those of his
early childhood in the timespan he chronicled, Tacitus had
first-hand experience of a wide range of imperial rulers. He
held office under the emperor Domitian, whom he viewed as
a tyrant, and then served as consul in 97 CE under Nerva, the
first of the 'Five Good Emperors' of the Nervan–Antonine
dynasty. (Ruling moderately, the reign of these men – each of
whom adopted as his son a senator to become his successor –
would be celebrated by the 18th-century English historian

Edward Gibbon – author of the seminal *History of the Decline and Fall of the Roman Empire* – as 'the period in the history of the world during which the condition of the human race was most happy and prosperous'.[8]) Yet, while he was acutely sensitive to the difference between good and bad emperors, Tacitus came to imply that the principate as an institution inherently tended to the destruction of liberty.

In the *Annals*, he dramatizes how senators who were proud of their republican heritage were brought under the thumb of the vicious emperors, as when Tiberius ascended to power after the death of Augustus Caesar in 14 CE: 'at Rome people plunged into slavery – consuls, senators, knights' (*Annals* 1.7).[9] The image of these men, who had nominally been elected to lead the republic, being effectively enslaved by a tyrannical emperor, marks a trenchant political condemnation. It forms a counterpoint to the Stoic theses we have considered, according to which no wise man is actually a slave, even if he is cast into chains as what the world calls a slave. The Roman Stoic philosophers extolled the freedom of every wise man, even if he were legally a slave. Tacitus, in contrast, condemned as slaves to imperial tyranny even those men whom the world counted as pre-eminently free.

He implies a further critique – not merely of bad sovereigns but of sovereigns altogether – in his *Dialogus De Oratoribus*, written after 101 CE, with a dramatic date of 74 CE. This dialogue explores the decision of a Roman writer to renounce oratory and law in favour of dramatic poetry. This was one model of coping with the pressures of the principate, but one that Tacitus himself adopted only in fits and starts (he withdrew from active political life at various points

but then took on certain roles over the years, while at the same time constructing another form of identity and autonomy relevant to his political and social standing, by writing his histories and other works).[10] Among those gathered are men who are senators and have held high elected offices: they have lived the full extent of political life that the principate allows. And yet, even when one of them celebrates his enjoyment of his oratorical powers in political life, he views the favour of the emperor as among the highest successes that he used them to win (7.1, 8.1–3).

Another participant looks back to the greater effectiveness of rhetoric under the republic, which, although torn by disagreement and civil strife, was genuinely governed by the convictions imparted to the people by its orators. He plays with the idea that in genuinely well-governed states there is no need for orators; orators reigned in Athens and Rhodes, not in Sparta or Crete (40.3). If a single wise monarch makes all the decisions, oratory would indeed be useless (41.4). The question is left open as to whether the *princeps* of the day qualifies as a single wisest monarch. If not, the picture of rhetoric under the principate as a matter of flattery and attention-seeking looks dark indeed. And, even if he does, is not liberty lost along with oratory, in the name of good government? That question Tacitus leaves provocatively unresolved.[11]

A Stoic Idealization of Sovereignty

While Tacitus would ruminate on the possible loss of liberty even under a good emperor, a Roman thinker of the previous

generation had pinned political hope on being able to cultivate a sovereign to rule well rather than badly. This was done
in a philosophical rather than an historical vein by Lucius
Annaeus Seneca, tutor and then political adviser to Nero
(who reigned 54–68 CE). A Stoic in philosophical adherence
who was also a playwright and man of letters, Seneca never
wrote a *De Re Publica* along the lines of the *Politeia* works
composed by the Stoic founders Zeno and Chrysippus (and
previously by Plato). Instead of delineating the constitution
or laws of an ideal commonwealth, he tellingly composed an
account of the idealized prince – a sign that the welfare of
the polity had already become overwhelmingly dependent
on the virtues or vices of a single man.

In the case of Nero, after the hopeful moment of his
accession at age sixteen that Seneca heralded with his treatise, the vices would predominate. Among other enormities,
Nero would eventually enjoy having Christians burned at
the stake and using the light to illuminate his garden, and
he would ultimately become so suspicious of Seneca's political intentions that he would order him to commit suicide.
But when Seneca wrote *De Clementia* (*On Mercy*) in 54, all
that was in the future, and Seneca's hopes lay in his effort
to shape Nero's reign for the good. He advises the prince
that 'your commonwealth [*rei publicae*] is your body and
you are its mind' (1.5).[12] As the animating mind of the commonwealth, the prince must model himself on the gods:
'because the gods ... are the best example for the prince ... he
should wish to be such to the citizens, as he would wish the
gods to be to him' (1.7). The prince here is given the most
exalted possible standard of conduct: the good order of the

commonwealth and even of the cosmos depends on his rectitude and virtue.

Of course, the idea of a good king or monarch was not new, and there were plenty of diverse intellectual resources in Greek and Roman thought and in the neighbouring societies with which they engaged on which Seneca could draw, even while maintaining his principal philosophical identity as a Stoic. The ideal of monarchy had never been absent from Greek political thought. We met it at various points in earlier chapters, including as one of the three basic kinds of constitution in Herodotus (Chapter 2); in the strands of Macedonian, Persian and other regime practices that Alexander the Great melded into the image of himself as a new kind of ruler; and in the Hellenistic ideals of the king as a living law that arose in the successor kingdoms in Alexander's wake (both, Chapter 6).

There were other important developments of a monarchical ideal too. Perhaps most important was that by Xenophon, a contemporary of Plato and friend of Socrates, who led almost as adventurous a life as Polybius. He wrote an encomium of the education of the earlier monarch Cyrus the Great of Persia, who had reigned in the 6th century BCE. That work articulated an ideal of kingship in the very heyday of classical Greek political theory that would be available for those reviving and inventing new practices of monarchical rule or sway to appropriate. Xenophon also wrote an epistle to Nicocles, the prince of Cyprus, on how to rule his subjects.

Yet Seneca's development of these ideas in a Roman context, composing a work of the kind that would become known as a 'mirror for princes' (understood as a highly

refracting mirror designed to make the prince see himself in a certain light), is still striking. The commonwealth, however autonomous it might have been under the republic, is now incapable of thinking or self-direction without its prince. That imposes on him a *noblesse oblige*. But it does so at the cost of divesting the citizens – even the high-status senators like Seneca himself – of meaningful political authority.

Political Ethics under Sovereign Rule

That approach is reflected in the tensions that Seneca himself experienced in living under a sovereign. The son of a prominent Roman citizen from Spain, Seneca was, like many sons of wealthy and ambitious provincial men, educated in rhetoric and philosophy in Rome. He made his reputation as an orator, served in high elected offices and joined the Senate, all as Cicero had done. Yet his life was threatened, and he was banished, because of the emperor Claudius' jealous suspicion of him; and, while he then returned to favour as tutor and adviser to Nero (the son of Claudius' wife Agrippina, who was adopted by her husband), he would eventually be suspected of conspiracy, and committed suicide upon Nero's orders in 65 CE. Such subjection to the arbitrary power of one man, without even the chance to battle for republican equality as Cicero had sought to do, marks a distinct break between a political life under the republic and one under the principate.

Seneca never gave up on the idea that the *patria* is to be counted among the primary goods for human beings (*Ep.* 66.36, 66.37), and that it is in his own *patria* that a citizen

should wish ideally to display his virtue (*Ep.* 85.40). But one could only serve the *patria* to the extent that it – or, rather, its new sovereign prince – would allow a political culture to exist in which it could be served. And in Seneca's day, that culture was deeply flawed. This was the reasoning by which he reconciled his sometime aversion to public life with his allegiance to a Stoic school whose founder had said that the wise man 'will go into public life, unless something impedes'.

Seneca goes so far as to argue that the effective implication of that injunction by Zeno is identical to the seemingly opposite Epicurean doctrine that the wise man 'will not go into public life, unless something interferes' (both as reported by Seneca in *De Otio* (*On the Private Life*) 3.2).[13] The more seemingly positive Stoic doctrine merges with the quietist Epicurean one when it is recognized that 'if the public realm is too corrupt to be helped, if it has been taken over by the wicked, the wise man will not struggle pointlessly nor squander himself to no avail' (all the more so, he adds, if the wise man also lacks sufficient health, authority or strength) (*De Otio* 3.3). The path of the wise man in a corrupt public realm is one of leisured withdrawal (*otium*), not active engagement (*negotium*).[14]

And yet Seneca does not leave it at that. For the withdrawal to *otium* in respect of the affairs of the commonwealth leaves the wise man open to serve what he calls a greater commonwealth. This is the use to which he now puts the Stoic idea of being a cosmopolitan citizen. For Seneca, this community of cosmopolitan citizens is not (as for the early Stoics) the perfected province of the wise. Nor is it, as for the orator Aelius Aristides quoted above, coterminous

with Rome. It is rather a fellowship of all potentially rational beings. Here is his expression of the implications of this idea in *De Otio* (4.1–2):

> We must grasp that there are two public realms, two commonwealths [*duas res publicas*]. One is great and truly common to all, where gods as well as men are included, where we look not to this corner or that, but measure its bounds by the path of the sun. The other is that in which we are enrolled by an accident of birth – I mean Athens or Carthage or some other city that belongs not to all men but only to a limited number. Some devote themselves at the same time to both commonwealths, the greater and the lesser, some only to the one or the other. We can serve this greater commonwealth even in retirement – indeed better, I suspect, in retirement – by inquiring what virtue is ...

Here we find a continuation of the idea of the *res publica* as the organizing conception for political life into the imperial period – together with its doubling into two: the *res publica* of any actual and particular political unit, versus the *res publica* of gods and men, coextensive with the cosmos. Both commonwealths may be served, but in different ways: the traditionally politically bounded one ('lesser' in size) with active political service, the 'greater' one in size by philosophizing in leisure or retirement (*otium*), withdrawing from worldly affairs (*negotium*) in order the better to serve one's larger commonwealth through philosophical contemplation. It is in this sense of philosophical service that Seneca enjoins that one should consider oneself 'a citizen and soldier of the cosmos' (*Ep.* 120.12).[15]

Chances to serve the lesser commonwealth – the actual Roman polity – were by contrast limited by the corruption of values and opportunities experienced within it. Despite the natural inclination to sociability that he as a Stoic recognizes, Seneca takes a bleak view of the crowded Roman forum and circus in which public life was variously lived: 'Life is the same here as in a school of gladiators – living together means fighting together' (*De Ira* (*On Anger*) 2.8).[16] In corrupt social conditions, the cruel, merciless social and political struggle for advancement, even for existence, makes it hard for anyone to live virtuously: 'our public madness makes this a difficult task; we drive each other into vice' (*Ep.* 41.9).[17] Public life is a source of conflict, corruption and temptation. It is better to watch elections in tranquillity than to participate in them (*Ep.* 118.3). Cicero and his brother Quintus had corresponded feverishly about how to win elections; Seneca notes how different he is from Cicero in preferring to keep away from them (*Ep.* 118.2).

Seneca's disillusioned stance was far from a universal view in a society where many people enthusiastically engaged in campaigns for local office, such as in Pompeii, where painted electoral 'posters' survive with dozens of voices, including women's, advocating their favourite candidates.[18] (The English word 'candidate' comes from the bleached white *toga candida* that those standing for public office wore.[19]) But to Seneca, from a stance of philosophical reflection (and despite his own history of being elected to high offices), striving for public honour is likely to lead to disappointment or even self-endangerment. '[P]ublic office' is, like money and the body, one of 'those things over which

chance exercises power', and therefore 'servile' (*Ep.* 66.23). It is not befitting of anyone whose ethical goal, as should be the ethical goal of everyone, is to be free. Freedom is no longer best embodied in political participation, though it is an idea originally modelled in political terms: now it resides in the conduct of the self.[20]

Ethics as One's Own Sovereign

If moral or ethical freedom is the most important value, and it can be attained only by the wise and virtuous man (the Stoic sage), how should one live to approach this goal? All of the Roman Stoic authors had much practical advice to give on this front. Indeed, to the extent that one withdrew from the public realm, the private realm of self-fashioning, of ruling one's own body and desires in place of attempting to rule over others, became a favoured domain for ethical practice. If one could not escape a wayward sovereign in the public realm, one could make oneself one's own sovereign in personal behaviour.[21]

For Seneca, the fundamental practice is a nightly self-examination of the good and bad deeds that he has performed, and the inclinations he has experienced, in the course of the day (*De Clementia* 3.36): he recommends a similar practice to the prince. The aim of such exercises is to maintain the rule of reason in one's soul, extirpating the everyday emotions, as they are not saturated by rational determination. By doing this, one can free oneself from fear of even the most terrible harm that one might ever face (such as being tortured on a rack, a common Roman punishment),

and therefore face good and bad fortune with the same equanimity. Seneca asks himself in a letter: 'are reclining at a dinner party and being tortured equal?', meaning, will a wise man consider these two possible fates with equal equanimity? He replies with an emphatic yes (*Ep.* 71.21).

Fundamental threats to self-rule came from the unregulated, irrational passions that go by the name of emotion in ordinary parlance (for Stoics, there were more rational responses that should replace them). For Seneca, one of the most important challenges was anger (an emotion in which as an aristocratic Roman he was perhaps freer to indulge from childhood than were those more servile to their patrons and betters). Dedicating a whole essay to this one emotion (*De Ira*), here, as in his other essays and letters, Seneca wrote, in part, to offer therapy to himself and his fellows. Not uniquely (Cicero had discussed the emotions in a similar way in the *Tusculan Disputations*), but characteristically, Seneca prescribes practical steps about 'how not to fall into anger ... on how to free ourselves from anger, and ... on how the angry should be restrained, pacified and brought back to sanity' (3.5).[22]

Seneca personifies anger as an enemy in war, which must be stopped at the 'city gates' of the mind rather than allowed to conquer and usurp the role of reason (1.8). Here the city walls have become internalized: the city for which we have responsibility is first of all our own mind (borrowing a Platonic image from the *Republic*). Developing in Stoic vein what was originally a Platonic challenge to the validity of the frequent anger that had animated Athenians' social and political struggles for respect, and now informed Roman ones,

Seneca insists again and again that anger is both useless and counter-productive, 'even in battle or in war. With its wish to bring others into danger, it lowers its own guard. The surest courage is to look around long and hard, to govern oneself, to move slowly and deliberately forward' (1.11).

Seneca was well aware of the castigation that would be launched against such a stance – it would be disparaged as unworldly and unnatural, even inhuman and vicious. To counter objections that anger is natural, admirable and befitting of ruling men, Seneca tells stories of the cruelty and self-destructive folly caused by the anger of kings. He recalls Alexander the Great's murder of a friend for showing too little flattery (*De Ira* 3.17). Closer to home, he recalls the action of the emperor Gaius, known as Caligula, who during his brief reign (37–41 CE) had torn down a villa in revenge for the fact that his mother had once been held there under house arrest. That angry act of destruction was self-defeating: it resulted only in drawing people's attention to the destruction and therefore to what had occasioned it: his mother's shame (3.22). According to Seneca all anger, like all conduct driven by passions rather than governed by reason, is self-defeating in an even more fundamental sense. By allowing oneself to be moved by passions, one fails to achieve the rational self-control that constitutes virtue. One allows oneself to be a slave rather than attaining the status of someone truly free.[23]

This Stoic stance was all the more compelling when voiced by someone who had been a slave himself. The Stoic Epictetus (*c.* 55–135 CE) has already been mentioned. He was born a slave in what is now Turkey, bought by a freedman

who was a secretary to Nero – so he, like Seneca, found himself at Nero's court in Rome. Having been freed by his master, he eventually established his own school in the Greek city of Nicopolis. His sayings were compiled in a book of *Dissertationes* (*Discourses*), along with a handbook to his philosophy (the *Enchiridion*), by his student Arrian.

Epictetus' emphasis on theory for the sake of practice was a departure, even something of an inversion, of the early Stoic insistence that ethics flowed out of physics. He stresses *ataraxia* (tranquillity) as the interpretation of the end of happiness, actively competing on the same turf as the Epicureans and Sceptics. But he still invokes the Stoic understanding of the cosmic order in explaining how one might best achieve tranquillity: by philosophizing in order to realize that freedom comes from wishing only what Zeus wills. Living in accordance with this norm-saturated nature will bring virtue and freedom.

If Seneca, contending with quarrelsome and ambitious courtiers, was especially preoccupied with the dangers posed by the emotion of anger, Epictetus was especially attuned – perhaps given the losses he had suffered in slavery – to the dangers posed by the emotion of grief. As reported in the *Discourses*, he chastised students who joined his school just to 'acquire a bookish disposition'; the worthwhile reason to study Stoicism is rather 'to work on eliminating from one's life grief and lamentation, the "Woe is me!" and "Alas, alack!" along with misfortune and bad luck' – so that one will not lament like Priam or Oedipus or any king in tragedy ('for tragedies are nothing but the sufferings of people who are impressed by externals, performed

in the right sort of meter').[24] He insists that each person has the capacity to make a moral choice in what he believes and desires that is free of 'hindrance, compulsion and impediment'. Even if threatened with death, one is not compelled to do what the threatener demands: 'It's not because you are threatened, but it's because you believe that it is better to do this or that rather than to die.' It is 'your opinion that compelled you', just as all action is determined by what we think. This is why emotions are at bottom only false beliefs.[25]

One of Epictetus' readers would become an emperor. Although not exclusively doctrinaire in his Stoicism, with a mix of philosophical inclinations including a strong current of Platonism, Marcus Aurelius likewise concerned himself with the practice of self-rule – even while he came to rule as emperor in Rome.[26] Marcus Aurelius is classed as the last of the 'Five Good Emperors' mentioned earlier (reigning first jointly, and then alone, in the course of the period 161–80 CE, during which he won important military campaigns and also lived an admirable domestic familial life). Writing in Greek, he composed a set of *Meditations* while at war that reveal the voice of an emperor beset with cares. Seneca had prescribed nightly self-examination; Marcus Aurelius begins Book 2 with the injunction to 'Say to yourself in the early morning: I shall meet today inquisitive, ungrateful, violent, treacherous, envious, uncharitable men' – but all of them act so only out of ignorance, and none of them can harm you, nor should you be angry with them (2.1).[27] (He seems not to have been one of life's natural early risers. Book 5 begins, 'At dawn of day, when you dislike being called ...' (5.1)[28])

The emperor is as suspicious of mere bookishness as was Epictetus. The goal of philosophy is to achieve genuine tranquillity: 'put away your thirst for books, so that you may not die murmuring, but truly reconciled and grateful from your heart to the gods' (2.3).[29] And he admonishes himself and his eventual reader against the fear of death, of course a constant concern for one commanding his troops in battle. He insists that no death is untimely, for each of us dies when nature ushers us out, 'as though the master of the stage, who engaged an actor, were to dismiss him from the stage' (12.36).[30] We were born not at our own behest, but in accordance with the divine plan infusing nature; so, too, we should accept our death will be so also. Hence one should not commit suicide, but otherwise there is nothing to resist or fear in death. Here again is the echo of Socrates, and an insistence that death is not to be feared that was shared for varying reasons by the Platonists, Stoics and Epicureans alike.[31] True tranquillity lies not in political institutions, but rather in this philosophical understanding.

By this stage, Stoics like Epictetus and Seneca had come for their own distinctive reasons to converge with the Epicurean view that one should focus primarily on one's private life: serving the political ruler when necessary, but not expecting that political service to supply the tranquillity that only a properly constituted mind can attain. Marcus Aurelius was in the unusual position of being an emperor, with duties to his people that it behoved him to fulfil. Yet his *Meditations* reveal that as important to him as was ruling his empire, it was even more fundamentally important to him to succeed in ruling over himself.

Freedom and Convention

The condemnation of the fear of death as unworthy of a rational being, and of the attractiveness of servile goods like money, body and public office, was, for Seneca and his fellow Stoics, part and parcel of their prizing of freedom as an individual virtue. In a world where law precisely defined the status of slave and free man in social relations, the Roman Stoics reiterated their school's teaching that there was a second and more fundamental scale on which these positions were to be judged: not social or legal, but ethical. Someone who is a legal slave (as Epictetus himself had been) may be ethically free – that is to say, free in the only truly meaningful sense of the word. Conversely, someone who is a legal self-master and so free man (*liber*) may be ethically and so, truly, a slave. The former legal slave Epictetus (his name in Greek, *Epiktetos*, simply means 'acquired', identifying him as someone who had been bought by a master) and the emperor Marcus Aurelius are equal candidates for ethical freedom. Social and legal standing neither excludes it for the one nor guarantees it for the other.

In the case of slavery, this analysis tended to be used by Roman Stoics in a politically quietist way, meaning so as not to make waves in established legal and political arrangements. For example, they accepted the continued existence of conventional legal slavery even while arguing that 'true' slavery was independent of the status dictated by that convention. But in the case of women, at least one Roman Stoic drew on this account of freedom and virtue to argue strongly against certain

gendered social conventions of the time (as the early Stoics, indebted to Cynic anti-conventionalism, had done more ubiquitously, as we saw in Chapter 6). This was Musonius Rufus, a considerably younger contemporary of Seneca, who survived banishment by Nero, becoming the teacher of Epictetus and a revered figure in Rome (he was specially exempted from a banishment of philosophers in 71 CE), and so forming an important link in the chain of Roman Stoic thought. He is also a paradigm of the debt to Socrates in Stoic thought.

Musonius Rufus' argument that women should practise philosophy runs along similar lines to Plato's *Republic*, but universalizes the claim there that only certain women and men are capable of philosophizing, in line with the Stoic view of the naturalness and universality of human rationality. He is quoted as saying:

> Women as well as men ... have received from the gods the
> gift of reason ... Likewise the female has the same senses
> as the male: namely, sight, hearing, smell, and the others.
> Also both have the same parts of the body, and one has
> nothing more than the other. Moreover, not men alone,
> but women, too, have a natural inclination towards virtue
> and the capacity for acquiring it ... If this is true, by what
> reason would it ever be appropriate for men to search out
> and consider how they may lead good lives, which is exactly
> the study of philosophy, but inappropriate for women?
> Could it be that it is fitting for men to be good, but not for
> women?[32]

Musonius Rufus presumes that most women will continue to play their traditional gender role in the Roman sense of

managing the household (a role that in Rome at the time could involve owning land and property in their own names, and engaging in commerce and in many aspects of public life, despite needing male representatives to carry out most legal transactions). That social role, however, will best be played by women who have exercised their divinely endowed capacity of reason to achieve virtue – which, for the Roman, will be done best 'by the woman who studies philosophy'.[33] Rufus argues further that getting married is compatible with practising philosophy. The natural strength of the bond between married spouses is a keystone of the development of the natural sociability that also supports the city and eventually the reproduction of the species.[34]

In these positions, which we might today call feminist,[35] we see how a Roman Stoic could practise the kind of sharp criticism of social conventions that we saw in the *Republic* of Zeno and of Chrysippus. But we also see the way in which he limited his attention to certain oppressive and irrational conventions while tacitly accepting others. One of Rufus' points in favour of marriage is that it needn't be an obstacle to philosophy insofar as the need to provide care for one's wife and children (here still picturing the philosopher as typically male) can largely be delegated to the house slaves that he presumes will be there to serve the philosopher.[36] Making freedom a matter of ethical achievement does not make it inherently incompatible with subordination of others. In some contexts, Stoic ethics could lead to a radical position, as for Musonius Rufus on gender; in others, as for the same figure on slavery, it could condone acceptance of existing inequalities.

Looking Back at the Republic

A final measure of the complex stance towards politics adopted by many thinkers under the empire may be taken by returning to a century before Marcus Aurelius, to an almost exact contemporary of Tacitus with whom the main part of this chapter began. We find there, in the late 1st to 2nd centuries CE, a biographer and philosopher who looked back to the lives of the Greek and Roman statesmen of the classical period – before the principate – even while accepting monarchy as a philosophical ideal in his own time.[37] This was Plutarch, a Greek from a small city on the outskirts of the empire (Chaeronea, in Boeotia).

Plutarch's life combined many of the themes of philosophy and politics that we have been considering. He became a philosophical Platonist by studying at the Platonic Academy in Athens. He was honoured with Roman citizenship, while living the life of a local magistrate and of a priest in the Temple of Apollo in Delphi (near his home town). At the same time, he lived out the tensions common to all educated and civically active Greeks under Roman hegemony. In an essay written around 100 CE, he advises a Greek friend seeking local public office to remember that 'you are subject as well as ruler ... you must make your cloak more humble, look out from your office to the proconsul's dais, don't puff yourself up at or trust too much in your crown (you can see the boots over your head).'[38]

It is to this man, Plutarch, that we owe many of the received images of the Greek and Roman legislators and politicians, which he transmitted to an eager posterity.

His portrait of Sparta, for example, in his life of Lycurgus, uniquely portrays the Spartan legislator as having prohibited the writing down of his laws in an effort better to instil values through practice and memory.[39] More generally, in his portraits of the political leaders of Athens and republican Rome especially, Plutarch also fashions a paradigm opposition between admirable statesmen and dangerous demagogues (while writing lives of men of both kinds). He sees demagogues as flattering and pandering the people, and statesmen as telling them what they needed to hear even when they didn't want to hear it. In this vein, he follows in Thucydides' view of Pericles as rule by the first man, calling him 'aristocratic and kingly' (*Per.* 14.2) once he had given up his initial experimentation with demagogic methods.

Like Pericles, many of these statesmen cultivated their virtue through exposure to philosophy, but what mattered was not whether they gained substantive knowledge (here Plutarch differed from his master Plato), but only whether philosophical training made them sufficiently moderate and self-disciplined. Philosophy in Plutarch's hands was primarily a mainstay of democratic and especially republican virtue, and so of political freedom.[40] If the Hellenistic schools ultimately emancipated philosophy from politics, at least on some points (as in their treatment of death), Plutarch turned philosophy into the handmaiden of politics, reconciling the two classical strands that we have been considering throughout this book.

Like many of his readers today, Plutarch lived in the shadow of the ideals of political liberty – able to hold office

in his Greek city, enjoying the prerogatives of Roman republican citizenship, but also knowing himself to be subject in crucial ways to rulers whose actions ordinary citizens could not fully control, and being keenly aware of Greek and Roman regimes in the past that he believed had included more complete experiences of political freedom and participation. The continuities and discontinuities of politics under imperial Rome with idealized Greek and Roman pasts included vaunted veneers alongside some real threads of similarity and influence. His struggle to take the measure of these political ideals of the past, and to reckon what they could mean in his changed political circumstances, is a predicament shared by his readers, and by readers of this book. The radical nature of late Roman sovereignty as a political idea in our own time lies in its posing the question of what self-rule really means whenever popular control seems more a promise or an illusion than a reality.

Futures of Greek and Roman Pasts

In canvassing eight of the many ideas of politics created by the ancient Greeks and Romans, we have scoured the speeches of lawyers alongside the speculations of philosophers, the reflections of ex-slaves and ardent scientists alongside the hits of the tragic and comic stages. A striking characteristic of classical antiquity is the proliferation of the kinds of writings and images that survive. Compared to the records surviving of many other ancient societies, the Greeks (especially the Athenians) and Romans have left tremendously detailed evidence of their ideas, and of the ways in which those ideas were forged and expressed in what they did and how they thought.

Part of the excitement of studying their ideas comes from this lived diversity. Writing near the dawn of writing, playing a multitude of roles in their relatively unprofessionalized societies, the Greeks in particular pioneered or advanced a whole host of intellectual disciplines while still keenly appreciating the connections between them. It may have been sheer luck that they enjoyed a sweet spot between advancing specific fields and maintaining an understanding of the whole of knowledge and value. Aristophanes' comic portrayal of philosophy, Plato's sense of political harmony

as mathematically expressible, Aristotle's situating of the human animal in a wide field of biological capacities of other species, Marcus Aurelius' ability to philosophize while on military campaign – all these testify to a seamlessness in the links between political ideas and other ideas and practices that can jolt a modern reader.

The sheer ambition of Greek and Roman exploration shows politics to have been only one of the many problems they were intent on finding new ways to solve. From the creation of the tragic drama and the secret ballot, to the astonishing mechanical calculator of astronomical phenomena found at Antikythera in Greece (in which researchers discern hints of a connection with the workshop of the great mathematician Archimedes), the inventiveness of these classical forebears took politics as only one of many interconnected fields to advance. Those tight links between politics and mathematics, science, poetry, engineering are both chastening and instructive for those who marvel at them today. It is never wise to fetishize politics as a separate, isolated field of study or practice: politics belongs to the larger life of a society, and can be fully understood only against that broader canvas.

This book has shown that political life for the Greeks, especially, was marked by tremendous internal diversity as well. The ongoing struggles for supremacy and survival that mutated in the hundreds of Greek city-states – from oligarchical wrangles with tyrants, to the tension of possible coups and counter-coups of oligarchs against democrats, all against a background of Persian and then also Macedonian kingship, and eventually Roman hegemony – left little room

for complacency in Greek thinking about politics. Just as advances in Greek science and logic may have been stimulated by the pressures of such competitive (and perhaps especially of democratic) politics, so the depth and seriousness of Greek political thinking was owed in part to the awareness of how high were the stakes and how real the rivals. Nor was an expanding Rome immune to the diversity of local populations, each with its own cultic practices and languages. As populations on the borders of the empire received bodies of laws to regulate their interactions with the Romans and among themselves, the diversity so engendered was a powerful force for political and intellectual innovation.

In Greece and Rome, diversity created a set of natural laboratories for elaborating and testing political ideas that goes far towards explaining how fertile those ideas proved at the time and have remained since. It is not that the Greeks or Romans possessed some secret political sauce from the get-go. Rather, by taking politics seriously as a life and death concern and as a part of their broader ambition to understand and change the world, the ground was laid for the astonishing productivity in political practices and ideas that we have surveyed here. Prominent among those products were certain polarizing dichotomies, which served (as another has argued) to construct the male Greek citizen in contrast with the unfree, minors, women, non-Greeks and the gods.[1] Although this book has focused primarily on the construction of the category of citizenship in relation to values like justice and to different kinds of constitutions, it is important to remember that the boundaries between the political and the purportedly non-political are themselves matters

317

for political inquiry and contestation. What it meant to be a slave or a woman or a metic or a conquered imperial subject is as much part of Greek and Roman political thinking as is what it meant to be a paradigmatic male citizen.

In presenting this survey, my ultimate aim is for readers to draw their own conclusions. It is as a prompt for that activity that I sketch out two of my own. The first is drawn from the history of Greek (and more specifically Athenian) democracy and the Roman republic, that is from the practices and institutions of the ancients; the second is drawn from the criticisms and challenges offered by their philosophers.

On the first set of conclusions, this book has tried to show that the Greeks and Romans are worth our interest even – or, rather, especially, when we give up on some of the received, exaggerated and simplistic ideas of what made their politics special. Not all Athenian citizens were eligible to hold all offices or free to decide all questions; not all or only Roman citizens served in the military. It can be a helpful corrective to stress the under-recognized similarities. The classical societies had at least basic forms of bureaucracy, delegation and even representation (though not in the modern sense of elected lawmakers). Hence they, like us, were deeply concerned with the ethics and institutional mechanisms of holding elected (and also allotted) officials accountable.

Yet that recognition only highlights a deeper and perhaps more important division. The Greeks and, in some ways, the Romans were deeply concerned with how to make popular power real. They didn't do so only or exactly in the ways that we sometimes imagine. But they experimented, variously, with other, even more compelling and interesting

mechanisms: popular juries unconstrained by judges, lay prosecutors, lottery for many official posts, the special role of the tribunes. And they recognized – and struggled with – the fundamental question of the social, economic and also military dimension of popular power.

While especially in Rome there was an unresolved conflict over where to draw the line, the idea that political freedom for the poor required certain social and economic protections and provisions was one that ancient regimes were again and again forced to recognize in practice. The Athenian democrats, for example, turned on its head the idea that a free society requires allowing the wealthy virtually unfettered influence in politics. They heaped special obligations on the wealthy, allowing them the kudos of serving the public while directing them very precisely as to what public benefit required.

At the same time, the Athenians protected and empowered the poor with pay for performing public services, as a condition of protecting the common citizenship and the liberty it made possible for all. They also regularized the position of immigrant foreigners, allowing them certain legal protections while requiring taxes and military service of them. The importance of citizenship for the Romans went further, in becoming the entitlement of a slave freed by certain procedures and eventually of all free men in the empire. But it also fell short of Athenian practices, in entrenching the political sway of a meritocratically chosen elite and in dramatically restricting the powers of office-holding, initiative, and, to some extent, the accountability and control that the ordinary people enjoyed.

Despite the significant differences between Athens and Rome, the political classes of both polities – drawn disproportionately but not solely from the landed wealthy – were regularly forced to recognize their dependence on popular opinion and popular tolerance to a certain extent. In Athens, a general lasted only as long as he was elected and not impeached for malfeasance by an impatient or suspicious public, an orator only as long as the people were willing to put up with his speeches and support his measures. In Rome, no one, however well born, could ascend the ladder of offices and arrive in the Senate without winning a series of elections (though the methods of grouping and counting votes lessened the impact of purely popular support there). This meant that politicians had always to have a close eye on their public support, and could not become too detached or complacent. Indeed, one of the crucial failings of the late republic was that political support became instead a matter of controlling armies and making backroom deals, cutting the electorate out of the picture. Their geographical heirs, 21st-century Greek and Italian politicians, are among those in many countries who have been painfully learning the dangers of complacently insulating themselves from the judgement of the people. The dangers of leaving a group of self-appointed political class in charge, who may well appear as a modern near-equivalent of ancient oligarchs, without proper scrutiny or accountability are ones of which the Greeks and Romans were far more acutely aware than many modern polities have been.

My second set of conclusions is drawn from the philosophers who were in varying degrees critics of the practices

of their regimes. Athens and Rome furnish vivid models of the strengths, if also the weaknesses, of democratic and republican regimes: they readily impress observers with the wealth and power that they gained at their zeniths; with their staying power as regimes, roughly 200 years in Athens and more like half a millennium in Rome; with the remarkable art, architecture, literature and scientific ingenuity that they attracted and produced. Yet, to the critical eyes of Plato and Aristotle especially, all this power was deployed to profoundly wrong ends. It was used to serve private ambition and public aggrandizement, rather than to cultivate ethical self-control and justice, or to pursue knowledge of how to live. The message of these philosophers is that with power comes responsibility. It is futile and often self-defeating to pursue power without a clear idea of the good that it can bring; to clarify that, however, requires the pursuit of knowledge of the good as the most fundamental aim of all.

That is why Virtue is as important an idea in this book as Democracy or Republic or any of the other purely political constitutional ideas. Indeed, for the classical thinkers shaped by the main line of philosophical ideas from Socrates to the Stoics, they were inextricably linked. To be free is to be in control of yourself – not just free from the arbitrary control of others, but also free from distracting impulses to pursue what most matters. Impatience with the tutelage and deference that these philosophers prescribed (and, to an extent, the Roman Senate itself embodied), and with the later tutelage and deference so long required by the Catholic Church's sway in European polities, modern political thinkers have discarded virtue from the main line of political ideas.

Yet if one message of this book is that democratic and republican rule is a matter of controlling one's rulers, another message is that such control of others is ultimately impossible or incoherent unless it also goes with control of oneself. Self-control is the prerequisite for any successful system of politics, and so, today, for a sustainable one. The spectrum of power and possibility that defines politics begins at home.

ACKNOWLEDGEMENTS

I could not have written this book without the generous support of Princeton University for sabbatical and additional leave of absence, and also for funding research assistance that was ably provided by Sarah Cotterill and Neil Hannan; the John Simon Guggenheim Foundation, for a 2012 Fellowship; and the Center for Advanced Study in the Behavioral Sciences (CASBS), Stanford University, for a 2012/13 Fellowship. CASBS provided a stunning space in which to write and all manner of logistical support, including the excellent library services of Tricia Soto and Amanda Thomas, and offered opportunities to talk through the ideas of the book with many people, including Deborah Tannen, who pressed me to define politics in the introduction, and Mark Vail, who read a first draft of my attempt to do so. For their enormous intellectual and temporal generosity in commenting on earlier drafts of this book, I am deeply indebted to Paul Cartledge and Malcolm Schofield, who each read the whole (and further still to Malcolm for reading a revised version of three chapters as well), and to Valentina Arena, Kinch Hoekstra, Jacob Lipton, Chaim Milikowsky and Victoria Pagán, who each read a substantial part. While their comments were invaluable in helping me to revise the book,

as was a reading of the book at copyediting stage by Neil Hannan, I take full responsibility for errors. I am more generally indebted to discussions of ancient Greek and Roman political ideas with too many friends, colleagues and students over the years to name here. It was a pleasure to work with my agent, Jonathan Conway, and the Penguin commissioning editor for Pelican, Laura Stickney, whose imagination and energy have helped to inspire and shape the book, and with Donna Poppy, who was a skilful and knowledgeable copyeditor. Finally I thank all the members of my extended family and family-like friends, above all Andrew Lovett, for all that he is, and gives, to me.

Glossary

NOTES ON CLASSICAL GREEK AND LATIN

As noted in the text, every syllable in Greek and Latin words should be sounded out (so a 'citizen' is *ho po-li-tēs*, as opposed to the plural of the English pronunciation of the word 'polite').

The transliterations of Greek in the main text of the book do not distinguish between two sets of Greek vowels that are sometimes marked by the absence or presence of a macron:

- the short epsilon (ε), pronounced alone roughly *eh*, as in 'evident', versus
- the long eta (η), pronounced alone roughly *ey*, as in 'hey'

- the short omicron (o), pronounced alone roughly as in 'obvious', versus
- the long omega (ω), pronounced alone roughly as in 'oh'

This is because readers who don't know Greek are more likely to find such macron marks distracting than illuminating, while those who do know it are likely to know which vowels are which without needing them. However, in this glossary, the long vowels are marked as such.

Greek nouns and certain other grammatical formations are preceded by short definite articles that decline according to gender, number and case. The list below omits definite articles except where the formulation is hard to construe without them, in which

case they are printed after the main word (so, *ta politika* in the text is found below as *politika, ta*).

Proper names are given in common anglicized forms, usually derived from Latin, with articles omitted (so, Epicurus, not *ho Epikouros*).

The information in the definitions and biographies below is drawn from *The Online Liddell–Scott–Jones Greek–English Lexicon*, Charlton Lewis's and Charles Short's *A Latin Dictionary*, the *Oxford Classical Dictionary* and *Brill's New Pauly*. These sources may be consulted for more in-depth descriptions of any terms or figures, as those presented here are deliberately brief and therefore sometimes partial or truncated.

BRIEF DEFINITIONS OF KEY GREEK [G.] AND LATIN [L.] TERMS

archē; plural, ***archas*** [G.] : office (in political context); can also mean 'origin'

archein [G.] : to rule or govern

aretē [G.] : excellence or virtue

boulē [G.] : will, deliberation or council (in Athens, can refer to the Council of 500, the Senate or agenda-setting body created by Cleisthenes (see below); see *ekklēsia* below)

civitas [L.] : political unit, roughly translatable as 'state' (in Roman political context, the most important unit of political activity)

Constitutio Antoniniana [L.] : edict of the emperor Caracalla, which granted almost all free people in the Roman empire citizenship in 212 CE

dēmokratia [G.] : literally 'power of the people'; origin of the English word 'democracy' (in political context, refers to a system of government where the *dēmos*, or 'people', hold significant power, with classical Athens being the most noted example of such a system)

dēmos [G.] : the people (in political contexts, often refers to the 'people' or common people in contrast with the elite; can also mean the whole body of citizens)

dikastēria [G., plural] : the law-courts

dikē, dikaiosunē [G.] : justice; *dikē* can also mean specifically trial, verdict or judgement

ekklēsia [G.] : assembly (in Athens, refers to the more general governmental body, in contrast with the more limited Council of 500, see *boulē* above; in later thought, refers to both political and religious bodies: thus one can speak of the *ekklēsia* as the community of members of a church or of the whole body of Christians)

ergon [G.] : deed or action; frequently contrasted in Greek thought and rhetoric with the words of a speaker (in singular, *logos*)

gerousia [G.] : Council of Elders (in Sparta, refers to the Senate or council)

honestas [L.] : honour, character or reputation, often contrasted with expediency, see *utilitas* below

hubris [G.] : insolence or wanton violence

imperium [L.] : command (in later political context, refers to the supreme power of the Roman emperor)

isos [G.] : the equal, sometimes translated as the just; related to *isotēs*, meaning 'equality'

Kallipolis [G.] : literally the 'Beautiful City' (in Plato's *Republic*, refers to the ideal city ruled by philosophers)

koinōnia [G.] : communion, association or partnership

kosmopolitēs [G.] : citizen of the world (in Stoic thought, refers to the idea that one should properly consider oneself a fellow citizen of every other rational being; gives rise to the idea that the truly significant political community is the world community)

kosmos [G.] : literally 'order'; often used to refer to the world-order or universe

kurios [G., adj.] : powerful or authoritative, sometimes translated as 'sovereign'

lex de imperio Vespasiani [L.] : literally the 'law concerning the command of Vespasian', which has been partially preserved in an inscription, and describes how the Roman emperor's authority derives from a legal grant by the people

libertas [L.] : freedom or liberty

monarchia [G.] : rule of one man; origin of the English word 'monarchy' (in political contexts, refers to a system in which a king rules)

nomos [G.] : law or custom (in political contexts, is frequently contrasted with nature, see *phusis* below)

officium [L.] : moral duty

oligarchia [G.] : rule of the few; origin of the English word 'oligarchy' (in political contexts, refers to a system in which the few wealthy citizens rule)

optimates [L., plural] : literally the 'best men' (refers to the Roman political faction in the late republic that supported the power of the elite (patricians and nobles, especially as represented in the authority of the Senate) against the plebeians, in contrast with the *populares*, below)

phusis [G.] : nature (in political contexts, is frequently contrasted with law and custom, see *nomos* above)

polis; plural, ***poleis*** [G.] : city-state (in Greek political context, the most significant unit of political activity)

politeia; plural, ***politeiai*** [G.] : citizenship, constitution or commonwealth (in general political contexts, refers both to a political community and to its form of government; in Aristotelian thought, can also refer to the well-governed form of rule by the many)

politēs; plural, ***politai*** [G.] : citizen

politika, ta [G.] : political affairs or affairs relating to citizens

politikos [G., adj.] : relating to citizens, civic or civil

populares [L., plural] : literally the 'men of the people' (refers to

the Roman political faction in the late republic that supported the concerns of the plebeians against the *optimates*, above)

princeps, princeps senatus, princeps civitatis [L.] : first man, first man of the Senate, first man of the state (title received by the first Roman emperor Octavian (see below), after his victory in the civil wars at the end of the Roman republic)

psychē [G., using *y* for the upsilon otherwise transliterated as *u*, as this produces a more recognizable English root in this case] : spirit or soul

res publica or ***re publica*** [L.] : public affair or concern; used to signify the commonwealth

rhētor [G.] : public speaker in political institutions

senatus [L.] : origin of the English word 'Senate'; the advisory and deliberative body of the Roman republic, which survived with increasingly symbolic role in the Roman empire

senatus consultum ultimum [L.] : literally 'ultimate decree of the Senate'; a declaration of a state of emergency by the Senate, giving the magistrates extraordinary powers, including the use of force, against enemies of the state

stratēgos; plural, ***stratēgoi*** [G.] : commander, governor or general

suffragio [L.] : ballot, vote or suffrage

telos [G.] : end or goal (in Aristotelian thought, can refer to the end to which an action, thing or person is directed; the source of the word 'teleological', which plays an important role in Greek ideas of ethics and politics)

turannos [G.] : an absolute ruler (in political context, refers to one who not only rules absolutely, but also rules without concern for the law or the common good)

utilitas [L.] : expediency, often contrasted with honour, see *honestas*, above

Zeus [G.] : ruler of the gods, frequently equated with the Roman god Jupiter

Athens Map Key

Agora: Center of Athenian political life
Areopagus: Hill of Ares, meeting place for aristocratic council of the same name
Dipylon: Western gateway to city
Eleusinion: Temple to Demeter
Eridanos: A small river
Ilissos: A principal river
Kolonos: Hill housing multiple religious sanctuaries
Lyceum: Park where Aristotle established his philosophical school
Mouseion: Sanctuary of the Muses
Nymphe: Sanctuary of the Nymphs
Olympieion: Temple of Olympian Zeus
Pnyx: Large hill, meeting place for the *ekklesia*, the people's assembly
Theatre: Space for public performances

Brief Biographies of Key Persons, Events and Places

Aeschylus (?525–456 BCE): Athenian tragic dramatist, whose works include the *Oresteia*, *Seven Against Thebes* and *Suppliants*

Alexander the Great (356–323 BCE): Macedonian king, who conquered the Persian empire and advanced through much of Central Asia and northern India before dying of a fever at Babylon, leaving his generals to fight over his kingdom; his death marks the beginning of the Hellenistic Age

Antigone: Titular character of the tragedy *Antigone* by Sophocles (see below), who prioritizes her duty to bury her brother Polyneices over the orders of her uncle Creon, the king of Thebes; having been sentenced to be buried alive, she commits suicide before Creon's attempt to commute the sentence reaches her

Aristophanes (d. 386 BCE): Athenian comic dramatist, whose works, including the *Clouds*, *Knights* and *Lysistrata*, explore tensions in Athenian democratic practice and society

Aristotle (384–322 BCE): Macedonian philosopher and student of Plato (see below), who established his own school at the Lyceum in Athens and produced many works, among which the *Politics* and *Nicomachean Ethics* hold particular importance in political thought

Athens: Greek *polis* located in Attica, noted for its democratic institutions, its wealth and its philosophical schools; major actor in both the Persian Wars (see below) and the Peloponnesian War (see below)

Augustus Caesar: see Octavian, below

Brutus, Marcus Junius (?85–42 BCE): Roman aristocrat and leader, along with Cassius (see below), of the conspiracy against Julius Caesar (see below); after the assassination, he gathered an army in Greece with the other conspirators and committed suicide after his defeat at the battle of Philippi; an ancestor of the same name ejected the last Roman king from power, thus initiating the republican period of Roman politics

Caesar, Julius (100–44 BCE): Roman general, who conquered Gaul (modern-day France) and fought a civil war against the *optimates*, the more aristocratic faction of the Senate, led by Pompey; he was victorious in this war, but his ambition alienated the other senators, and he was assassinated on the Ides of March in 44 BCE

Cassius (?80–42 BCE): Roman aristocrat and leader, along with Marcus Junius Brutus (see above), of the conspiracy against Julius Caesar (see above); after the assassination, he gathered an army in Greece with the other conspirators, and committed suicide after his defeat at the battle of Philippi

Chrysippus (280–207 BCE): Stoic philosopher, who became the head of the Stoa, or Stoic school, in 232 BCE; heavily influenced by the thought of Zeno of Citium (see below), he wrote extensively and developed Stoic thought

Cicero, Marcus Tullius (106–43 BCE): Roman orator and politician, who was both a major political figure of the late Roman republic and the author of various philosophical writings, including *De Oratore*, *De Re Publica* and *De Officiis*; a noted supporter of the Senate, he was proscribed and executed during the instability that followed the assassination of Julius Caesar (see above)

Cleisthenes (late 6th c. BCE): Athenian politician, who made popular reforms, including the reorganization of the Athenian people into political units called demes and the creation of ostracism, which helped to establish the institutions of Athenian democracy

Cleon (d. 422 BCE): Athenian politician, who came from a wealthy but non-aristocratic family; he was a strong supporter of the Athenian multitude's political power and concerns, participated as both a politician and general in the Athenian decisions during the Peloponnesian War (see below), and was criticized for his methods and outlook by Thucydides and Aristophanes

Diogenes the Cynic (Diogenes of Sinope) (?412–324 BCE): Cynic philosopher, who lived much of his life in Athens and strove to live his life according to nature; he thus owned almost no property or possessions, and showed no shame at performing all acts publicly, including those normally considered private

Diogenes of Oenoanda (2nd c. CE): Author of an Epicurean inscription on a portico in Lycia that contains selections from the works of Epicurus (see below) and other Epicurean maxims, as well as the author's own writings

Ephialtes (5th c. BCE): Athenian politician and reformer, who initiated reforms to increase the power of the people; he was supported by Pericles (see below) and other democratic leaders, but the contentiousness of his policies led to his eventual murder

Epictetus (mid 1st–2nd c. CE): Stoic philosopher and former slave; he was taught by Musonius Rufus (see below) and heavily influenced by the thought of Chrysippus (see above), and his writings, including *Discourses* and the *Manual*, influenced in turn the Roman emperor Marcus Aurelius (see below)

Epicurus (341–270 BCE): Founder of Epicureanism, which generally holds, among other doctrines, that the soul is not immortal, that all matter is composed of an infinite

arrangement of atoms and that pleasure, particularly the
pleasure of a quiet life with friends, is the proper end of life

Euripides (?484–406 BCE): Athenian tragic dramatist, whose
works include *Alcestis*, *Medea* and *Trojan Women*; although he
lived most of his life at Athens, he eventually left the city and
spent the end of his life writing at the court of the Macedonian
king Archelaus

Herodotus (*c*. 484–430 BCE): Greek historian, originally from
Halicarnassus, whose *Histories* offers a thorough account of
the wars between the Greek cities and the Persian empire; in
this account, he examines, in part, the differences between
the political constitutions of the Greeks and the Persians,
frequently contrasting Greek freedom with Persian despotism

Hesiod (8th–7th c. BCE): Early Greek poet, whose surviving
works, including the *Theogony* and *Works and Days*, offer a rare
perspective on early Greek mythology, culture and values

Lycurgus (?11th–7th c. BCE): Legendary founder and lawgiver of
Sparta, who is said to have instituted both the Spartan way of
life and the mixed Spartan constitution, which included two
kings, a council, or *gerousia* (see above), and an assembly

Marcus Aurelius (121–80 CE): Roman emperor, who was the
successor to Antoninus Pius and the last of the subsequently
named 'Five Good Emperors'; heavily influenced by his tutors and
the works of Epictetus (see above), he lived both by Stoic and by
Platonic precepts and produced his own philosophical *Meditations*

Musonius Rufus (?30–101 CE): Stoic philosopher and Roman
equestrian, who was a teacher of Epictetus (see above); his
writings survive largely as brief sayings and dialogues

Nero (37–68 CE): Roman emperor and noted patron of the arts,
whose reign began well, but descended into vice and disorder;
his notorious behaviour, including the assassination of his
mother and the ordering of his adviser Seneca (see below)
to commit suicide, led the Senate eventually to resist him,
leading to his own suicide

Octavian (63 BCE–14 CE): Heir of Julius Caesar (see above) and first emperor of Rome; following his victories in civil wars, first against the assassins of Julius Caesar and then against Mark Antony, the Senate named him *princeps* and gave him the title Augustus

Peloponnesian War (431–404 BCE): War primarily between alliances led by Athens (see above) and Sparta (see below) respectively; Athenian military superiority on the sea and Spartan military superiority on land created a long stalemate, which eventually concluded with an Athenian defeat

Pericles (495–429 BCE): Athenian politician, who led Athens both before and during its early involvement in the Peloponnesian War (see above); his democratic support gave him a near-dominant position in Athenian politics – although this did not prevent him from being tried for embezzlement – and he remained influential until his death from the plague that struck Athens in the early 420s BCE

Persian Wars (490, 480–479 BCE): Refers to the two failed attempts of the Persian empire, led by the emperors Darius and Xerxes, to conquer mainland Greece; many of the Greek *poleis*, most notably Sparta (see below) and Athens (see above), allied to successfully repel these invasions

Plato (424–348 BCE): Athenian philosopher, student of Socrates (see below) and founder of the Academy, whose writings take the form of dialogues, many of which include Socrates as a main speaker; among the most politically significant of these are the *Apology of Socrates*, *Crito*, *Gorgias*, *Republic*, *Statesman* and *Laws*

Plutarch (?50–120 CE): Greek philosopher and biographer, whose writings include moral treatises, rhetorical works and, most famously, his *Parallel Lives*, a series of biographies that frequently pairs Roman and Greek historical figures

Polybius (?200–118 BCE): Greek politician and historian, sent from the Achaean League to Rome as a hostage; he became a

close friend of Scipio Aemilianus (see below) and wrote his *Histories* in order to explain Rome's swift rise to power

Rome: Capital of the Roman republic and subsequent Roman empire, located in central Italy, and noted for martial and dutiful culture; through its military power and inclusive institution of citizenship, it maintained political control of the lands around the Mediterranean Sea for several centuries

Scipio Aemilianus (?185–129 BCE): Roman politician and general, who captured Carthage in 146 BCE and was a dominant conservative presence in the Roman politics of his period; he was a student and close friend of Polybius (see above), and he appears posthumously as an ideal Roman statesman in the philosophical writings of Cicero (see above)

Seneca, Lucius Annaeus (?1–65 CE): Stoic philosopher, who served first as tutor, then as adviser to the Roman emperor Nero, until ordered by the emperor to commit suicide; his writings include both dramas and various ethical treatises outlining Stoic thought

Socrates (469–399 BCE): Athenian philosopher, who frequently challenged his fellow Athenians on their moral beliefs and was tried and condemned to death by the Athenian democracy; his thought survives primarily in the writings of his followers Plato (see above) and Xenophon (see below)

Solon (*c.* 630–*c.* 560 BCE): Athenian politician, lawgiver and poet, who made several political reforms, including debt-forgiveness and a reorganization of political offices, which have led many to regard him as a founder of the Athenian democracy, or at least of its precursor institutions

Sophocles (?496–406 BCE): Athenian tragic dramatist, whose plays include *Oedipus Turannos*, *Antigone* and *Oedipus at Colonus*; he was additionally an active participant in Athenian political life, serving in multiple public offices

Sparta: Greek *polis* located in the Peloponnesus, famous in antiquity for its austere, martial culture, its mixed constitution

and its exploitation of local populations as helot serfs; long-time rival of Athens (see above), which it fought during the Peloponnesian War (see above)

Tacitus, Publius Cornelius (?55–118 CE): Roman historian, who acerbically catalogued the history of the early Roman empire in his *Histories* and *Annals*, and who denounced both the vices of the earlier emperors and the servility of the Senate in the face of these vices

Thucydides (?460–400 BCE): Athenian politician and historian, who served as an Athenian general during the Peloponnesian War (see above) and authoritatively documented this war in his *History*, in which he examines both the causes of the war and the conduct of the belligerent parties

Xenophon (430–354 BCE): Athenian soldier and follower of Socrates (see above), who spent much time away from the city, first as a mercenary commander in Persia and then in or near Sparta; among his many writings are the *Anabasis*, an account of his expedition in Persia, and *Memorabilia*, *Apology* and *Symposium*, which recount the conversations and speeches of Socrates

Zeno of Citium (The Stoic) (355–263 BCE): Founder of Stoicism, a philosophical school that generally holds, among other doctrines, that one should strive to live by nature, that virtue is the only good and that one should consider oneself a fellow citizen of the entire world community

Reference List and Abbreviations

Greek and Latin are cited from the Oxford Classical Texts where not otherwise specified, or other scholarly editions or compilations where specified. A widely available resource for Greek and Latin texts and translations is the online library of Greek and Latin literature at www.perseus.tufts.edu. Capitalization in Latin titles in this book follows English rather than Latin conventions.

References to primary sources use the standard Greek and Latin numbering systems common to most editions and translations of a given work (these vary greatly for different ancient authors, so that Euripides, for example, is cited by line numbers; Plato and Aristotle by 'Stephanus' and 'Bekker' numbers respectively, both of which take the form of a number followed by a letter; and Herodotus by book and section number). Certain modern editions also have their own conventions (so West's collection of archaic poetry organizes fragments into sections by ancient author, within which they are then cited by fragment number only).

ABBREVIATIONS USED FOR PRIMARY TEXTS AND ANCIENT AUTHORS CITED

Alex.	Plutarch, *Life of Alexander*
AP	Aristotle or his school, *Athenaion Politeia* (*Constitution of the Athenians*)
Apophth.	Plutarch, *Apophthegmata Laconica* (*Sayings of Spartans*)
B. Civ.	*Bellum Civile* (*Civil War*) (One work of this title written by Appian, another by Julius Caesar)
Cic.	Plutarch, *Life of Cicero*
D	Epictetus, *Dissertationes* (*Discourses*)
DL	Diogenes Laertius, *Lives of Eminent Philosophers*
De Alex. Fort.	Plutarch, *De Alexandri Magni Fortuna aut Virtute* (*On the Fortune or the Virtue of Alexander*)

De Leg.	Cicero, *De Legibus* (*On the Laws*)
De Rep.	Cicero, *De Re Publica* (*On the Commonwealth*) (Also given as *De Republica*; contrast *Rep.* = Plato, *Republic*)
EN	Aristotle, *Ethica Nicomachea* (*Nicomachean Ethics*)
Ep.	Seneca, *Epistulae Morales* (*Moral Letters*)
Fin.	Cicero, *De Finibus* (*On Moral Ends*)
Grg.	Plato, *Gorgias*
Lacae.	Plutarch, *Lacaenarum Apophthegmata* (*Sayings of Spartan Women*)
Met.	Aristotle, *Metaphysica* (*Metaphysics*)
Off.	Cicero, *De Officiis* (*On Duties*)
Or.	Aelius Aristides, *Orationes* (*Orationes*)
Per.	Plutarch, *Life of Pericles*
Phoen.	Euripides, *Phoenissae* (*Phoenician Women*)
Pol.	Aristotle, *Politikon* (*Politics*)
Rep.	Plato, *Politeia* (*Republic*)
	(English title, from Latin title *Respublica*; Greek title is *Politeia*; contrast *De Rep.* = Cicero, *De Re Publica*)
WD	Hesiod, *Erga kai Hemerai* (*Works and Days*)

In cases where only a single work of an ancient author is widely cited, no title is given; this is the case for Herodotus, Thucydides and Polybius, for example, all of whom are cited by abbreviation (Hdt., Thuc., Polyb. respectively) and section numbers, or, where it is clear which author's work is meant, by section numbers alone.

ABBREVIATIONS USED FOR COLLECTIONS OF PRIMARY TEXTS

DK = Diels, Hermann, and Kranz, Walther. 1992. *Die Fragmente Der Vorsokratiker: Griechisch Und Deutsch*. Zurich: Weidmann.

EGPT = Gagarin, Michael, and Woodruff, Paul (eds.). 1995. *Early Greek Political Thought from Homer to the Sophists*. Cambridge and New York: Cambridge University Press.

KRS = Kirk, G. S., Raven, J. E., and Schofield, M. 1983. *The Presocratic Philosophers: A Critical History with a Selection of Texts*. 2nd edition. Cambridge: Cambridge University Press.

LS = Long, A. A., and Sedley, D. N. (eds.). 1987. *The Hellenistic Philosophers. Vol. 1: Translations of the Principal Sources with Philosophical Commentary; Vol. 2: Greek and Latin Texts with Notes and Bibliography*. Cambridge:

Cambridge University Press. (When translations from LS are cited in the endnotes, they are always taken from Vol. 1.)

Perseus = Online free library of Greek and Latin texts and translations. Editor-in-chief, Gregory R. Crane, Tufts University. http://www.perseus.tufts.edu/hopper/

SEG = Hondius, J. J. E., et al. Ongoing from 1923. *Supplementum Epigraphicum Graecum*. Leiden: Sijthoff.

TGF = Snell, Bruno, and Nauck, August (eds.). 1986. *Tragicorum Graecorum Fragmenta*. Göttingen: Vandenhoeck & Ruprecht.

TLG = *Thesaurus Linguae Graecae*, online subscription-based library of Greek texts, *TLG* project of the University of California, Irvine. http://stephanus.tlg.uci.edu/inst/fontsel

W = West, M. L. 1989. *Iambi et Elegi Graeci ante Alexandrum Cantati*. 2nd edition. Oxford: Oxford University Press.

OTHER EDITIONS, COLLECTIONS AND TRANSLATIONS OF PRIMARY SOURCES

Aristides, Aelius. 1976. *P. Aelii Aristidis Opera Quae Exstant Omnia*, edited by F. W. Lenz and C. A. Behr. Lugduni Batavorum: E. J. Brill.

—. 1981. *The Complete Works*, edited and translated by Charles A. Behr. 2 vols. Leiden: Brill.

Aristotle. 1984. *The Complete Works of Aristotle: The Revised Oxford Translation*, edited by Jonathan Barnes. 2 vols. Princeton, NJ: Princeton University Press.

—. 1998. *Politics*, edited and translated by C. D. C. Reeve. Indianapolis, IA: Hackett.

Bion. 1976. *Bion of Borysthenes: A Collection of the Fragments*, edited by Jan Fredrik Kindstrand. Uppsala: Acta Universitatis Upsaliensis.

Cicero, Marcus Tullius. 1991. *On Duties*, edited by M. T. Griffin and E. M. Atkins. Cambridge: Cambridge University Press.

—. 1999. *'On the Commonwealth' and 'On the Laws'*, edited by James E. G. Zetzel. Cambridge: Cambridge University Press.

—. [named in French as Cicéron]. 2002a. *Discours: Sur la loi agraire. Pour C. Rabirius*, edited and translated by André Boulanger. Paris: Les Belles Lettres (Budé Édition, Vol. 9).

—. [named in French as Cicéron]. 2002b. *Discours: Philippiques I–IV*, edited and translated by André Boulanger and Pierre Wuilleumier. Paris: Les Belles Lettres (Budé Édition, Vol. 19).

Cicero, Quintus Tullius. 2001. *Commentariolum Petitionis*, edited, translated

and with commentary by Günther Laser. Darmstadt: Wissenschaftliche
Buchgesellschaft.

—. 2012. *How to Win an Election: An Ancient Guide for Modern Politicians*,
translated by Philip Freeman. Princeton, NJ: Princeton University Press.

Digest of Justinian. 1985. Edited by Theodor Mommsen with Paul Krueger,
and translated by Alan Watson. Philadelphia, PA: University of
Pennsylvania Press.

Diogenes Laertius. 1925. *Lives of Eminent Philosophers*, translated by
R. D. Hicks. Cambridge, MA: Harvard University Press; London: William
Heinemann Ltd.

Inwood, Brad, and Gerson, Lloyd P. (trans., introduction and notes). 1997. *Hellenistic
Philosophy: Introductory Readings*. 2nd edition. Indianapolis, IN: Hackett.

— (trans.). 2008. *The Stoics Reader: Selected Writings and Testimonia*.
Indianapolis, IA: Hackett.

J. Paul Getty Museum. Online catalogue of objects. http://www.getty.edu/art/

Marcus Aurelius. 1989. *The Meditations of Marcus Aurelius Antoninus; with
Introduction and Notes, and Selection from the Letters of Marcus and Fronto*,
edited by R. B. Rutherford, translated by A. S. L. Farquharson (*Meditations*)
and R. B. Rutherford (*Letters*). Oxford: Oxford University Press.

Musonius Rufus. 1947. 'Musonius Rufus: The Roman Socrates', edited by Cora
Lutz, *Yale Classical Studies*, Vol. 10, pp. 3–147.

'Old Oligarch'. 2008. *The 'Old Oligarch': The Constitution of the Athenians
Attributed to Xenophon*, translated and edited by J. L. Marr and P. J. Rhodes.
Oxford: Oxbow.

Philodemus. 1996. *On Piety*, edited with translation and commentary by Dirk
Obbink. Oxford and New York: Oxford University Press.

Plato. 1997. *Complete Works*, edited by John M. Cooper, with associate editor
D. S. Hutchinson. Indianapolis, IN: Hackett.

Plutarch. 1931. *Moralia*, Vol. 3, translated by Frank Cole Babbitt. London:
William Heinemann.

—. 1949. *Moralia*, Vol. 10, translated by Harold North Fowler. Cambridge, MA,
and London: Harvard University Press and William Heinemann.

—. 1973. *The Age of Alexander*, translated by Ian Scott-Kilvert. Baltimore, MD:
Penguin Books.

—. 1988. *The Life of Cicero*, edited and translated by J. L. Moles. Eastbourne:
Aris & Phillips.

—. 2005. *Plutarch on Sparta*, edited and translated by Richard J. A. Talbert. 2nd
edition. London: Penguin.

Polybius. 1962. *The Histories of Polybius*, translated by Evelyn S. Shuckburgh.
Bloomington, IN: Indiana University Press.

— [= Budé Polybius]. 2004. *Histoires*, edited and translated by Éric Foulon, with commentary by Michel Molin. Paris: Les Belles Lettres.

Seneca, Lucius Annaeus. 1995. *Moral and Political Essays*, edited by John M. Cooper and J. F. Procopé. Cambridge: Cambridge University Press.

—. 2007. *Seneca: Selected Philosophical Letters*, translated and edited by Brad Inwood. Oxford: Oxford University Press.

Smith, M. F. (ed.). 1974. *Thirteen New Fragments of Diogenes of Oenoanda*. Wien: Verlag der Österreichischen Akademie der Wissenschaften.

—. 1993. *The Epicurean Inscription*. Napoli: Bibliopolis.

—. 1996. *The Philosophical Inscription of Diogenes of Oenoanda*. Wien: Verlag der Österreichischen Akademie der Wissenschaften.

—. 2003. *Supplement to Diogenes of Oenoanda, The Epicurean Inscription*. Napoli: Bibliopolis.

Tacitus, Cornelius. 2003. *'The Annals' and 'The Histories'*, edited by Moses Hadas, translated by Alfred John Church and William Jackson Brodribb. New York: Modern Library.

SECONDARY SOURCES

Allen, Danielle S. 1996. 'A Schedule of Boundaries: An Exploration, Launched from the Water-Clock of Athenian Time', *Greece & Rome*, Second Series, Vol. 43, pp. 157–68.

—. 2000. *The World of Prometheus: The Politics of Punishing in Democratic Athens*. Princeton, NJ: Princeton University Press.

—. 2006. 'Talking about Revolution: On Political Change in Fourth-century Athens and Historiographic Method' in *Rethinking Revolutions through Ancient Greece*, edited by Simon Goldhill and Robin Osborne, pp. 183–217. Cambridge and New York: Cambridge University Press.

—. 2010. *Why Plato Wrote*. Chichester: John Wiley & Sons.

Anderson, Greg. 2005. 'Before *Turannoi* were Tyrants: Rethinking a Chapter of Early Greek History', *Classical Antiquity*, Vol. 24, pp. 173–222.

Ando, Clifford. 1999. 'Was Rome a Polis?', *Classical Antiquity*, Vol. 18, pp. 5–34.

Appiah, Anthony. 2006. *Cosmopolitanism; Ethics in a World of Strangers*. New York; W.W Norton.

Arena, Valentina. 2012. *Libertas and the Practice of Politics in the Late Roman Republic*. Cambridge and New York: Cambridge University Press.

Balot, Ryan K. 2006. *Greek Political Thought*. Malden, MA: Blackwell.

Baronowski, Donald Walter. 2011. *Polybius and Roman Imperialism*. London: Bristol Classical Press.

Benson, Thomas W., and Prosser, Michael H. (eds.). 1972. *Readings in Classical Rhetoric*. Bloomington, IN: Indiana University Press.

Bloom, Allan. 1991. 'Interpretive Essay' in Plato, *The Republic of Plato*, translated by Allan Bloom. 2nd edition. New York: Basic Books.

Bobonich, Christopher. 2002. *Plato's Utopia Recast: His Later Ethics and Politics*. Oxford: Oxford University Press.

Bosher, Kathryn. 2012. 'Infinite Variety: Ancient Greek Drama in Sicily' in *Theatre Outside Athens: Drama in Greek Sicily and South Italy*, edited by Kathryn Bosher, pp. 111–13, 116–21. Cambridge: Cambridge University Press.

Bosman, P. R. 2008. 'Traces of Cynic Monotheism in the Early Roman Empire', *Acta Classica*, Vol. 51, pp. 1–20.

Bradley, Keith. 2011. 'Slavery in the Roman Republic' in *The Cambridge World History of Slavery*, edited by Keith Bradley and Paul Cartledge, Vol. 1, pp. 241–64. Cambridge: Cambridge University Press.

Brunt, P. A. 1977. 'Lex de Imperio Vespasiani', *Journal of Roman Studies*, Vol. 67, pp. 95–116.

—. 1988. *The Fall of the Roman Republic and Related Essays*. Oxford and New York: Oxford University Press.

—. 1993. *Studies in Greek History and Thought*. Oxford and New York: Oxford University Press.

Burnyeat, M. F. 1980. 'Aristotle on Learning to be Good' in *Essays on Aristotle's Ethics*, edited by Amélie Oksenberg Rorty, pp. 69–92. Berkeley: University of California Press.

Cammack, Daniela. 2013. 'Aristotle on the Virtue of the Multitude', *Political Theory*, Vol. 41, pp. 175–202.

Carter, L. B. 1986. *The Quiet Athenian*. Oxford and New York: Oxford University Press.

Cartledge, Paul. 2001. *Spartan Reflections*. London: Duckworth.

—. 2002. *The Greeks: A Portrait of Self and Others*. 2nd edition. Oxford and New York: Oxford University Press.

—. 2009. *Ancient Greek Political Thought in Practice*. Cambridge: Cambridge University Press.

Clay, Diskin. 2007. 'The Philosophical Inscription of Diogenes of Oenoanda' in *Greek and Roman Philosophy 100 BCE–200 CE*, edited by Robert W. Sharples and Richard Sorabji, Vol. 1, pp. 283–91. London: Institute of Classical Studies, University of London.

Constant, Benjamin. 1988. 'The Liberty of the Ancients Compared with that of the Moderns' in *Political Writings*, edited by Biancamaria Fontana, pp. 308–28. Cambridge and New York: Cambridge University Press.

Cooper, John M. 2012. *Pursuits of Wisdom: Six Ways of Life in Ancient Philosophy from Socrates to Plotinus*. Princeton, NJ: Princeton University Press.

—, and Procopé, J. F. 1995. 'General Introduction' in Lucius Annaeus Seneca, *Moral and Political Essays*, edited by John M. Cooper and J. F. Procopé, pp. xi–xxxii. Cambridge and New York: Cambridge University Press.

Denyer, Nicholas. 1983. 'The Origins of Justice' in ΣΥΖΗΤΗΣΙΣ: *Studi sull'epicureismo greco e romano offerti a Marcello Gigante*, Vol. 1, pp. 133–52. Naples: Biblioteca della Parola del Passato.

Downing, Francis Gerald. 1992. *Cynics and Christian Origins*. Edinburgh: T & T Clark.

Dorandi, Tiziano. 1999. 'Chronology' in *The Cambridge History of Hellenistic Philosophy*, edited by Keimpe Algra, Jonathan Barnes, Jaap Mansfeld and Malcolm Schofield, pp. 32–54. Cambridge and New York: Cambridge University Press.

Drogula, Fred K. 2007. 'Imperium, Potestas and the Pomerium in the Roman Republic', *Historia: Zeitschrift Für Alte Geschichte*, Vol. 56, pp. 419–52.

Dunn, John. 2005. *Setting the People Free: The Story of Democracy*. London: Atlantic Books.

Evans, J. A. S. 1981. 'Notes on the Debate of the Persian Grandees in Herodotus 3.80–82', *Quaderni Urbinati di Cultura Classica*, Vol. 7, pp. 79–84.

Finley, M. I. 1985. *The Ancient Economy*. 2nd edition. London: Hogarth Press.

Flower, Michael A. 2002. 'The Invention of Tradition in Classical and Hellenistic Sparta' in *Sparta: Beyond the Mirage*, edited by Anton Powell and Stephen Hodkinson, pp. 191–217. Swansea and London: The Classical Press of Wales and Duckworth.

Fornara, Charles W. 1971. *Herodotus: An Interpretative Essay*. Oxford: Oxford University Press.

Forsdyke, Sara. 2005. *Exile, Ostracism, and Democracy: The Politics of Expulsion in Ancient Greece*. Princeton, NJ: Princeton University Press.

Foucault, Michel. 2010. *The Government of Self and Others*. Basingstoke, Hants, and New York: Palgrave Macmillan and St Martin's Press.

Frank, Jill. 2005. *A Democracy of Distinction: Aristotle and the Work of Politics*. Chicago: University of Chicago Press.

Fritz, Kurt von. 1954. *The Theory of the Mixed Constitution in Antiquity: A Critical Analysis of Polybius' Political Ideas*. New York: Columbia University Press.

Gabrielsen, Vincent. 1981. *Remuneration of State Officials in Fourth Century BC Athens*. Odense: Odense University Press.

Gagarin, Michael. 1986. *Early Greek Law*. Berkeley and London: University of California Press.

—. 2008. *Writing Greek Law*. Cambridge: Cambridge University Press.

Garnsey, Peter. 1996. *Ideas of Slavery from Aristotle to Augustine*. Cambridge: Cambridge University Press.

—. 2007. *Thinking about Property: From Antiquity to the Age of Revolution*. Cambridge: Cambridge University Press.

Gibbon, Edward. 1837. *The History of the Decline and Fall of the Roman Empire*. London: T. Cadell.

Gill, Christopher. 2007. 'Marcus Aurelius' in *Greek and Roman Philosophy 100 BCE–200 CE*, edited by R. W. Sharples and Richard Sorabji, Vol. 1, pp. 175–87. London: Institute of Classical Studies, University of London.

Goldhill, Simon. 1986. *Reading Greek Tragedy*. Cambridge and New York: Cambridge University Press.

Griffin, Miriam. 2013. 'Latin Philosophy and Roman Law' in *Politeia in Greek and Roman Philosophy*, edited by Verity Harte and Melissa Lane, pp. 96–115. Cambridge: Cambridge University Press.

Hadot, Pierre. 1995. *Philosophy as a Way of Life: Spiritual Exercises from Socrates to Foucault*. Oxford and New York: Blackwell.

Hall, Jonathan M. 2014. *A History of the Archaic Greek World, ca. 1200–479 BCE*. 2nd edition. Chichester: John Wiley & Sons.

Hansen, Mogens Herman. 1991. *The Athenian Democracy in the Age of Demosthenes: Structure, Principles and Ideology*, translated by J. A. Crook. Oxford: Blackwell.

—. 1993. 'The Polis as a Citizen-state' in *The Ancient Greek City-State: Symposium on the Occasion of the 250th Anniversary of the Royal Danish Academy of Sciences and Letters, July 1–4, 1992*, edited by Mogens Herman Hansen, pp. 7–29. Copenhagen: Munksgaard.

—. 2005. 'Direct Democracy, Ancient and Modern' in Mogens Herman Hansen, *The Tradition of Ancient Greek Democracy and Its Importance for Modern Democracy*, Historisk-filosofiske Meddelelser 93, pp. 45–69. Copenhagen: Royal Danish Academy of Science and Letters.

— (ed.). 1998. *Polis and City-state: An Ancient Concept and Its Modern Equivalent: Symposium, January 9, 1998*. Acts of the Copenhagen Polis Centre, Vol. 5. Copenhagen: Munksgaard.

—, and Nielsen, Thomas Heine. 2004. *An Inventory of Archaic and Classical Poleis*. Oxford: Oxford University Press.

Harries, Jill. 2006. *Cicero and the Jurists: From Citizen's Law to the Lawful State*. London: Duckworth.

Harris, Edward M. 2002. 'Did Solon Abolish Debt-Bondage?', *Classical Quarterly*, Vol. 52, pp. 415–30.

Harte, Verity. 1999. 'Conflicting Values in Plato's *Crito*', *Archiv Für Geschichte Der Philosophie*, Vol. 81, pp. 117–47.

—, and Lane, Melissa. 2013. 'Introduction' in *Politeia in Greek and Roman Philosophy*, edited by Verity Harte and Melissa Lane, pp. 1–12. Cambridge: Cambridge University Press.

Hatzistavrou, Antony. 2005. 'Socrates' Deliberative Authoritarianism', *Oxford Studies in Ancient Philosophy*, Vol. 29, pp. 75–113.

Hesk, Jon. 2007. 'The Socio-political Dimension of Ancient Tragedy' in *The Cambridge Companion to Greek and Roman Theatre*, edited by Marianne McDonald and J. Michael Walton, pp. 72–91. Cambridge: Cambridge University Press.

Hirschman, Albert O. 1991. *The Rhetoric of Reaction: Perversity, Futility, Jeopardy*. Cambridge, MA: Belknap Press.

Hoekstra, Kinch. Forthcoming. 'Athenian Democracy and the People as Tyrant' in *Popular Sovereignty in Historical Perspective*, edited by Richard Bourke and Quentin Skinner. Cambridge: Cambridge University Press.

Hornblower, Simon. 2006. 'Herodotus' Influence in Antiquity' in *The Cambridge Companion to Herodotus*, edited by Carolyn Dewald and John Marincola, pp. 306–18. Cambridge: Cambridge University Press.

Humfress, Caroline. 2005. 'Law and Legal Practice in the Age of Justinian' in *The Cambridge Companion to the Age of Justinian*, edited by Michael Maas, pp. 161–84. Cambridge: Cambridge University Press.

Inwood, Brad. 2005. 'Seneca on Freedom and Autonomy' in Brad Inwood, *Reading Seneca: Stoic Philosophy at Rome*, pp. 302–21. Oxford: Oxford University Press.

—. 2007. 'Introduction' in *Seneca: Selected Philosophical Letters*, translated and edited by Brad Inwood, pp. xi–xxiv. Oxford: Oxford University Press.

Kapust, Daniel J. 2011. *Republicanism, Rhetoric, and Roman Political Thought: Sallust, Livy, and Tacitus*. Cambridge: Cambridge University Press.

Keane, John. 2009. *The Life and Death of Democracy*. London: Simon & Schuster.

Kraut, Richard. 1984. *Socrates and the State*. Princeton, NJ: Princeton University Press.

Krentz, Peter. 1982. *The Thirty at Athens*. Ithaca, NY: Cornell University Press.

Laks, André. 1990. 'Legislation and Demiurgy: On the Relationship between Plato's *Republic* and *Laws*', *Classical Antiquity*, Vol. 9, pp. 209–29.

Lane, Melissa. 1998a. 'Argument and Agreement in Plato's *Crito*', *History of Political Thought*, Vol. 19, pp. 313–30.

— [as Lane, M. S.]. 1998b. *Method and Politics in Plato's Statesman*. Cambridge: Cambridge University Press.

—. 1999. 'Plato, Popper, Strauss, and Utopianism: Open Secrets?', *History of Philosophy Quarterly*, Vol. 16, pp. 119–42.

—. 2001. *Plato's Progeny: How Plato and Socrates Still Captivate the Modern Mind*. London: Duckworth.

—. 2007. 'Virtue as the Love of Knowledge in Plato's *Symposium* and *Republic*' in *Maieusis: Essays in Ancient Philosophy in Honour of Myles Burnyeat*, edited by Dominic Scott, pp. 44–67. Oxford: Oxford University Press.

—. 2010. 'Persuasion et force dans la politique platonicienne', translated by D. El Murr, in *Aglaïa: autour de Platon. Mélanges offerts à Monique Dixsaut*, edited by A. Brancacci, D. El Murr and D. P. Taormina, pp. 165–98. Paris: Vrin.

—. 2011. 'Ancient Political Philosophy' in *The Stanford Encyclopedia of Philosophy*, edited by Edward N. Zalta. http://plato.stanford.edu/archives/fall2011/entries/ancient-political/

—. 2011/2012. *Eco-Republic*. Oxford: Peter Lang (2011); Princeton, NJ: Princeton University Press (2012). Each edition has its own subtitle.

—. 2012. 'The Origins of the Statesman – Demagogue Distinction in and after Ancient Athens', *Journal of the History of Ideas*, Vol. 73, pp. 179–200.

—. 2013a. 'Founding as Legislating: The Figure of the Lawgiver in Plato's Republic' in *Dialogues on Plato's Politeia (Republic): Selected Papers from the Ninth Symposium Platonicum*, edited by Noboru Notomi and Luc Brisson, pp. 104–14. Sankt Augustin: Academia Verlag.

—. 2013b. 'Lifeless Writings or Living Script? The Life of Law in Plato, Middle Platonism and Jewish Platonizers', *Cardozo Law Review*, Vol. 34, pp. 937–64.

—. 2013c. 'Platonizing the Spartan *Politeia* in Plutarch's *Lycurgus*' in *Politeia in Greek and Roman Philosophy*, edited by Verity Harte and Melissa Lane, pp. 57–77. Cambridge: Cambridge University Press.

—. 2013d. 'Political Expertise and Political Office in Plato's *Statesman*: The Statesman's Rule (*archein*) and the Subordinate Magistracies (*archai*)' in *Plato's Statesman: Proceedings of the Eighth Symposium Platonicum Pragense*, edited by A. Havlíček, J. Jirsa and K. Thein, pp. 49–77. Prague: OIKOYMENH.

—. 2013e. 'Claims to Rule: The Case of the Multitude' in *The Cambridge Companion to Aristotle's Politics*, edited by Marguerite Deslauriers and Pierre Destrée, pp. 247–74. Cambridge: Cambridge University Press.

—. Forthcoming. '"Popular Sovereignty" in Ancient Greek Democracy? Aristotle on Rule as Control of Magistrates' in *Popular Sovereignty in Historical Perspective*, edited by Richard Bourke and Quentin Skinner. Cambridge: Cambridge University Press.

Lear, Jonathan. 1988. *Aristotle: The Desire to Understand*. Cambridge: Cambridge University Press.

Ley-Pineda, Miguel. 2009. 'The Royal Expert: Plato's Conception of Political Knowledge', dissertation submitted for the degree of Doctor of Philosophy, University of Cambridge, and deposited in the University Library.

Lintott, Andrew. 1999. *The Constitution of the Roman Republic*. Oxford: Oxford University Press.

Long, A. [Alexander]. 2013. 'The Political Art in Plato's *Republic*' in *Politeia in Greek and Roman Philosophy*, edited by Verity Harte and Melissa Lane, pp. 15–31. Cambridge: Cambridge University Press.

Long, A. A. [Anthony A.]. 1995. 'Cicero's Politics in *De Officiis*' in *Justice and Generosity: Studies in Hellenistic Social and Political Philosophy: Proceedings of the Sixth Symposium Hellenisticum*, edited by André Laks and Malcolm Schofield, pp. 213–40. Cambridge: Cambridge University Press.

McCormick, John P. 2011. *Machiavellian Democracy*. New York: Cambridge University Press.

Mackay, Christopher S. 2004. *Ancient Rome: A Military and Political History*. Cambridge: Cambridge University Press.

McPherran, Mark. 2002. 'Elenctic Interpretation and the Delphic Oracle' in *Does Socrates Have a Method? Rethinking the Elenchus in Plato's Dialogues and Beyond*, edited by Gary Alan Scott, pp. 114–44. University Park, PA: Pennsylvania State University Press.

Manin, Bernard. 1997. *The Principles of Representative Government*. Cambridge: Cambridge University Press.

Marr, J. L., and Rhodes, P. J. 2008. 'Introduction' in *The 'Old Oligarch': The Constitution of the Athenians Attributed to Xenophon*, translated and edited by J. L. Marr and P. J. Rhodes, pp. 1–29. Oxford: Oxbow.

Meier, Christian. 1990. *The Greek Discovery of Politics*. Cambridge, MA: Harvard University Press.

—. 2011. *A Culture of Freedom: Ancient Greece and the Origins of Europe*. Oxford: Oxford University Press.

Millar, Fergus. 2002. *The Roman Republic in Political Thought*. Hanover, NH: University Press of New England.

Moles, John. 2000. 'The Cynics' in *The Cambridge History of Greek and Roman Political Thought*, edited by C. J. Rowe and Malcolm Schofield, pp. 415–34. Cambridge: Cambridge University Press.

Monoson, S. Sara. 2000. *Plato's Democratic Entanglements: Athenian Politics and the Practice of Philosophy*. Princeton, NJ: Princeton University Press.

—. 2011. 'Recollecting Aristotle: Pro-slavery Thought in Antebellum America and the Argument of *Politics*, Book I' in *Ancient Slavery and Abolition: From Hobbes to Hollywood*, edited by Edith Hall, Richard Alston and Justine McConnell, pp. 247–78. Oxford: Oxford University Press.

—. 2012. 'Dionysius I and Sicilian Theatrical Traditions in Plato's *Republic*: Representing Continuities between Democracy and Tyranny' in *Theatre Outside Athens: Drama in Greek Sicily and South Italy*, edited by Kathryn Bosher, pp. 156–73. Cambridge: Cambridge University Press.

Morgan, Kathryn. 2013. 'Imaginary Kings: Visions of Monarchy in Sicilian Literature from Pindar to Theokritos' in *Sicily: Art and Invention between Greece and Rome*, edited by Claire L. Lyons, Michael J. Bennett and Clemente Marconi, pp. 98–105, 108–9. Los Angeles: J. Paul Getty Museum.

Morris, Sarah. 2003. 'Imaginary Kings: Alternatives to Monarchy in Ancient Greece' in *Popular Tyranny: Sovereignty and Its Discontents in Ancient Greece*, edited by Kathryn A. Morgan, pp. 1–24. Austin, TX: University of Texas Press.

Morwood, James. 2012. 'Euripides' Suppliant Women, Theseus and Athenocentrism', *Mnemosyne*, Vol. 65, pp. 552–64.

Nails, Debra. 2002. *The People of Plato: A Prosopography of Plato and Other Socratics*. Indianapolis, IN: Hackett.

Nehamas, Alexander. 1998. *The Art of Living: Socratic Reflections from Plato to Foucault*. Berkeley: University of California Press.

Nightingale, Andrea. 1993. 'Writing/Reading a Sacred Text: A Literary Interpretation of Plato's Laws', *Classical Philology*, Vol. 88, pp. 279–300.

—. 1999. 'Plato's Lawcode in Context: Rule by Written Law in Athens and Magnesia', *Classical Quarterly*, Vol. 49, pp. 100–122.

North, J. A. 1990. 'Democratic Politics in Republican Rome', *Past & Present*, No. 126, pp. 3–21.

Nussbaum, Martha Craven. 1994. *The Therapy of Desire: Theory and Practice in Hellenistic Ethics*. Princeton, NJ: Princeton University Press.

Ober, Josiah. 1989. *Mass and Elite in Democratic Athens: Rhetoric, Ideology, and the Power of the People*. Princeton, NJ: Princeton University Press.

—. 1998. *Political Dissent in Democratic Athens: Intellectual Critics of Popular Rule*. Princeton, NJ: Princeton University Press.

—. 2000. 'Quasi-rights: Political Boundaries and Social Diversity in Democratic Athens', *Social Philosophy and Policy*, Vol. 17, pp. 27–61.

—. 2005. 'Aristotle's Natural Democracy' in *Aristotle's Politics: Critical Essays*, edited by Richard Kraut and Steven Skultety, pp. 223–43. Lanham, MD: Rowman & Littlefield.

—. 2008a. *Democracy and Knowledge: Innovation and Learning in Classical Athens*. Princeton, NJ: Princeton University Press.

—. 2008b. 'The Original Meaning of Democracy: Capacity to Do Things, Not Majority Rule', *Constellations*, Vol. 15, pp. 3–9.

—. 2013. 'Democracy's Wisdom: An Aristotelian Middle Way for Collective Judgment', *American Political Science Review*, Vol. 107, pp. 104–22.

Ogilvie, R. M. 2011. *The Romans and Their Gods*. London: Random House.

Pagden, Anthony. 1995. *Lords of All the Worlds: Ideologies of Empire in Spain, Britain and France, c. 1500–c. 1850*. New Haven, CT: Yale University Press.

Paine, Thomas. 2000. *Rights of Man* in *Paine: Political Writings*, edited by Bruce Kuklick. Cambridge: Cambridge University Press.

Patterson, Orlando. 1991. *Freedom. Vol. 1: Freedom in the Making of Western Culture*. New York: Basic Books.

Raaflaub, Kurt A. 2007. 'The Breakthrough of *Dēmokratia* in Mid-fifth-century Athens' in *Origins of Democracy in Ancient Greece*, edited by Kurt A. Raaflaub, Josiah Ober and Robert W. Wallace, pp. 105–54. Berkeley: University of California Press.

Reydams-Schils, Gretchen. 2005. *The Roman Stoics: Self, Responsibility, and Affection*. Chicago: University of Chicago Press.

Rhodes, P. J. 1981. *A Commentary on the Aristotelian Athenaion Politeia*. Oxford and New York: Oxford University Press.

Richter, Daniel S. 2011. *Cosmopolis: Imagining Community in Late Classical Athens and the Early Roman Empire*. Oxford: Oxford University Press.

Rihll, T. E. 2011. 'Classical Athens' in *The Cambridge World History of Slavery*, edited by Keith Bradley and Paul Cartledge, Vol. 1, pp. 48–73. Cambridge: Cambridge University Press.

Roberts, Paul. 2013. *Life and Death in Pompeii and Herculaneum*. London: British Museum Press.

Rousseau, Jean-Jacques. 2001. *Letter to Beaumont, Letters Written from the Mountain, and Related Writings*, edited by Eve Grace and Christopher Kelly, translated by Christopher Kelly and Judith R. Bush. The Collected Writings of Rousseau, Vol. 9. Hanover, NH: University Press of New England.

Rowe, Christopher, and Schofield, Malcolm (eds.). 2000. *The Cambridge History of Greek and Roman Political Thought*. Cambridge: Cambridge University Press.

Ryan, Alan. 2012. *On Politics: A History of Political Thought from Herodotus to the Present*, 2 vols. New York: Liveright Publishing Corporation.

Sacks, David. 1995. *A Dictionary of the Ancient Greek World*. Oxford: Oxford University Press.

Sailor, Dylan. 2008. *Writing and Empire in Tacitus*. Cambridge: Cambridge University Press.

Saxonhouse, Arlene W. 1975. 'Tacitus' *Dialogue on Oratory*: Political Activity under a Tyrant', *Political Theory*, Vol. 3, pp. 53–68.

—. 1992. *Fear of Diversity: The Birth of Political Science in Ancient Greek Thought*. Chicago: University of Chicago Press.

Schofield, Malcolm. 1991. *The Stoic Idea of the City*. Cambridge: Cambridge University Press.

—. 1999a. *Saving the City: Philosopher-Kings and Other Classical Paradigms*. London: Routledge.

—. 1999b. 'Social and Political Thought' in *The Cambridge History of Hellenistic Philosophy*, edited by Keimpe Algra, Jonathan Barnes, Jaap Mansfeld and Malcolm Schofield, pp. 739–70. Cambridge: Cambridge University Press.

—. 2003. 'The Presocratics' in *The Cambridge Companion to Greek and Roman Philosophy*, edited by David Sedley, pp. 42–72. Cambridge: Cambridge University Press.

—. 2006. *Plato: Political Philosophy*. Oxford: Oxford University Press.

Schwartzberg, Melissa. 2010. 'Shouts, Murmurs and Votes: Acclamation and Aggregation in Ancient Greece', *Journal of Political Philosophy*, Vol. 18, pp. 448–68.

Sedley, David. 1997. 'The Ethics of Brutus and Cassius', *Journal of Roman Studies*, Vol. 87, pp. 41–53.

Sen, Amartya. 1982. 'Equality of What?' in *Choice, Welfare, and Measurement*, Vol. 1, pp. 353–69. Cambridge, MA: MIT Press.

Sinclair, R. K. 1991. *Democracy and Participation in Athens* (1st edition, 1988). Cambridge: Cambridge University Press.

Staveley, E. S. 1972. *Greek and Roman Voting and Elections*. Ithaca, NY: Cornell University Press.

Stein, Peter. 1999. *Roman Law in European History*. Cambridge: Cambridge University Press.

Strauss, Leo. 1964. *The City and Man*. Chicago: Rand McNally.

Tarnopolsky, Christina. 2010. 'Mimêsis, Persuasion and Manipulation in Plato's *Republic*' in *Manipulating Democracy*, edited by John Parrish and Wayne S. LeCheminant, pp. 135–56. New York: Routledge.

Thomas, Rosalind. 2005. 'Writing, Law and Written Law' in *The Cambridge Companion to Ancient Greek Law*, edited by Michael Gagarin and David Cohen, pp. 41–60. Cambridge: Cambridge University Press.

Viroli, Maurizio. 1992. *From Politics to Reason of State: The Acquisition and Transformation of the language of Politics, 1250–1600*. Cambridge: Cambridge University Press.

Vlassopoulos, Kostas. 2007. *Unthinking the Greek Polis: Ancient Greek History beyond Eurocentrism*. Cambridge: Cambridge University Press.

Walbank, F. W. 1957. *A Historical Commentary on Polybius*. Oxford: Oxford University Press.

—. 1962. 'Introduction' in *The Histories of Polybius*. Indiana University Greek and Latin Classics. Bloomington: Indiana University Press.

—. 1981. *The Hellenistic World*. Brighton: Harvester Press; Atlantic Highlands, NJ: Humanities Press (reprinted with amendments, 1992).

Waldron, Jeremy. 1995. 'The Wisdom of the Multitude: Some Reflections on Book III, Chapter 11, of Aristotle's *Politics*', *Political Theory*, Vol. 23, pp. 563–84.

Wallace, Robert W. 2007. 'Revolutions and a New Order in Solonian Athens and Archaic Greece' in *Origins of Democracy in Ancient Greece*, edited by Kurt A. Raaflaub, Josiah Ober and Robert W. Wallace, pp. 49–82. Berkeley: University of California Press.

Wallach, John R. 2001. *The Platonic Political Art: A Study of Critical Reason and Democracy*. University Park, PA: Pennsylvania State University Press.

Weiss, Roslyn. 1998. *Socrates Dissatisfied: An Analysis of Plato's Crito*. New York: Oxford University Press.

—. 2006. *The Socratic Paradox and Its Enemies*. Chicago: University of Chicago Press.

White, Stephen A. 1995. 'Thrasymachus the Diplomat', *Classical Philology*, Vol. 90, pp. 307–27.

Whitmarsh, Tim. 2005. *The Second Sophistic*. Oxford: Oxford University Press, published for the Classical Association.

Williams, Bernard. 1993. *Shame and Necessity*. Berkeley: University of California Press.

Williams, J. M. 1983. 'Solon's Class System, the Manning of Athens' Fleet, and the Number of Athenian Thetes in the Late Fourth Century', *Zeitschrift Für Papyrologie Und Epigraphik*, Vol. 52, pp. 241–5.

Wilson, James Lindley. 2011. 'Deliberation, Democracy, and the Rule of Reason in Aristotle's *Politics*', *American Political Science Review*, Vol. 105, pp. 259–74.

Winton, Richard. 2000. 'Herodotus, Thucydides and the Sophists' in *The Cambridge History of Greek and Roman Political Thought*, edited by C. J. Rowe and Malcolm Schofield, pp. 89–121. Cambridge : Cambridge University Press.

Zetzel, James E. G. 1999. 'Introduction' in Marcus Tullius Cicero, '*On the Commonwealth*' and '*On the Laws*', edited by James E. G. Zetzel, pp. vii–xxiv. Cambridge: Cambridge University Press.

Notes

INTRODUCTION: POSSIBILITIES OF POWER AND PURPOSE

1. Rousseau, 'Ninth Letter from the Mountain', published in 1764, as translated in Rousseau 2001, pp. 292–3.
2. Ibid., p. 293.
3. Viroli 1992.
4. Figures for territory size are conveniently summarized in Ober 2008a, pp. 43–8, 84–6, who draws on a range of sources, including the important inventory of 1,035 different *poleis*, the plural of *polis* (or, strictly, communities that were 'definitely, probably or possibly' to be classed as such, in Hansen and Nielsen 2004 (quotation, p. 53)).
5. This translation is coined by Hansen 1993, pp. 7–29.
6. On the different forms of manumission in Rome, noting that only those involving civil procedures (as distinct from merely the wilful decision of the master) conferred citizenship, see Arena 2012, pp. 16–19, and Bradley 2011, pp. 254–5.
7. On Athenian water-clocks, Allen 1996; on Roman augurs, Ogilvie 2011.

CHAPTER 1: JUSTICE

1. *WD* 189: the phrase translates a single Greek word, *cheirodikai*, literally 'hand-justice', meaning the justice imposed by force of fists. For this gloss and translation, see *EGPT*, p. 15.
2. This is also observed by Ryan 2012, Vol. 1, p. 13.
3. On Solon's achievement, see Wallace 2007.
4. In the *Constitution of the Athenians* produced by Aristotle or his school in the mid to late 4th century, and rediscovered in the late 19th century,

which offers an interpretative political history and analysis of Athenian political arrangements, this is described as abolishing 'lending on the body' (*AP* 6.1). I follow Harris 2002 in interpreting this as the abolition of debt-slavery between individuals, while still allowing debt-bondage understood as the obligation to work at a creditor's will until a debt is paid off, but this is a matter of scholarly debate (for the view that Solon rather abolished debt-bondage, see Finley 1985, p. 166 and *passim*; I am grateful to Paul Cartledge for discussing these matters with me, though we don't fully agree). Debt-slavery for debts to the *polis* persisted in any case. Also debated is the meaning of the more general abolition of private and public debts, the so-called *seisachtheia* (or shaking off of burdens, from the same root as 'seismic tremors', or earthquakes) with which Solon is also credited in the same section of the text.

5. Patterson 1991, p. xiii ('freedom was generated from the experience of slavery') and p. xv ('freedom, as a core value, was first socially constructed in ancient Athens'); these conclusions are especially striking, given the broad historical and ethnographic sweep of Patterson's study.

6. Florentinus, *Digest* 1.4.5.1, as translated in Garnsey 1996, p. 14.

7. For authoritative overviews of slavery in classical Athens and republican Rome, see the chapters by Rihll 2011 and Bradley 2011 in *The Cambridge World History of Slavery*, Vol. 1. A useful brief discussion is in Hansen 1991, pp. 120–23; on p. 124 he notes that the public slaves (*demosioi*) could bring suits before the courts.

8. Ober 2000, Vlassopoulos 2007.

9. On Athens into the 4th century, Rihll 2011, p. 54, citing the 'Old Oligarch' 1.10; on Rome, Bradley 2011, p. 261, citing Appian, *B. Civ.* 2.122.

10. J. Paul Getty Museum object 85.AA.352.

11. Bernard Williams 1993, pp. 111–17, 124–9.

12. Less accepted in theory, perhaps, but just as ingrained in practice, are the modern forms of bondage prevalent in many parts of the world that apply to certain groups of domestic workers, sex workers and various kinds of indentured labourers, especially those trafficked or brought into foreign countries.

13. *Tereus*, TGF, p. 591, in the translation given in EGPT, p. 56.

14. Cartledge 2002, p. 148.

15. Hansen 1991, pp. 116–20.

16. *Nomos* is the word usually translated as 'law', but it can also mean 'rule', 'custom' or 'way of life': all of these are intimately related in ancient Greek thought.

17. My translation. This passage is also quoted in Balot 2006, p. 21; Balot

sees justice and the oppression it remedies as central to Greek political thinking, as is also argued here.

18. KRS 101A, for Greek text and translation.

19. These enthusiasts 'supposed ... the whole heaven to be an attunement and a number', so Aristotle later reported: KRS 430, quoted and discussed by Schofield 2003, p. 55. Not all Greek thinkers agreed that justice ordered the cosmos. One dissident was the philosopher Empedocles, born in Sicily not far from the Pythagorean settlements, who claimed that love rather than justice was what fundamentally unified the conflict-stricken cosmos.

20. For an overview of the political context and contribution of Greek tragedy, see Hesk 2007, or, at greater length, Goldhill 1986.

21. Having stipulated in advance that a tie will count as an acquittal, Athena can be described as casting the deciding vote in the sense that her vote, coming twelfth, is the sixth to find Orestes innocent.

22. Gagarin 1986, pp. 12–14, 19–20, and *passim*.

23. Gagarin 2008, p. 155.

24. Euripides, *Phoen.* 536–8, my translation. The word translated here as 'Fairness' is actually *isoteta*, which is literally 'equality'. The mathematical precision of what is *ison* favours a translation of 'equality', but sometimes words involving *ison* are used in a broader sense of fairness.

25. The ties of kinship between brother and sister were thought by the Greeks to be especially deep. Herodotus (3.119) tells the story of a Persian woman who is given the choice by King Darius of saving just one of her male kinsman from death. Out of her brother, husband and sons, she chooses her brother, on the grounds that she could remarry and bear more children, but with her parents dead, she could never have another brother. The king honours her choice by sparing the life of her eldest son as well as her brother.

26. Not all of those whom we call sophists presented human justice and law as having no roots in divine intentions. Protagoras, for example, took a version of the Hesiodic approach, recounting in a myth the origins of justice as a gift from Zeus together with 'awe' (*aidos*). Justice sets the terms of fairness among humans; awe makes humans fear the gods and feel shame in breaching the laws and customs in which justice is embodied. Together, awe and justice 'bring order to cities and [are] the communal bonds of friendship' (this is the view ascribed to Protagoras in Plato, *Protagoras* 322c, as translated by Lombardo and Bell in Cooper 1997).

27. As described in Garnsey 1996, pp. 75–6, who notes that he was perhaps defending the Messenian helots, many of whom achieved freedom from their Spartan overlords in 369 BCE.

As Garnsey also notes there, Aristotle refers to a group of people who think this way in *Pol.* 1253b20–23, but he names no names.

28. We know that this was the view of the sophist Lycophron as reported by Aristotle, *Pol.* 1280b10–12, and it was also apparently that of the sophist Antiphon: DK 87 B44. We will see in Chapter 4 that it is the view put forward for refutation in Book 2 of Plato's *Republic*.

29. This is the argument of Denyer 1983.

30. *Rep.* 359a, translated by Grube, revised Reeve, in Cooper 1997.

31. Ober 2008b.

CHAPTER 2: CONSTITUTION

1. The imperial *constitutiones* were given the force of law (*lex*) by Hadrian in the 2nd century CE: Stein 1999, p. 28. They were collected into a single codex by Justinian in 529 CE and revised in 534 CE into a definitive second edition: Humfress 2005, pp. 162–6.

2. *Pol.* 1295a40.

3. Ibid., 1290a7–8.

4. Hdt. 9.33. More precisely, this is the 'first extant occurrence [of *politeia*] in a non-fragmentary text of known authorship', as put in Harte and Lane 2013, p. 1, on which this paragraph draws more generally.

5. I owe these points to Schofield 2006, pp. 30–35, discussing the surviving fragments of Critias' prose and verse writings titled *Politeia of the Spartans*; Xenophon's prose work of the same name; and Hippodamus of Miletus' account of the 'best *politeia*'.

6. For an influential analysis, see Fornara 1971.

7. Hornblower 2006, p. 306.

8. Winton 2000, p. 102.

9. Hornblower 2006, pp. 306–7.

10. There can be no doubt that the specific vocabulary of ideas and institutions used in this debate, especially in the speech by Otanes about popular regimes, are 5th-century Greek rather than 6th-century Persian, contrary to Keane 2009. For a judicious discussion of the possibility of some kernel of 6th-century Persian concern with equality among nobles, and for the best way to interpret the related passage of Hdt., 6.43, in that context, see Evans 1981.

11. See Chapter 3, and Hoekstra forthcoming.

12. The dates of the three seemingly earliest surviving writings to use

demokratia – by the 'Old Oligarch', Herodotus and Democritus – are all contested, but probably all date from about the 430s or soon afterwards in terms of their composition and circulation: see Raaflaub 2007, p. 108, though he suggests other indirect evidence for a circulation of the term in Athens from the 460s.

13. Morwood 2012, pp. 557–8.
14. As translated in *EGPT*, modifying *ison* from 'fair' to 'equal' and adjusting syntax accordingly.
15. As translated in *EGPT*.
16. Hdt. 5.78, using a word from the same root as the verb 'to speak in the assembly' and the noun *agora*, a place of assembly.
17. The phrase is due to the analysis of modern political and ideological debate in Hirschman 1991.
18. Alcaeus, fragments 70.10–11, as translated in Anderson 2005, p. 182.
19. Morris 2003, p. 1.
20. The most powerful and influential Spartan kings were Cleomenes I, ruling from *c.* 590 to 490, and Agesilaos II, ruling from 399 to 360.
21. There was also a lineage of Greek kings governing the colony of Cyrene, established in the area of modern-day Libya, which ruled (though under the thumb of the Persians from the last quarter of the 6th century onwards) until being deposed in favour of a democracy in about 440 BCE: Sacks 1995, pp. 73–4. And there seems to have been a monarchy in Taras, in southern Italy, a city that identified itself as a Spartan colony: Hall 2014, pp. 116–20.
22. I am drawing on, but going somewhat beyond, Anderson 2005, who asserts at p. 177: 'For most of the archaic era, a *turannis* was not a "regime" at all. The term referred rather to a conventional, if unusually dominant style of leadership that flourished in early Greek oligarchies.'
23. Anderson 2005, pp. 211–14.
24. See Monoson 2012.
25. Plutarch, *Nicias* 29.2–3, cited in Bosher 2012, p. 116.
26. This *Constitution of the Athenians*, discovered in the late 19th century and identified with Aristotle's school, should not be confused with the more polemical text written by the anonymous author now called the 'Old Oligarch', which is also sometimes titled *Constitution of the Athenians* (especially in older scholarship, in which it was often credited to Xenophon, among whose writings it was preserved).
27. The evolution of the democracy in Athens will be considered in more detail in Chapter 3.
28. Hoekstra forthcoming.
29. As we saw in Chapter 1, the exclusion of slaves and foreigners from

citizenship, and the problematic and partial exclusion of women, was practised by all Greek regimes, including even full-blown democracies.

30. 2.18–19, Greek in *TLG*, translated as in Benson and Prosser (1972), modified: I translate 'all those sharing in the constitution', as opposed to their 'all those sharing in citizenship': their translation of this phrase cannot be correct, since the conclusion of the extract quoted is that the multitude in an oligarchy will be citizens but will be excluded from office. I have made other small modifications to their translation as well. This text is now believed to be the work of Anaximenes of Lampsacus. For further discussion, see Lane forthcoming.

31. Gabrielsen 1981, p. 113.

32. Thuc. 5.84.3.

33. For an overview of the distinctiveness of the Spartan constitution, see Cartledge 2001, pp. 21–38.

34. Some of the inhabitants of Laconia (the *perioikoi*), however, enjoyed local forms of self-government under Spartan dominance.

35. Notice that, contrary to the prevalent myth of an unchanged Spartan constitution, Herodotus mentions at least one law introduced at a particular time in the middle of the Persian Wars: that one of the two kings had to stay home when the other was out on military campaign (5.75). Scholars argue that many of the other customs described by Plutarch as Lycurgan were still later innovations of the 3rd century BCE: see Flower 2002.

36. Crete, too, which shared Doric kinship with Sparta, had common meals (indeed, Lycurgus is said to have borrowed many of the laws he imposed from Crete). Aristotle, in the *Politics* (1271a–1272a), contrasts the method of providing such meals by individual contributions in Sparta unfavourably with the method of having common lands and supplies in Crete, which made such meals more genuinely 'of the common'.

37. Plato and Aristotle noted in the 4th century that this ban hadn't worked, with Spartans secretly hoarding money, perhaps accumulated on military campaigns abroad. See for example Aristotle, *Pol.* 1271b5.

38. *Apophth.* and *Lacae.*, cited in this paragraph, can both be found in Plutarch 1931.

39. I follow here the dating suggested by Marr and Rhodes 2008, p. 5, with reference to certain earlier scholars' arguments, although they themselves acknowledge the wide range of dates suggested by others (pp. 31–2). The text was preserved along with writings by Xenophon, and was from later in antiquity attributed to him; its author is therefore sometimes referred

to as 'pseudo-Xenophon', though most scholars today (including Marr and Rhodes 2008, pp. 6–12) consider Xenophon unlikely to have been the author.

40. As translated by and according to the Greek text in Marr and Rhodes 2008.

41. Ibid.

CHAPTER 3: DEMOCRACY

1. For the view of Athenian democracy as a form of popular sovereignty, see Lane forthcoming.

2. For measures of Athens' economic and cultural influence, see Ober 2008a.

3. The details of the new property qualification are disputed; for a brief overview, see Williams 1983.

4. In fact, scholarly opinion is divided about whether this is the best answer: Christian Meier 1990, pp. 82–4, and Kurt Raaflaub 2007, for example, have argued that the beginning of 'democracy' is better credited to the 460s and the reforms of Ephialtes, described below.

5. Post-Cleisthenes, citizens were identified as members of their demes, for example, 'Antigenes of Xypete', mentioned in Lycurgus' speech prosecuting Leochares. Another way in which Cleisthenes is said in the AP to have extended democracy was by introducing ostracism: this is discussed below.

6. In addition, a hero of the battle of Marathon in the Persian Wars, Aristides, is credited in the AP with having subsequently instituted public pay for soldiers, sailors and certain magistrates, all funded by imperial tributes. This gave the ordinary Athenian a financial stake in the empire.

7. *Per.*, 37.

8. On the facts and significance of methods of voting in Athens and to a lesser extent Sparta, see Schwartzberg 2010.

9. Staveley 1972, pp. 93–4, and 78–100, for Athenian voting procedures generally.

10. Hansen 1991, pp. 153, 166–7.

11. As noted in Lane forthcoming, the phrase 'dead letter' is used by Rhodes 1981, p. 146 (AP 7.4), Sinclair 1991 (1988 edition), p. 17, n. 64, and Hansen 1991, pp. 88, 107, 227. But both the passages on which all of these authors lean heavily – AP 7.4 and 47.1 – suggest that the ban on the lowest class (*thetes*) holding office had some life to it as an official policy, even if it was sometimes or often evaded in practice.

12. *The Quiet Athenian* is the title of Carter 1986.

13. Ober 1989.

14. Isocrates 20.5–6; see Allen 2000 for a discussion of anger in democratic Athens.

15. Ober 1989 and 1998.

16. Diodotus' advice narrowly carried the day: the assembly decided to rescind the order to put the men to the sword. To do so, it sent out a second ship with that countermanding order, which overtook the first ship with murderous instructions in the nick of time.

17. The decision was made to consider the guilt of the Arginusae generals as a group, rather than individually, which violated proper procedures; Socrates says in the *Apology* that he protested against this in his role as member of the council at the time.

18. For one account, see Dunn 2005.

19. Paine 2000, p. 180.

20. In contrast, Hansen considers Athens and some other Greek democracies (though he notes, not all of them) to have been forms of 'direct democracy in which every major political decision automatically has to be debated and voted on by the people' (2005, p. 46). While the role of the open popular assembly in Athenian decision-making is vital, I think that labelling it 'direct democracy' is unhelpful and has become misleading, for the reasons given in the main text.

21. Hansen 1991, p. 230.

22. On election as anti-democratic, see Manin 1997, though one must remember that the Athenians, too, chose to elect certain officials.

23. To pass the scrutiny (*dokimasia*) prior to taking up a post to which he had been appointed by lottery, a citizen had to prove that he was properly enrolled as a citizen and to establish 'whether he does well by his parents, fulfils his tax obligations and has served as a soldier when required' (*AP* 55.3).

24. Constant 1988.

25. For a valuable discussion of Athenian religion and politics in the context of Socrates' trial, see Cartledge 2009, pp. 76–91.

26. I follow Forsdyke 2005, pp. 281–4 (Appendix 1), who reviews the arguments for and against attributing the introduction of Athenian ostracism to Cleisthenes, and suggests that, on balance, its Cleisthenic origins can be defended, while at the same time pointing out that other cities, and Athens itself, already had elite practices of exile that bear similarity to ostracism without being identical to it.

27. This is argued by Forsdyke 2005, pp. 144–204.

28. Endangered in his exile in Argos by Spartan plotting, Themistocles

eventually left Greece altogether and ended his life – ironically – in the service of the Persian king.

29. Ober 2000.

30. As translated by and according to the Greek text in Marr and Rhodes 2008.

CHAPTER 4: VIRTUE

1. *Grg.* 452e, translation by Zeyl in Cooper 1997.

2. Ibid., 452d, 452e.

3. Translation by Grube in Cooper 1997.

4. Krentz 1982, p. 65: 'The excluded (those outside the 3,000 [who remained on the citizen rolls under the oligarchy]) were banned from living in the city.'

5. Weiss 2006 brings out this perspective well, though her argument does not exhaust what the dialogues are doing.

6. He seems to go further, suggesting that knowledge is not only necessary but also sufficient for virtue: whether and how he argues for this is a disputed matter among scholars.

7. On Socrates as more apparently virtuous than any others of his generation, Plato, *Phaedo* 118a, discussed by Nehamas 1998 and Lane 2007.

8. Monoson 2000 details Plato's intellectual debts to Athenian democracy (with Saxonhouse 1992 specifically on frank speaking also); Wallach 2001 argues that he is no more critical of Athens than of other regimes; while Ober 1998 suggests that he should be understood contextually as one of a circle of radical 'rejectionist' critics of Athens.

9. Translation by Grube in Cooper 1997.

10. There is a large and contentious literature on how to read the *Apology*; I am developing my own reading here. For one perspective on key elements in the text, see McPherran 2002. For a distinctive reading of Socrates as committed to following an expert rather than his own judgement, see Hatzistavrou 2005.

11. There is also a large and contentious literature on how to read the *Crito*, in particular as to how the speech of the 'Laws' imagined by Socrates in the *Crito* relates to his own views. The most influential reading of that speech in recent English-language literature is Kraut 1984. For various challenges to the broad view accepted by Kraut that the views of the 'Laws' and those of Socrates coincide, see Harte 1999, Lane 1998a and Weiss 1998.

12. Xenophon, in *Hellenica* 1.7, records the illegality – of sanctioning all six generals collectively rather than considering their deeds individually – and

Socrates' opposition. It's worth noting that Socrates must have let his name go forward in order to be chosen by lot to serve as a member of his deme's council contingent for that year.

13. DL 3.46.

14. Even in the *Laws*, there is an Athenian Visitor whom some think a disguised portrait of either Socrates or of Plato himself.

15. The essential reference work about Plato's characters by Debra Nails 2002 dates his birth 424/423.

16. I owe the identification and exploration of this connection to Allen 2010.

17. On Thrasymachus, a real person and rhetorician who is serving as an ambassador from Chalcedon to Athens in the moment that he is purportedly a participant in the discussion of the *Republic*, see White 1995.

18. Translation by Grube, revised Reeve, in Cooper 1997.

19. From here on, I will often use the conventional translation 'soul' for *psyche*, in common with many English translations and discussions.

20. The centrality of guarding in the *Republic* is emphasized by A. [Alexander] Long 2013.

21. Lane 2011/2012.

22. On the 'noble lie', see Schofield 2006, pp. 292–309, and Tarnopolsky 2010.

23. See Lane 2001. In the case of communism, as Garnsey 2007 has shown, the *Republic*'s case for depriving some of property was misreported by Aristotle in his *Politics* as a case for abolishing private property in favour of common ownership by all in a city. That misunderstanding (perhaps fostered by Plato's *Laws* 739c–e, in which communism of property and family for all is called the first-best regime) led to a long legacy of Plato being thought of as the father of positive communism – in which all own property in common – and serving as the inspiration for Thomas More in his *Utopia* (1516) and for French revolutionaries like Gracchus Babeuf. In fact, Plato's argument in the *Republic* is for only a limited negative communism, in which none of the rulers own anything, but ownership relations are not abolished overall.

24. *Rep.* 517a, translation by Grube, revised Reeve, in Cooper 1997.

25. There is an alternative reading of the *Republic* claiming that its point is rather to show that philosophical rule and its requirements are impossible (Strauss 1964, Bloom 1991). I have argued in Lane 1999 that this interpretation discounts the explicit analysis of possibility offered by Socrates in Book 5; for more on Platonic ideas of possibility, see Laks 1990.

26. Lane 2007.

27. Ley-Pineda 2009.

28. Lane 2001.

29. Lane 1998b and Lane 2013d.

30. Lane 2013a.

31. On the second-best status of the city of the *Laws*, Laks 1990. At *Laws* 739c–e, the best city is said to abolish property and family for all citizens (unlike what is proposed for Kallipolis in the *Republic*).

32. Translation by Saunders in Cooper 1997.

33. On self-rule in the *Laws*, see Bobonich 2002, criticized in part by Lane 2010. On law and writing, see Nightingale 1993 and 1999.

34. For a judicious assessment of the status of the text, see Brunt 1993, pp. 282–342.

35. As translated in Plutarch 1973, p. 119.

36. Once: Diodorus Siculus; twice: Cornelius Nepos; three times: the 'Seventh Letter' and Plutarch. Unfortunately none of the works by historians of Sicily on which the later writers themselves were drawing has survived.

37. The argument of this paragraph draws on and is indebted to Allen 2010.

CHAPTER 5: CITIZENSHIP

1. This is the project of, among others, Ober 2005.

2. For an excellent overview of Aristotle highlighting this starting point, see Lear 1988.

3. *EN* 1103b, closely following but modifying the translation in Barnes 1984.

4. For an excellent analysis of this aspect of Aristotle's ethics, see Burnyeat 1980.

5. On the ways in which the family and household are encompassed within the *polis*, see Cooper 2012, pp. 70–143.

6. Here I draw on and follow Schofield 1999a, pp. 115–40.

7. On the use of Aristotle in the Spanish conquest in the Americas, Pagden 1995; in the antebellum South, Monoson 2011.

8. The question was famously put in this form by Amartya Sen 1982.

9. For a valuable discussion of the ways in which the family and household are for Aristotle encompassed within the *polis*, see Cooper 2012, pp. 70–143.

10. Lane 2013e, Lane forthcoming. Note that I consider this worth counting as a conception of popular sovereignty, even though it is articulated without the legal vocabulary of the rights of the people to control and manage their own affairs and interests that characterizes the theory of popular sovereignty developed in Cicero (Schofield 1999a, pp. 178–94).

11. *Pol.* 1281a–b, as translated in Reeve 1998.

12. Collective feasts in Athens were generally provided by collective monies of a panel of citizens; in cities like Crete by the city's general funds; in Sparta by individual contributions of foodstuffs, both levies of basic provisions and also occasional gifts of hunted meat or side-dishes. For a reading focused on aggregation of quantity, see Lane 2013d, versus the usual reading of the passage as primarily about potluck meals and more generally about qualitative diversity, which is influentially found in Waldron 1995 and well defended in Wilson 2011 and Ober 2013. For a related line of scepticism to my own, see Cammack 2013.

13. On the contribution of Plato and Aristotle to articulating the ideal of the 'rule of law', see Allen 2000.

14. *Pol.* 1282b, as translated in Reeve 1998.

15. Ibid., 1323a, 1323b for the quotations respectively.

16. The approach taken here is influenced by Frank 2005.

CHAPTER 6: COSMOPOLITANISM

1. Aristotle does talk at one point about the prospects that the Greeks could rule all the other neighbouring peoples, should they chance to develop 'a single *politeia*' (*Pol.* 1327b31–3). But, while it is enticing to read this as along the lines of Alexander's imperial vision, as does Meier 2011, p. 41, it is better interpreted to mean all Greek cities adopting the same constitution rather than merging into a single city (with Reeve 1998, p. 202, n. 31).

2. Schofield 1991, pp. 104–11, argues that Plutarch is here misconstruing Zeno's idea of something like the Spartan *politeia* by assimilating it to the political programme of Alexander the Great. However, for my limited purposes in making this introductory point, the absence of distinctive city walls and laws would hold true also of Schofield's own reconstruction of Zeno as defining a *politeia* in terms of shared social norms (Schofield 1991, p. 73).

3. New fragment 21.1.4–14, quoted here in LS 22S translation. The inscription (ironically, carved into the city walls, covering in toto about 100 metres) was commissioned by Diogenes of Oenoanda in about 200 CE (he is not to be confused with Diogenes of Sinope, the Cynic). This is among the fragments highlighted by the overview and review of Clay 2007, p. 288; it is published in Smith 2003.

4. Alexander's generals would break up his empire into parts after his death, making themselves rival monarchs and elaborating ideals of kingship that had some continuity with Alexander's aspirations to empire. For

an overview of the history and politics of the Hellenistic period, see Walbank 1981.

5. See Moles 2000.

6. Alexander is said to have been accompanied by another Cynic philosopher, Onesicritus, and other Cynics in later periods were also court-philosophers, however improbable this may sound. Kindstrand 1976, pp. 14–15, discusses this in the context of the relation between Bion, a philosopher born a slave who studied in the old Academy at the end of the 4th century and became a popular, Cynic-identified teacher, and Antigonus Gonatas, the general ruling Macedon.

7. Indeed the counter-cultural aspect of the parables about Jesus have led some scholars to speak – controversially – of 'Jesus the Cynic'. We can identify the Cynic life as one of the powerful inherited images within which some understandings of the life of Jesus – and later the preaching of Paul – were fashioned. See Bosman 2008 and Downing 1992.

8. *Alex.* 14.

9. These accounts of Chrysippus' writings are found in Plutarch, *On Stoic Self-Contradictions* 1044F–1045A, as translated in LS 67F; Sextus Empiricus, *Outlines of Pyrrhonism* 3.247–8, as translated in LS 67G.

10. The approach here and in the account of the Stoics in this chapter generally owes much to Schofield 1991.

11. This account of Zeno, presented by his critics, is in DL 7.32–3, as translated in LS 67B.

12. The general account of the Stoics in DL is usefully collected and translated in sequence in Inwood and Gerson 2008.

13. Arius Didymus, as reported by Eusebius: passage excerpted and translated in LS 67L.

14. *D* 2.10.7–12.

15. Ibid., 2.10.3, as translated in Text 144 (p. 200), Inwood and Gerson 2008.

16. Appiah 2006.

17. DL 10.117–20, as translated in LS 22Q.

18. DL 10.119, as translated in Inwood and Gerson 1997, p. 42.

19. Ammianus Marcellinus, 30.4.3 (51 Usener), as translated in Inwood and Gerson 1997, p. 96.

20. Reported in Porphyry, *On Abstinence* 1.71.–9.4, as translated in LS 22M.

21. DL 10.139–54, as translated in Inwood and Gerson 1997, p. 35.

22. The early Stoics, too, had celebrated friendship among the sages, classing it as among those things that are to be 'chosen for their own sakes' (according to *Fin.* 3.70, as translated in Inwood and Gerson 1997, p. 242) rather than merely as a means to something else. Still, they tended to stress

the commonality and community among sages more than the particular ties of friendship.

23. Epicurus, *Key Doctrines* 7. 27, as translated in LS 22C, 22E.

24. Cicero, *Fin.* 1.66–70, as translated in LS 22O.

25. Ibid.; followed by DL 10.120, as translated in LS 22Q.

26. According to Seneca, *Ep.* 19.10, as translated in LS 22I.

27. New fragment 21.1.4–14, as translated in LS 22S.

28. Fragments 3.2.7–3.6.2, Smith. This is among the fragments highlighted in the overview and review of Clay 2007, pp. 286–7; it is published in Smith 1993.

29. All translations from *De Re Publica* are from Cicero 1991, according to the system of numbering the fragments used there, which are not always printed in numerical order, so I shall cite fragment numbers together with page numbers; here 3.33, at pp. 71–2. As with other incompletely surviving ancient texts, many of the fragments are quoted or reported by later ancient sources and may be shaped by the agendas of the latter.

30. All translations in this paragraph are from 3.21a, in Cicero 1991, p. 63.

31. Ibid., 3.13.

32. Ibid., 3.17, p. 65.

33. Ibid.

34. Ibid., 3.24b, p. 66.

35. Admittedly, the shadowy figure of Pyrrho – a contemporary of Epicurus and Zeno, whose life and teachings recounted by his student Timon were appropriated by the later Sceptic Aenesidemus as a forebear – was said to have applied the theory in a more radically incautious way, 'going out of his way for nothing, taking no precaution, but facing all risks as they came, whether carts, precipices, dogs, or what not' (DL 9.11, as translated by Hicks in Diogenes Laertius 1925). But Pyrrho was more dogmatic in his Scepticism than some of his later self-proclaimed 'Pyrrhonist' followers.

CHAPTER 7: REPUBLIC

1. On the meaning of *res publica*, I draw on Schofield 1999a, pp. 178–94, though in then eliding this with 'republican' for my own purposes I depart from his more cautionary approach.

2. Brunt 1988, p. 283, and generally pp. 281–350.

3. McCormick 2011 offers a democratic and populist reading of republican Rome, one that he finds in Machiavelli's reflections on Livy's history.

4. Polyb. 1.1.5. I have made my own translations from the Budé text: Polybius 2004. The standard English translation is by Evelyn S. Shuckburgh (Polybius 1962), which I have also consulted and sometimes followed or adapted.

5. For an overview of Polybius' life on which this account draws, see Walbank 1962.

6. Baronowski 2011, pp. 2–3.

7. The last three sentences of this paragraph draw on Schofield 1999b, p. 746.

8. Polybius uses no such shorthand label, but describes the equilibrating of the elements of the regime at length. His idea would be better described as 'balanced' than as 'mixed'; as Paul Cartledge vividly suggested to me, it is more 'seesaw' than 'pudding'.

9. Thuc. 8.97.2.

10. Plato, *Laws* 691e. The translations from the *Laws* in this paragraph are by Saunders in Cooper 1997.

11. Ibid., 693d.

12. The relevance of this Aristotelian passage is noted (pp. v–vi) in the course of the general helpful guide to Polybius on the mixed constitution in Fritz 1954.

13. For the later influence of the Roman constitution in the history of political thought, see Millar 2002.

14. Drogula 2007.

15. The translation is in Arena 2012, p. 201, who also cites the two sources using the phrase: Caes., *B. Civ*. 1.5, and Livy 3.4.9.

16. For a review of the debate, see North 1990.

17. *Cic*. 3.7, translated by J. L. Moles in Plutarch 1998.

18. Zetzel 1999, p. vii.

19. *Off*. 1.77, as translated by Margaret Atkins in Cicero 1991.

20. As translated by J. L. Moles in Plutarch 1988.

21. Zetzel 1999, p. viii.

22. *Cic*. 42. 2–8.

23. For the Latin text of Quintus' instructions, see Q. T. Cicero 2001, and for an accessible recent translation, Q. T. Cicero 2012.

24. Cicero adds the caveat that rhetoric is elevated above moral philosophy (ethics) only, not above the whole of philosophy; and we may add the caveat that Plato's *Phaedrus* includes a qualified defence of rhetoric, in contrast with his *Gorgias*.

25. *De Rep*. 1.1 and 1.12, for the respective quotations, as translated in Cicero 1999, p. 6.

26. On Cicero's Latin philosophical vocabulary and the influence of Roman law in shaping it, see Griffin 2013.

27. This is the translation offered in Schofield 1999a, p. 183, omitting the clause numbering that he introduces; his account of the passage influences mine here and in what follows. In Cicero 1999, the fragment is numbered 1.39a.

28. Interestingly, however, for a paragon of republican statesmanship, Scipio expresses a personal endorsement for monarchy over the other two simple forms if one must choose one simple form of the original three, comparing it with the single master of a household, and Platonically to the rule of reason in the mind.

29. This fragment is numbered thus in Cicero 1999, p. 56.

30. Similar efforts had been made before and would be made again: Julius Caesar would succeed in passing two agrarian laws in 59, despite the vehement opposition of Cicero, Cato and others.

31. My translation, from *De Lege Agraria*, second speech, 2.7.17, 2.7.16, for the respective quotations in this sentence (Latin in Cicero 2002a); the ideas expressed in the preceding two sentences are found in the first speech of the three. For the broader context in which the *optimates*, including Cicero, opposed land redistribution as an attack on liberty, see Arena 2012, pp. 220–43.

32. Cicero's *De Legibus* is also clearly modelled on Plato's *Laws*, though the relationships posited in their respective texts on law to their respective texts on commonwealth and constitution are not identical.

33. 'Party walls and gutters' is the pungent phrasing in Harries 2006, p. 15, of this quotation from *De Leg.* 1.14.

34. *De Leg.* 1.20, as translated by Zetzel in Cicero 1999.

35. *De Leg.* 1.23, my translation.

36. *Off.* 1.21, my translation.

37. *Off.* 2.73, my translation.

38. My translation, from the Latin text in Cicero 2002b.

39. All quotations in this section from this work, unless otherwise marked, are as translated by Atkins in Cicero 1991.

40. This paragraph draws on and is closely related to my account in Lane 2011. There I quote the telling remark by A. A. [Anthony A.] Long 1995, p. 240: 'The *De officiis*, not the *De re publica*, is Cicero's *Republic*.'

41. See Cic. 41. 3–4 in Plutarch 1988.

42. These claims are challenged in Chapters 16 and 18 of *The Prince* respectively; the intermediary Chapter 17 of *The Prince* targets not any work by Cicero but rather Seneca's *De Clementia (On Mercy)*, a text to be discussed in Chapter 8.

CHAPTER 8: SOVEREIGNTY

1. Here I follow Mackay 2004, p. 165, quoting his translation of Octavian's new title.
2. Mackay 2004, pp. 167–8. The key moment in Octavian's defeat of Cleopatra and Mark Antony was the battle of Actium in 31 BCE; in extinguishing the Ptolemaic dynasty in Egypt, this also marked the fall of the last of the Hellenistic kingdoms that had been set up by Alexander's generals, after which Egypt became a province of the Roman empire.
3. Mackay 2004, pp. 183, 185.
4. Brunt 1977, who explains that this is better understood as a *senatus consultum* though presented as a *lex*.
5. On the significance of this speech 'To Rome' by Aelius Aristides, which has been variously dated between 144 and 155 CE, see Ando 1999 and Richter 2011. For the text, see Lenz and Behr 1976, and for a translation, see Behr 1981, Vol. 2.
6. The *Histories* chronicle 68–96 CE; the *Annals*, charting 14–68 CE, were written after the *Histories* as a kind of prequel. Both survive only in parts.
7. Tacitus wrote other works that would significantly shape later political thought, including his *Germania*, describing the customs of the German groups on the outskirts of the empire in his day, and a book about his father-in-law, the eponymous *Agricola*, a Roman who had become governor of Britain.
8. Gibbon 1837, p. 30 (Chapter 3). In fact, Gibbon accorded this accolade to a longer period including this one: from 'the death of Domitian to the accession of Constantine'.
9. As translated in Tacitus 2003, pp. 6–7.
10. See Sailor 2008, pp. 33–6, on different paths to protecting autonomy and social standing in Tacitus' time, including his own distinctive combination of historiographical and political activities.
11. On the *Dialogue on Oratory*, see Saxonhouse 1975 (an article devoted to this theme) and Kapust 2011, pp. 122–33.
12. Translation of *De Clementia* here and below by J. F. Procopé in Seneca 1995.
13. Translation of *De Otio* here and below (title often translated as *On Leisure*, but in this edition as *On the Private Life*) by J. F. Procopé in Seneca 1995.
14. It is in this sense that it is right to say that Seneca, despite being an adviser to an emperor, was 'apolitical': Cooper and Procopé 1995, p. xxiv.
15. Translation of this and all other letters of Seneca mentioned are by Brad Inwood in Seneca 2007.

16. Translation of *De Ira* here and below by J. F. Procopé in Seneca 1995.

17. As this letter is not included in Inwood's edition of selected letters, it is quoted here from the translation in Inwood and Gerson 2008.

18. Roberts 2013, pp. 25–8.

19. Ibid., p. 144.

20. Inwood 2005, pp. 303, 319.

21. For an influential perspective on this practice, though one stressing self-fashioning more than self-rule, see Foucault 2010.

22. I say 'in part' to register Brad Inwood's perceptive admonition that Seneca wrote not only as a therapist or 'spiritual and moral guide', but also as a 'man of letters'. See Inwood 2007, p. xviii. On Stoic and other Hellenistic therapies, see Nussbaum 1994, and on ancient philosophy generally as a way of life, see Hadot 1995 (emphasizing spiritual exercises) and Cooper 2012 (emphasizing philosophical argument).

23. For an overview of the Roman Stoics on the theme of self-rule and society, see Reydams-Schils 2005.

24. *D* 1.4.23, 1.4.26 respectively, as translated in Text 139 (p. 196), Inwood and Gerson 2008.

25. *D* 1.17.23 ('hindrance' . . .), 1.17.24 ('it is not because' and 'your opinion', as translated in Text 140 (p. 198)), Inwood and Gerson 2008.

26. Gill 2007, p. 175.

27. Translation here and below by A. S. L. Farquharson (*Meditations*) and R. B. Rutherford (*Letters*) in Marcus Aurelius 1989. Here, at p. 10.

28. Ibid., p. 34.

29. Ibid., p. 11.

30. Ibid., p. 118.

31. Platonism would animate one of the last consuls in the Western empire, the Christian Boethius (he held the consulship in 510 CE, his sons in 522), in his own search for philosophical consolation while imprisoned awaiting execution.

32. Musonius Rufus, Fragment [Lecture] 3, as translated in Lutz 1947, pp. 38–41.

33. Ibid.

34. Fragment [Lecture] 14 is titled 'Is marriage a handicap for the pursuit of philosophy?', and is quoted here as translated in Lutz 1947, pp. 90–97.

35. Clearly the first position would be called feminist today; whether the second would also depends on what today is taken to be a feminist position on marriage, a controversial question. In context in Roman and Greek philosophical debates, to support married philosophers was to oppose ascetic stances that in practice tended to denigrate the value of concerning oneself with women (*qua* wives) and children.

36. Fragment [Lecture] 14, as above.
37. This is from section 827BC of a fragment entitled in Greek *Peri Monarchias kai Demokratias kai Oligarchias* (*On Monarchy, Democracy and Oligarchy*); its Latin title in the traditional corpus of Plutarch's works is much longer, beginning with the words *De Unius*, by which the fragment is typically identified. Its authenticity is disputed, but it can be found in Plutarch 1949.
38. *Praecepta Gerenda Reipublicae* (*Political Advice*) 813E (Plutarch 1949), quoted in the translation given in Whitmarsh 2005, p. 12.
39. On Plutarch's *Lycurgus*, Lane 2013c; and for a comparison to Jewish Platonizers, Lane 2013b.
40. The discussion of Plutarch on statesmen and demagogues draws on and summarizes Lane 2012.

CONCLUSION: FUTURES OF GREEK AND ROMAN PASTS

1. Cartledge 2002, p. 4.

Index

T ───────────────────────

V ───────────────────────

W ───────────────────────

X ───────────────────────

Z ───────────────────────

D0713214